American Democracy

American Democracy

From Tocqueville to Town Halls to Twitter

Andrew J. Perrin

polity

First published in 2014 by Polity Press
Reprinted 2014

Polity Press
65 Bridge Street
Cambridge CB2 1UR, UK

Polity Press
350 Main Street
Malden, MA 02148, USA

ISBN-13: 978-0-7456-6232-9
ISBN-13: 978-0-7456-6233-6(pb)

A catalogue record for this book is available from the British Library.

Typeset in 11 on 13 pt Sabon by
Servis Filmsetting Ltd, Stockport, Cheshire
Printed and bound in the USA by Edwards Brothers Malloy, Inc.

For further information on Polity, visit our website: www.politybooks.com

For Jonah and Daniel

Contents

Acknowledgments

Like citizenship, intellectual life is profoundly collective, and this book is a great example. I've been privileged to learn the theory and practice of citizenship from many people. The ideas I pursue here have developed through conversations, arguments, and question-and-answer sessions with mentors, teachers, colleagues, students, and loved ones.

I have been very fortunate to be on the faculty at the University of North Carolina, Chapel Hill, which embodies the rigor, collective mission, and broad access that make truly public flagship universities absolutely central to democracy. This book started out with stimulating discussions about democracy and representation at UNC's magnificent Institute for the Arts and Humanities (IAH), and continued at our Cultural and Political Sociology Workshop and in first-year seminars on "Citizenship and Society" and "Difficult Dialogues" in which great students discussed, considered, and debated many of these issues. My colleagues in sociology and across campus, and in particular those who give of their time and energy to be outstanding University citizens, are a great source of energy and ideas. I am grateful to Andy Andrews, Chris Bail, Susan Bickford, Neal Caren, Matt Cone, Gregg Flaxman, George Huba, Mosi Ifatunji, Charles Kurzman, Michael Lienesch, Abigail Panter, and Debra and Michael Simmons for their comments on the project. John McGowan went above and beyond to give wonderful advice on the manuscript itself.

Acknowledgments

The ideas here crystallized in my Philip and Ruth Hettleman Lecture in 2010, as well as a 2011 panel I organized at IAH on civility and incivility in politics. I have learned greatly from the audiences for these talks, as well as those at Duke University's Kenan Center for Ethics; Swarthmore College; the University of California, Berkeley; UNC's School of Journalism and Mass Communication; UNC's Program in the Humanities and Human Values; Wake Forest University; and Yale University's Center for Cultural Sociology; as well as conferences in Paris and Trento.

I am also extremely grateful for the love and support of my family. My parents, Jim and Ellen Perrin, are consistently supportive of, and interested in, my pursuits, and actively fostered engagement in politics and citizenship at a young age. My wife, Eliana, has improved virtually everything I've written, very much including this book. She read every word and her insights have made the book immeasurably better. She is an extraordinary thinker and an incredible partner in every possible way: generous, wise, tolerant, and helpful. Andrea and Norman Miller are loving, supportive, and intellectually engaged, not to mention model citizens themselves. I am lucky to have them as in-laws. Norman read and provided very thoughtful comments on drafts of the entire book. My wonderful sons, Jonah and Daniel, keep me grounded and make me happy daily. I dedicate the book to them for the boys they are already and the men they are becoming: curious, kind, responsible, helpful, and committed. May they be part of a new generation of citizens to make the world better.

Parts of chapter 2 appeared as "Why You Voted", *Contexts*, Fall, 2008.
Parts of chapter 4 appeared as "Social Theory and Public Opinion" by Andrew J. Perrin and Katherine McFarland, *Annual Review of Sociology* 37 (2011).

Introduction

One witty friend, when I said I was writing a book about democracy, joked that it must be a work of historical fiction. Like all true wit, my friend's quip contains more than a grain of truth. In the United States and around the world, a host of indicators give people reason to be worried or even cynical about the way their democracy is working.

Americans have increasingly lost confidence in their government. Voter participation is low, rarely reaching much beyond 50 percent, and has remained so for over a century. A recent poll showed that Congress had only a 9 percent favorability rating, lower than Brussels sprouts, root canals, traffic, and even lice (Jensen 2013). Cynical, manipulating political actors can trick citizens into voting against their own interests (Frank 2004), and declining education and cultural marginalization exacerbate that (Bageant 2007). In a 2010 poll, 57 percent of Republicans said that President Obama was a Muslim; 45 percent that he "was not born in the United States," 38 percent that he is "doing many of the things that Hitler did," and even 24 percent that he "may be the Antichrist." Beyond the United States, democracy is "under pressure in many parts of the world," with more countries becoming less democratic than are becoming more so (Economist Intelligence Unit 2011).

Public "conversation" is just as worrisome. The media depict a landscape of an America deeply divided, "red state" vs. "blue state" as different cultures, different outlooks, entirely

1

Introduction

different kinds of people. Media commentators on newly partisan cable television trade charged accusations and barbs in place of substantive, thoughtful discussion and information. Most Americans prefer not to talk about politics at all, and those who do tend to talk about politics with people they already agree with. Dialogue across lines of disagreement seems all too rare, and when it happens it is often uncivil, generating more heat than light.

The sheer amount of money needed to run for a major office in the United States means that all but the wealthiest candidates spend a disproportionate percentage of their time raising money, a problem exacerbated by the Supreme Court's *Citizens United* decision. Many candidates end up paying more attention to a few very wealthy donors than to the bulk of their constituents. Lawmakers seek to pursue their constituents' own interests, or their own party's concerns, without regard to the common good of the country (Mann and Orenstein 2012).

New presidential powers exercised by the George W. Bush administration after the September 11 attacks dramatically expanded the power of the president, thereby diminishing the public's ability to oversee and object (Scheppele 2006). Observers at the time worried that these expanded powers would be all but impossible for future presidents to renounce, since any president would always prefer more power to less. Indeed, the Obama administration maintained many of these new powers, further eroding the influence of public and congressional oversight (Spitzer 2012), and laying the groundwork for the revelations of government surveillance leaked by Edward Snowden in 2013.

In short, there are plenty of reasons to be skeptical of democracy's progress and pessimistic about its future. Many of these concerns have to do with the technical aspects of democracy: the structures of electoral and legislative processes that lawyers and political strategists hold in the foreground when talking about politics and democracy. Others deal with the changed media environment and the cultural disposition toward division and incivility.

This book offers a new way to think about democracy: a distinctly *sociological* perspective. Conventional accounts of democracy tend to focus on the institutions, rules, and systems of government. While these are important, the sociological perspective examines how these interact with social and cultural practices and beliefs. It studies the *polity*, not just the *government*. And while there are plenty of reasons to be worried, that sociological angle also offers reasons for optimism: for responding to my friend's cynicism with a degree of hope. I attempt to follow the advice of the great French sociologist Pierre Bourdieu: to "steer between 'never-been-seen-before' and 'the-way-it-always-has been'" (Bourdieu 1999), avoiding both the breathless sense that everything is topsy-turvy and the blasé view that nothing is really new. To people who throw up their hands in despair at the state of contemporary democracy, I hope to offer reasons for optimism. For those who view democracy as, if not ascendant, at least safe, I hope to show some of the perils for real representation we face. The unique synergy of mobility, technology, and money that characterizes the late twentieth and early twenty-first centuries is enough to make a committed democrat wring his hands in despair. It should also be enough to spur optimism for new ways of practicing and experiencing democracy.

As widespread as cynicism toward democracy is – and as justified as it is for various reasons – I believe American democracy isn't nearly so badly off as it seems, and democracy worldwide is also reasonably healthy. Furthermore, although an attentive, cynical citizenry may be good for keeping government in check, excessive cynicism about democracy has the potential to become a self-fulfilling prophecy: if citizens are generally disillusioned about their government, that government's performance itself may suffer.

In the United States, voter participation has returned to mid-1960s levels after years of fretting about decreasing turnout. And the public pressure to vote is sufficient to encourage as many as 20 percent of Americans who didn't vote to actually *lie* to survey interviewers, claiming that they *did* vote. Around the world, support among ordinary people for the principles of democracy is very high (Tessler and Gao 2005; Andersen 2012).

Mounting evidence shows that when we compare governmental

policies with public opinion polls, most of the time governments do what the people want them to do. Government decisions generally align fairly well with public opinion as measured in polls (Brooks and Manza 2013; Manza and Cook 2002), although there remains a large bias in favor of the wealthy (Gilens 2012; Schlozman et al. 2012). While the low level of trust in government can make citizens cynical and disengaged (Hetherington 2005), it also serves to gather people into "attentive publics," paying close attention to government, ready to speak up if they don't like government activities (Arnold 1990).

The sociological approach I present here justifies some optimism. This book is unabashedly centered on *American* democracy, and the particular historical, cultural, and institutional dynamics of the United States. Some examples are pulled from elsewhere in the world, but the main thrust of the book is a sociological account of democracy in the United States, with only passing references to other countries' experiences.

Thinking Sociologically About Democracy

The French aristocrat Alexis de Tocqueville visited the young United States in 1831, sent by the French government to investigate the American prison system. The work he produced, *Democracy in America*, became a classic. *Democracy in America* is most often remembered for its identification of America as "a nation of joiners" and for its celebration of the young nation's citizens' tendency to assemble voluntarily to solve problems:

> Americans of all ages, all conditions, and all minds are constantly joining together in groups. In addition to commercial and industrial associations in which everyone takes part, there are associations of a thousand other kinds: some religious, some moral, some grave, some trivial, some quite general and others quite particular, some huge and others tiny. Americans associate to give fetes, to found seminaries, to build inns, to erect churches, to distribute books, and to send missionaries to the antipodes. This is how they create hospitals, prisons, and schools. If, finally, they wish to publicize a truth or foster

a sentiment with the help of a great example, they associate. Wherever there is a new undertaking, at the head of which you would expect to see in France the government and in England some great lord, in the United States you are sure to find an association.

In America I came across types of associations which I confess I had no idea existed, and I frequently admired the boundless skill of Americans in setting large numbers of people a common goal and inducing them to strive toward that goal voluntarily. (Tocqueville 2004 [1835], 595)

Tocqueville's analysis went well beyond joining. It emphasized the cultural roots of democracy in America. Americans were democratic, he claimed, because of the *ways they tended to associate*, their "habits of the heart" (331) and their rejection of old-fashioned hierarchies in favor of hierarchy based on accomplishments.

The men who inhabit the United States were never separated by privilege of any kind. They never knew the reciprocal relation of inferior and master, and since they neither fear nor hate one another, they never felt the need to call upon the sovereign to manage the details of their affairs. The destiny of the Americans is singular: they took from the aristocracy of England the idea of individual rights and the taste for local liberties, and they were able to preserve both because they had no aristocracy to fight. (799)

Tocqueville identified the foundation as well as the perils of political democracy in the *cultural practices* that characterized nineteenth-century American life. Alongside the tendencies to voluntarism and joining, he worried that the lack of moral regulation would lead toward internal strife and unfettered materialism (Kaledin 2011). Americans' *culture* formed both the promise and the peril of political democracy.

In focusing on the cultural and social elements of democracy, Tocqueville pioneered the sociology of democracy. American political *institutions* have changed enormously since Tocqueville. But the *cultural* configuration of American society – the tension between the individual and the collective, the tendency to reject

Introduction

hierarchy and snobbery, the willingness to take voluntary action – has remained more or less intact through nearly two centuries. This book focuses on those sorts of questions: the *cultural* and *social* dynamics of democratic citizenship, particularly in the United States, and the ways political representation and electoral systems shape and are shaped by those dynamics.

In early democracies in Athens, in France, and in the early United States, rule by "the people" was understood to be collective: "the people" was not just the agglomeration of otherwise unrelated individuals, but what we might now call the *public*: a collective, culturally bound and socially related, that shares a common experience, orientation, or concern. Suppressed under regimes and in cultures where there was no literal or figurative space between the government, the economy, and people's private lives, the public emerged when such opportunity opened (Habermas 1962).

The German term *Öffentlichkeit*, translated literally as "publicness," describes the cultural precondition for democratic politics. People – not necessarily everyone, but some people – have to be able to think and talk in public terms. So important is the idea of a separate set of public concerns, distinct from concerns of family life, economic necessity, and governmental power, that *Öffentlichkeit* has sometimes been translated directly as "democracy," as if publicness and democracy were the same thing (Jasanoff 2005, 74). It has been variously translated as "openness," "publicness," "publicity," "public opinion," and "public sphere" (Nowotny 2003). Its meaning is difficult to render in English, but at its core is the idea of an arena of human activity and concern devoted to collective life – the "civil sphere" (Alexander 2006) in which matters of common concern can be worked out and communicated. The sociology of democracy, therefore, is a sociology of *Öffentlichkeit*: a sociology of publics, their construction, and their effects: what the French political historian Pierre Rosanvallon refers to as "how an epoch, a country, or a social group may seek to construct responses to what, with greater or less precision, they perceive as a *problem*" (Rosanvallon 2006, 62).

Introduction

A sociological study of democracy must consider what cultural environments and practices foster publicness and successful democratic citizenship, since democracy is best understood as a cluster of cultural elements around political practices. Indeed, as Tocqueville worried, apparently democratic political systems can encourage antidemocratic cultures and behaviors. I suggest (especially in chapter 5) that precisely this is happening currently: that the democratic system of press freedom – certainly a core democratic value – is combining with privatizing communications technologies and industrialized media to result in a less democratic public culture. The opposite can also be true: "lively political activity and experiences of citizenship may actually thrive under conditions in which, perhaps even because, the state is fragile and national identification limited" (Wedeen 2008, 99). Neither of these is a reason to abandon democratic structures and institutions, of course. But they do press us to expand the scope of our thinking to examine the cultural and social dynamics of democracy as separate from, though dependent on, its formal processes, structures, and institutions.

This idea undermines what political scientists call the "minimalist" definition of democracy: that leadership is selected in competitive elections in which the outcome is uncertain (Schumpeter 1950; see also Wedeen 2008, 105–13). The minimalist conception misses what is most important about democracy: the interplay between democratic culture and democratic structure. Archibugi goes a bit further, emphasizing that democracy "may be summed up as *nonviolence*, popular *control*, and political *equality*" (Archibugi 2008, 26). Instead, I suggest that we understand the construction, maintenance, and characteristics of publics – including, but not limited to, "the public," the collectivity of the entire country – as sociological questions in which political structures like elections, legislation, and rules are important actors but far from the principal focus.

Since the late 1980s, sociologists have developed and refined a conception of culture as a system of shared beliefs, practices, styles, skills, and habits that serve at once to motivate, constrain, and explain human action (Swidler 2001; Johnson-Hanks et al. 2011; Vaisey 2009). *Culture in the mind* – the shared ways people within a culture think about issues – helps explain how societies produce *culture in the world*: the physical, technological, and textual artifacts that shape human behavior and, over time, refine and change culture in the mind. Culture in the mind helps explain why groups of people make some decisions and not others, why they think of some opportunities as more attractive than others, and why these decisions tend to be shared among groups of people. Culture in the world helps explain how these groups develop, use, and experience artifacts in the world: everything from media messages to communication technologies and voting systems. Cultural sociology offers the best tools for understanding democracy not just as a political system but as a social, cultural, and historical accomplishment.

I will therefore examine three interlocking areas to understand how publics form, persist, and die, and where they get their features. These are citizenship *practices*, *technologies*, and *institutions*. Practices are the everyday behaviors and habits of life: talking, reading, paying attention, voting. *Technologies* are patterned tools for accomplishing things: developed by humans for performing tasks, they enable some actions and constrain others, and so have important social and organizational effects. We naturally think of high technologies like computers and mobile phones, but the fixed line telephone, the voting booth, and the public opinion poll are also technologies. Technologies don't just determine what people do and don't do; people interpret technologies differently and use them in different ways (Orlikowski 1992, 2000). Finally, *institutions* are the organized rules and structures that govern democratic life: the electoral system, the legislative system, and the law, for example. Like technologies, these constrain and enable citizenship actions in particular ways. Traditional political science treatments of democracy focus on institutions and behaviors to the exclusion of practices and technologies. This book shows how practices, technologies, and institutions work together to represent publics, and how that process also helps to form and shape those publics.

Introduction

The Obama Citizenship Doctrine

Because I focus on the cultural aspects of democratic citizenship, ideas and rhetoric from leaders about why people should be involved and how they should make political decisions play a key role. Republicans and Democrats alike have, at times, put forward ideals of citizenship that tend to privatize and individualize: to make voting and participation into things people do for themselves and their own interests. At other times, both have put forward fundamentally *public* reasons for participation and engagement.

Building on his background in constitutional law, community organizing, and pragmatist social theory (Kloppenberg 2011), President Barack Obama has articulated more clearly a rhetoric and theory of the duties and rights of American citizenship than has any president since Kennedy. Consider, for example, the defiant speech that launched his career, at the 2004 Democratic convention nominating John F. Kerry for president:

> The pundits like to slice and dice our country into red states and blue states: red states for Republicans, blue states for Democrats. But I've got news for them, too. We worship an awesome God in the blue states, and we don't like federal agents poking around our libraries in the red states. We coach little league in the blue states and, yes, we've got some gay friends in the red states. There are patriots who opposed the war in Iraq, and there are patriots who supported the war in Iraq. We are one people, all of us pledging allegiance to the stars and stripes, all of us defending the United States of America. In the end, that's what this election is about. Do we participate in a politics of cynicism, or do we participate in a politics of hope? (Obama 2004)

Nine years later, after having been elected twice as president himself, Obama repeated these themes of unity, duty, and rights in his State of the Union Speech:

> We are citizens. It's a word that doesn't just describe our nationality or legal status. It describes the way we're made. It describes what we believe. It captures the enduring idea that this country only works when we accept certain obligations to one another and to future

9

generations; that our rights are wrapped up in the rights of others; and that well into our third century as a nation, it remains the task of us all, as citizens of these United States, to be the authors of the next great chapter in our American story. (Obama 2013)

These are the cultural themes that have persisted in American political culture for generations (Morone 1998): the tension between the common good and individual rights and interests; the combination of liberty with duty. Obama's intellectual style has been to call on that tension to enroll citizens in the culture of citizenship.

Seeking to build on this connection between unity and diversity, several times during his candidacy and early presidency he suggested that "we can disagree without being disagreeable." This emphasis on trying to bridge differences and interact with civility – although not entirely successful – is part of the doctrine of citizenship Obama has sought to articulate.

Leaving aside the question of whether Obama's policy proposals are desirable, his cultural logic emphasizes the cultural over the systemic elements of democracy. In asking Americans to think in terms of common citizenship, it is particularly attractive for the approach I take in this book because it evokes Americans' cultural and social practices and styles, not the systems of government that express those styles.

Plan for the Book

The first chapter of the book sets democracy in international and historical context. Democracy has been "invented" in several different places and at different times, and it has meant different things through history. In the American context and around the world, "the people" has meant something very different at different historical moments. Chapter 1 traces some of the big historical junctures that have produced the vision of democracy we work with today.

Chapters 2 and 3 focus on the practices of representation in

American democracy. Chapter 2 deals with "micropolitics": the decisions individual citizens make about participation in political and public life, and how these decisions are structured. Chapter 3 takes the same question from the other end, looking at the systems of electoral and legislative representation and how they represent and shape the public.

Next, chapters 4 and 5 deal with specific technologies of representation. Chapter 4 examines the practice of public opinion polling, whose ubiquitous use has shaped the ways Americans think about democracy, opinion, and participation. Chapter 5 examines the media, both traditional mass media and contemporary "social" media. Both of these chapters ask how publics are formed around technologies and their practices, and how these publics can best be represented in a democratic fashion.

Finally, chapter 6 offers conclusions about how to think about democracy sociologically, and the benefits of this approach. It also presents some reasons to think twice about popular reforms to the electoral and legislative systems, and suggests one reform that is rarely considered but might be worth considering.

Overall, the book's main point is that democracy – and its close cousin, representation – are *first* cultural, social concepts, *then* political ones. That has been the magic of the practices Americans and democrats worldwide have cherished for years.

1

History and Theory of Democracy

What do we think of when we hear the term "democracy"?

For now, Abraham Lincoln's famous phrase at Gettysburg – "government of the people, by the people, for the people" (Lincoln 1865) – is as good a place as any to begin. The most important feature of democracy is that the people's ideals and preferences should direct decisions taken by government. A democratic government's decisions should reflect the people's desires. Simple, right? A closer look reveals that this concept actually raises more questions than it answers.

This book offers an unusual angle on democracy: a *sociological* angle. It owes much to political science, the discipline devoted to understanding and documenting political ideas, institutions, and behavior. But the book's overall case is this: *democracy is best understood as the back-and-forth interactions among citizens and institutions of government, structured through rules, ideas, and technologies.* Citizens learn to act within constraints set by governmental and other powerful institutions and to use resources that are particularly useful with those institutions. Institutions, for their part – particularly democratic institutions – adapt to and structure citizens' opportunities and desires for action: their "democratic imaginations" (Perrin 2006). The sociological perspective is uniquely helpful for understanding how institutions *in general* adapt to and help create their environments (Aldrich 1999) and how culture and society *in general* structure the opportunities, constraints, and imaginations for individual and group action. Less- and non-democratic societies have fewer opportunities for citizens to form into publics, to voice opinions and ideas, and to monitor and learn from the decisions and outcomes of their governments.

Democracy, in other words, is not only, or even primarily, a political phenomenon. It is also a deeply social, institutional, cultural, and historical phenomenon. This sociological treatment of it highlights the ways social, institutional, cultural, and historical forces interact with political ones to produce modern political democracy. Tocqueville understood as much when he identified democracy in Americans' "habits of the heart": the unstated assumptions, habits, and manners that made their everyday interactions different from the aristocratic ones of France (Tocqueville 2004 [1835]; Torpey 2006).

Looking back after a quarter-century, 1989 was a very good year for democracy. That spring, the world watched as pro-democracy students faced down government tanks in Tiananmen Square in Beijing, China. Later that year, the authoritarian regimes of the old Soviet bloc ushered in unprecedented changes in openness and freedom in response to increasing international pressure and popular uprisings. In November of that year perhaps the most visible symbol of the Cold War – the Berlin Wall – was opened, and East Germans were allowed to visit West Berlin and West Germany freely. Meanwhile, another of the twentieth century's thorniest problems – the *apartheid* regime in South Africa and its occupation of neighboring Namibia – was changing swiftly. Democratic leader Nelson Mandela's release from prison was negotiated, as was Namibia's independence. Largely successful democratic transitions in both countries followed. At the other end of the African continent, North and South Yemen unified into a single country in 1990, ushering in a widely discussed transition to democracy (Wedeen 2008). In short, in 1989 it looked like the world was moving swiftly toward increasing democracy, and that these new democracies would embody a newly energetic, creative view of democratic practice (Blokker 2009). In many ways that was true. The world of 1990 looked dramatically different for democracy than it had in 1988, though many of the same thorny questions that had arisen before 1989 remained unsolved. The demise of the Soviet Union and its allies left the door open for chaos and antidemocratic forces, with tragic results in several cases. And democratic uprisings elsewhere had to wait much longer. In December 2010, a wave of uprisings across the Arab world brought major changes to governments in that area, and conflict between autocratic leaders and the populations continues.

What does it mean for the world to move toward democracy? And how was the stage set for these sweeping changes? To start to unravel these questions, we turn toward a history of some of the key ideas and practices of democracy, particularly in the United States but around the world as well. We'll then use that history to understand the turning point in 1989, the differences between kinds of democracy, and how we can best evaluate democracies' performance.

A Partial History of Democracy

This is not by any means a full or comprehensive history of American democracy; there are far better such histories already written (e.g., Wilentz 2005). Instead, it offers a relatively brief examination of strains of thought and practice at the roots of democracy as we currently understand it. It pays particular attention to the history of American democracy, but since American democracy is thoroughly connected with practices of democracy worldwide, I include other connections and approaches when those are helpful to our understanding.

The roots of democracy can be traced as far back as ancient Athens, the first stable democracy, which flourished around 500 BC. By our standards, Athenian democracy was very exclusive: many people subject to the laws of the city had no voice in making those laws. These included people who were excluded because of sex (women), status (slaves), and wealth (debtors). Those who *were* allowed to participate assembled into large bodies to discuss and vote on important matters. Athenian democracy was notable for the fact that it was relatively direct: participating citizens had a direct impact on the decisions that were made. By contrast, modern democracy tends to be representative: participating citizens elect representatives whose job is to make those decisions. Citizens may communicate with, criticize, monitor, and even recall those representatives, but with certain exceptions they are not able to take the decision making into their own hands.

The term "democracy" itself comes from Greek, and probably emerged in Athens. The second part of the word, "-cracy," means *power*. The first part, "demo-," refers to the *demos*, or the people: the same idea Lincoln evoked over 2,000 years later at Gettysburg. In democracy, then, power is vested in the people. But which people? What if they can't agree? How is power vested in the people? What if a majority of the people infringes upon the legitimate needs and rights of a minority? What if the people make the wrong decision for the common good due to misunderstanding, malice, selfishness, or ignorance? As democrats[1] wrestle with these questions, they bring innovative ideas to the table that refine the relationships between majorities and minorities, between rights, responsibilities, and publics. These innovations, in turn, form the practices and groups we think of as democracies and publics.

For centuries after the fall of Athens, democracy was not only out of favor but literally unthinkable throughout most of the world. It would be over 1,000 years before forms of modern democratic practices re-emerged in places like England and Venice in the thirteenth and fourteenth centuries. It was several hundred more years before the European Enlightenment and the development of industrial capitalism gave rise to a wave of democratic revolutions across the West. These revolutions – in particular the American Revolution of 1776 and the French of 1789 – signaled a new way of conceptualizing the rights, responsibilities, and characteristics of a citizen. These eighteenth-century developments literally changed the world and set us on the path to current democratic practices.

Throughout the European Middle Ages, the authority of monarchs (kings and queens) and the lesser nobles who paid fealty to them was largely unchallenged. To be sure, questions of *which* royalty would rule over a given territory were very much open; but the idea that sovereignty could be held by anyone other than a sovereign was virtually unthinkable. Most people were *subjects* of the sovereign, and the normal mode of life was to live under the economic and political protection of the sovereign and provide him (or, rarely, her) with the products of agricultural life – crops, raw materials, etc. – in return. That slowly began to change as trade and transportation made business and commerce more possible, and by the eighteenth century the *citizen* became the way people understood their role in society. The citizen belonged to a state or culture, but was much less dependent upon the sovereign than subjects had been before. Whereas before, kings and queens provided comprehensive protection in return for comprehensive loyalty, citizens began to view the demands of the feudal monarchies as excessive. It's not too much of an exaggeration to say that citizen-traders' frustrations with the monarchy were responsible for the invention of the modern citizen and civil society, two key elements of modern democracy.

The concept of *citizen* contains both a sense of belonging to a polity and obligation to it, and at the same time a sense of the practices of citizenship: participation, obligations, and civic duty. The element of civic duty is older, based on the idea that "the best form of state is based on two supports . . . : good civic behaviour and a republican form of state" (Heater 2004, 4). In other words, good government depends both on having strong democratic institutions and on having citizens who act responsibly and democratically. By the nineteenth century, the burden had shifted and citizenship was held out more as an obligation governments owed to their citizens, but the importance of educating citizens to be responsible members of the polity has remained and grown in recent years (Heater 2004, 5, 130–1).

These developments went far beyond the economic realm; they took place in the realm of culture as well. Literary and cultural worlds – previously reserved largely for nobles – were available more to the *bourgeoisie*, the ascendant class of people who depended on trade for their livelihood and cherished autonomy from the nobles. The lively intellectual atmosphere of eighteenth-century *salons* encouraged the discussion of matters of substance across lines of status and wealth: in Jürgen Habermas' memorable phrase, "a public sphere constituted by private people putting reason to use" (Habermas 1962, xviii). This, in turn, "produced not merely a change in the composition of the public but amounted to the very generation of the 'public' as such" (Habermas 1962, 39).

Meanwhile, on the other side of the Atlantic, when the Continental Congress met at Philadelphia they understood how new and remarkable the republic they were designing would be. But they probably had no idea just how enormous the forces they unleashed were. They were doing no less than putting into place a new way of imagining the relationship between a government and its people. In fact, the demands for democracy at that time were quite moderate by our standards. The representatives to the Continental Congress – like those who eventually made up the Constitutional Convention – were very much elites themselves: European, white, male landowners, many of them slaveholders, and many of whom knew each other through the elite institutions they frequented (Schudson 1998, 42–3). Furthermore, their complaints were rooted as much in economic liberty as they were in democratic representation. The colonists who carried out the famous Boston Tea Party of 1773, for example, were angry over the British monarchy's assertion of its right to tax them (even though that system would have lowered the overall price of tea; Lepore 2010, 76–7). The protests over the monarchy's right to tax the colonies without providing them a voice in Parliament – taxation without representation – helped cement the idea that the citizenry was separate from the monarchy and could have ideas, preferences, and interests at odds with those of the monarchy.

In the wake of the successful American Revolution, the high-minded debates between the Federalists and the Anti-Federalists worked through many of the thorny issues that became central to the design and practice of democracy. These were heady, high-stakes times. Although the so-called "Founding Fathers" were far from representative in the way we think of representation now, they shared a commitment to self-government and to the idea that the people could and should govern themselves. "The remarkable debate about sovereignty and liberty that took place between 1761, when James Otis argued the writs of assistance case, and 1791, when the Bill of Rights was ratified, contains an ocean of ideas," writes historian Jill Lepore. "You can fish almost anything out of it" (Lepore 2010: 64). These ideas were not divorced from day-to-day concerns. Rather, the American constitutional designers debated the structures of government – elections, legislative bodies and rules, judiciary forms, rights – as ways of implementing ideas about self-government.

These debates took place through the publication of papers by the Founders – generally called the Federalist Papers and the Anti-Federalist Papers – in newspapers, pamphlets, and other available venues of the time. The papers are far from unanimous. They contain the intellectual back-and-forth of a remarkable group of people seeking to work out the contours of a new form of government, and there is great disagreement within them about the ways to balance it. They are far more than discussions about government structures; they are theories about the relationship of private, public, and governmental life, and how these three spheres are best balanced over time and across space.

It's important to remember that, in the eighteenth century, the very concept of democracy was highly controversial. Edmund Burke, a British philosopher, observed the French Revolution's insistence on popular sovereignty with great horror, arguing that durable virtues such as loyalty and morality should not be subject to the whims of the unsophisticated populace (Burke 1790 [1993]). However, the success of the French and American Revolutions put these views on the defensive. Indeed, the Federalists in the American debate, who were deeply influenced by Burke and his conservative allies, did not dispute the basic right of the people to govern themselves: the cornerstone of democracy. That ship, as they say, had sailed. The question was how self-government was to be set up, and with what rights, privileges, and protections.

The people allowed to self-govern were, of course, much fewer than our contemporary ideals of democracy dictate. The most important restriction the Constitution endorsed was allowing the continued practice of slavery, a monumental injustice and one that severely limited the reach of democratic representation. If people were allowed to own other people, how could those who were owned by others be understood to hold power (the *-cracy* in democracy)? The historic "three-fifths compromise," in which American slaves were counted in states' populations as three-fifths of their actual number, only compounded the problem by officially separating the people to be represented from the people actually allowed to participate in that representation. The decision to endorse slavery in the early Republic was an extension of what seemed "obvious" to scholars and democrats at the time: "The assumption of nonwhite intellectual inferiority was widespread" (Mills 1997: 60), although perhaps not universal. The need for compromise itself was an indication that questions like this were in dispute. Still, even those colonies that had outlawed slavery did not allow free African Americans to vote, suggesting that opposition to slavery did not necessarily imply a thorough commitment to equality or true democracy as we understand it now.

The compromise over slavery was only the most glaring of several exclusions that, from a twenty-first-century viewpoint, are obviously problematic. Women were not allowed to vote, a rule that would not be rescinded until the early twentieth century. Voting was restricted to property-owners, the belief of the Founders being that such men were the only ones sufficiently committed to and wisest about the common good of the society. So while the American Founders imagined a republic governed by the consent of the people – and, in so imagining, opened the door for an explosion of growth in democratic representation – their design was limited even as it provided the vocabulary and opportunity for extraordinary future democratic development. The limits, from our twenty-first-century vantage point, are clear. What made the design revolutionary was its future promise: the Founders evoked the idea of "the people" without explicitly defining it or putting clear boundaries on the concept. They thereby gave a gift to generations of future democrats who worked to expand, mold, and manipulate the idea of "the people." Tocqueville predicted the expansion of voting rights long before it became the universal assumption, although he doubted the wisdom of it:

The more broadly voting rights are extended, the more one feels the need to extend them still further, for with each new concession, the forces of democracy increase, and its demands grow with its newfound power. The ambition of those who remain below the qualification level is spurred in proportion to the number who stand above it. At last the exception becomes the rule; concessions follow one upon the other, and there is no stopping until universal suffrage is achieved. (Tocqueville 2004 [1835], 64)

As sociologist Michael Schudson demonstrates, the Founders didn't really trust the people – even those who were allowed the vote – to be actively engaged in public matters: "they . . . disapproved of general public discussion [even] among the propertied white males. They were far from sharing a pluralist vision, still attached as they were to the notions of consensus, property, virtue, and deference that came naturally to them" (Schudson 1998: 55). But through the vigorous, innovative thinking of the Federalist–Anti-Federalist debates and the US Constitution and Bill of Rights, they set in motion a historical process developing ideas and forms of "the people" that led eventually to the expansive notion of popular sovereignty that blossomed at the end of the twentieth century.

The Founders' limitations on democracy took place in a social, cultural, and political environment very different from the one we live in, even as their work helped foster and develop our current environment. In addition to their exclusive view of "the people," the design they came up with entrusts that collectivity as the best source of decisions as what we might now call *epistemic democracy* (Cohen 1986). The essence of this idea is that the reason to consult the people is that the people as a collectivity are most likely to come up with the objectively best decision. The Founders assumed that there was always a correct decision in the interests of the public or the common good. The problem they were trying to solve was how best to figure out what that correct decision was. Democratic representation was the best way to reveal the authentic, objective best decision for a government to take; monarchy and other non-democratic systems were less likely to reveal the common good because they didn't leverage the collective wisdom of the people. Democracy, in this conception, is the best means to realize the right end, not a matter of citizens' right to participate in their own fate (participatory democracy), to discuss and convince others about public matters (deliberative democracy), or to defend their interests against the interests of opponents (agonistic democracy). Democracy was important because of the end it yielded, not because of the means it enabled.

In the generations since, democracy has come to be seen as the only truly legitimate way to govern a country. The people, we are now prone to believe, have an inherent *right* to govern themselves, and decisions made democratically are legitimate *even if they are incorrect*. Thus we have moved from an epistemic to a combination of participatory, deliberative, and agonistic approaches to democracy: democratic representation is charged with balancing the interests of different groups within society, insuring that each of these groups is represented in governmental decisions, and encouraging widespread participation in political discussions and decision making. We will return to these ideas of representation and democracy later in the chapter.

Reconstruction and Social Change

The nineteenth century in Europe and the United States saw these societies transform from mostly rural, agricultural ones into much more urban, industrial countries (figure 1). In the United States in particular, the industrial North grew increasingly distant from the agricultural South, which depended on slave labor for its economic system. Meanwhile, urbanization and industrialization transformed Europe as well, giving rise to new movements and demands for representation. The idea of one correct decision, to be arrived at through considered deliberation among propertied elites, was no longer tenable. In mid-century these differences increasingly strained the Constitutional compromise over slavery. An extensive social movement emerged to challenge the institution of slavery, including leaders who had been former slaves (such as Frederick Douglass) and white abolitionists like William Lloyd

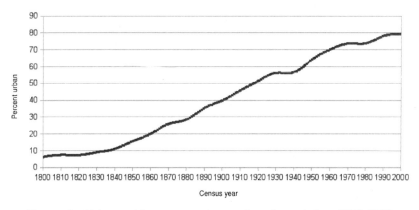

Figure 1   Urban residents as percentage of total population, 1800–2000

Garrison. While the abolitionists, as they were called, had mixed motives, including some based on their own racism (Allen 2007), their popular mobilization helped introduce a culture of political engagement in major issues in the United States. The abolitionist movement helped establish "democratic discourses" for American politics even as they were far from unanimous themselves (Bennett 2005, 5–6). An enormous social and political change had been brought about through popular involvement.

Through the same time period, women's movements were struggling as well to achieve women's right to vote. Women's suffrage campaigners argued for the vote based on basic fairness and representation as well as claims that women's special points of view would improve democratic governance in general. Like that of the abolitionists, the movement for women's suffrage was an important source for popular democracy, an early social movement that helped develop the idea of ordinary people organizing for political changes.

The strain of slavery, and of the difference between industrial and agricultural economies, drove the American Civil War. The war and its aftermath spawned a new, flourishing dialogue about democracy and the people, one product of which was Lincoln's memorable phrase at Gettysburg, "of the people, by the people, for the people." Because of the centrality of race and slavery to the

22

war, this dialogue focused largely on those issues, and the question of women's suffrage was largely sidelined.

In the aftermath of the war, congress asserted the power of the federal government, in the service of both racial equality and retribution on the former Confederate states (Foner 1989). This period – called "Reconstruction" – saw passage of the 13th, 14th, and 15th Amendments to the US Constitution, the "Reconstruction Amendments," which redefined the nature and focus of citizenship (Ackerman 1991; Cottrol 1991; Foner 1999). The amendments went well beyond abolishing the practice of slavery, itself an enormous accomplishment given the history of the country up to that point. They established the principle of universal suffrage, fulfilling Tocqueville's prediction in theory albeit not in practice. The principle was that all citizens were eligible to vote, although the implementation of that principle, both for African Americans and for women, took far longer and hit plenty of roadblocks along the way. The amendments greatly expanded "the people" both in terms of *who* was included and in terms of *how* the people could be represented. Indeed, "the Radical Republicans [who championed the Reconstruction Amendments] did not simply tinker with the Constitution, but fundamentally changed it from a pro-slavery document into a pro-equality document" (Newman and Gass 2004, 2).

Before the Reconstruction Amendments, "the people" of the Constitution was a unified whole: a society whose best interests could be discerned and managed through the wisdom of social elites. The Civil War had changed all that: conflict *within* American society was at least as important as conflict *between* American society and others, and the depths of the conflicts (racial, economic, social) couldn't be ignored. "Reconstruction represented less a fulfillment of the Revolution's principles than a radical repudiation of the nation's actual practice for the previous seven decades" (Foner 1999: 2006). Americans turned to the Constitution and its democratic sensibilities to manage the newly revealed social pressures. The Reconstruction Amendments provided the opportunity to do that. The 13th Amendment outlawed slavery. The 14th and 15th laid out specifically the rights of all citizens to vote, determined who was a citizen ("All persons born or naturalized in the United States"), and outlawed discrimination based on race. The fundamental principle of democracy thus became *inclusion*: citizens had to be able to participate in the political life of the country in order to achieve representation. This change had been brewing for some time, and its application was both very slow to materialize and very uneven, as we will see shortly. But the very idea that "the people" of the country was to be made up of the collection of individual men (and, later, women) who lived in the country emerged from the struggle for racial liberation of the abolitionists and was legally enshrined in the Reconstruction Amendments (Foner 1999, 2004).

The other major change of the nineteenth century was a social one, resulting from the enormous immigration into the United States, from Europe in particular (figure 2). America's big cities became bustling metropolises in which rich and poor intermingled, mixing ethnicities, classes, and races (Daniels 2002). Each of these groups had a legitimate claim to being part of "the people," and sought to make these claims through early labor

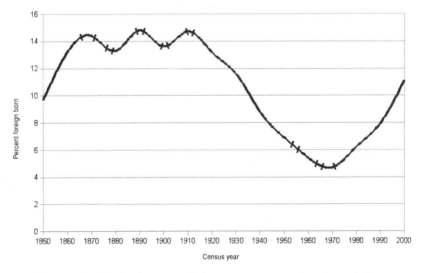

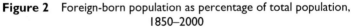

Figure 2 Foreign-born population as percentage of total population, 1850–2000

movements like the Knights of Labor (Voss 1993) and ethnic clubs such as the Polish-American and Irish-American clubs. With these increasing demands for representation came two important changes in the American idea of democracy. First was the very idea that "the people" included citizens beyond the elites: the very logic the Founders had used to demand independence from monarchy acquired a new power in breaking down the privilege property-owners had previously enjoyed. The second change was the idea that different groups of people held different, even contradictory, interests. Workers in factories wanted different things from government than did factory owners, farmers, and cultural elites, and different ethnic groups sought to improve their positions in the cities (Kaufman 1999). In part this was a recognition of the groups' different material interests; in part, it was the product of elites' work in carving out "highbrow" culture as separate from working classes' mass taste (DiMaggio 1982).

By 1875, then, the United States looked enormously different from the United States of 1825. The liberation of African slaves and the immigration of European immigrants with widely varying appearances and backgrounds made the people look hugely different. The shift from an agricultural to an industrial economy made the cities bigger, more important, more bustling, more exciting, and more dangerous than they had been before. These developments produced ugly backlashes as well, including anti-immigrant discrimination and violence. In fact, in the election of 1874 the voters replaced the Republican pro-civil-rights majority with a virulently racist Democratic majority in Congress, bringing an end to Reconstruction, willful neglect of the Reconstruction Amendments, and the beginning of Jim Crow, the legally enforced racial segregation prevalent in the South for 80 years (Valelly 2004; McConnell 1994).

The political result of the nineteenth century's upheavals was a lively, exciting, participatory (albeit deeply unequal) system of patronage politics in most of the country's large cities. Political parties mobilized their ethnic and economic bases to keep them in power; in exchange, voters loyal to these parties got civic services and access to basic government resources and civil service jobs.

Participation in politics in the late nineteenth century was public, engaging, collective, and social. Political life brought in citizens of different class and ethnic backgrounds, although it was based also on important exclusions of African Americans, women, and others. This pattern of requiring party affiliation for access to basic government services – which we now appropriately see as corrupt – offered representation and opportunities for participation to vast numbers of people who would not have been involved or even considered in eighteenth-century democratic thought and practice.

The people of the Founders was a unified whole. Other languages have better words for this concept: in German it is *Volk*; in Greek a *demos*. Both of these concepts connote a collective, combined people, not just a collection of individuals (Weiler 1995), a distinction explored by Jeffrey Olick (1999). By the late nineteenth century, the American conception of the people had morphed into a collection of individuals instead of a combined collectivity. In the language of the political philosopher Jean-Jacques Rousseau, the image of the people began to shift from the *"volonté générale"* (the general will, or the common good), to the *"volonté de tous"* (the will of the people, or the collected individual preferences) (Rousseau 1913, 203). This nineteenth-century development is crucial, as it marks the point at which the increasing freedom and autonomy of the individual overtook the collective nature of the public.

Industrialization and the Progressive Era

Through the late nineteenth and early twentieth centuries, industrialization continued, and the ongoing movement of Americans and immigrants into cities continued to generate ethnic diversity and conflict and, increasingly, economic poverty. These social ills inspired a generation of reformers and social radicals committed to visions of fairness, equality, and rationality. Their political visions varied considerably, but they shared a number of elements that gelled into a truly revolutionary change in the early

26

twentieth century. First, they were committed to on-the-ground social service and reforms. Jane Addams, for example, ran Hull House, the famous Chicago settlement house that provided food, shelter, and educational opportunities to poor residents, many of them recent immigrants. Reformers like Addams, along with John Dewey and Horace Kallen, brought an intellectual sensibility along with practical reform and a faith in knowledge and science. Among their innovations is the philosophy of *pragmatism*, or the idea that truth and correct outcomes can be determined through observation and experimentation – practice – more than through abstract ideas and thoughts. Pragmatism is certainly the most important American contribution to world philosophy; it has also been the driving force in American political thought and practice since the beginning of the twentieth century (McGowan 2012).

Pragmatism's faith in science and rationality offered the philosophical basis for the most important social movement of the time, the Progressive movement. The Progressives detested the corruption and insider patronage of the urban political machines, and also the increasing power of very large corporations and trusts. To combat these threats to individuals' freedom and popular sovereignty, they advocated for the government to regulate and break up the large trusts to increase competition and consumer freedom. And to break the machines' stranglehold on government, they pushed for an array of reforms to make government more accountable, more rational, fairer, and more responsive to the popular will.

Among the most important of these reforms was the secret ballot, also called the Australian Ballot (Friedman 1968). In nineteenth-century America, voting was a very public practice: citizens would obtain a ballot, pre-printed with the names of members of one or another party, from the party itself. They would then take that pre-printed ballot and deposit it in the ballot box, demonstrating to the assembled observers that they had voted and for whom (Bensel 2004). Progressive reformers were convinced (correctly) that this public process made it all but impossible for citizens to express their genuine preferences and hold politicians accountable. As more vulnerable citizens such as poor and lower-status people became eligible to vote, it was particularly important to provide protection from intimidation so their authentic beliefs could be represented by the vote. To that end, Progressive reformers insisted on a secret ballot. This ballot, printed by the government and provided to voters to fill out and submit privately, put power in the hands of the citizen.

Progressives also had close ties to the suffragette movement, which championed the right of women to vote. That right was eventually implemented in American law through the 19th Amendment in 1920. And struggles of black and immigrant citizens for recognition and inclusion also called upon Progressive ideas and allies. Different Progressive groups and leaders supported each of these, and the movement was certainly not unified on broad rights to participation – Progressives could be just as resistant as the rest of society to marginalized groups. But in terms of a *theory* of democracy, theirs was at once inclusive and individualistic. That vision has largely won out in the century since.

Civil service reforms required that all citizens have the opportunity to apply for government jobs and to be awarded those jobs by experience and qualifications instead of loyalty and patronage. So-called "sunshine laws" required that governments provide information about their operations to the public to avoid back-room deals. Similar reforms, such as referendum elections to decide major public issues and the possibility of recalling public officials by popular election, sought to return power and fairness to citizen elections.

Like the Founders and the Reconstruction-era reformers, the Progressives too faced major opposition from people concerned about offering too much power to the people. Indeed, the birth of what we now understand as American conservatism had its origins during the Progressive era, as conservatives worried about threats to religious and traditional values (Lienesch 2007) and the privileges of race and wealth that came with expanding individual rights and ending systems of special privileges. These questions continue to the present day, but overall Progressive logics of transparency, fairness, and popular power have largely won the ideological battle. Few present-day politicians or commentators call for *less* popular involvement, government transparency, or accountability.

There is an important, unfortunate lesson to be learned from the Progressive era as well. That lesson is: all reforms, even well-intentioned and well-considered ones, have consequences that can't be fully understood beforehand. The Progressive reforms certainly made American democracy fairer and returned power to the population. At the same time, they made political involvement less exciting – no more party carnivals and social events – and much more confusing. All a voter needed to know to vote in 1875 was which party he favored; the party would take care of the rest. In a post-reform world, a voter needed to know the name of each candidate he intended to vote for. And in states where referenda were common, such as California, he also needed to know whether to favor or oppose each of these referenda. Little wonder, then, that voter turnout dropped in the wake of the reforms (Valelly 1990). By insisting that each campaign be run separately instead of as a party operation, the reforms also increased the cost of campaigning, as each campaign had to do its own work to reach voters and convince them to vote for its candidate. Thus two of the thorniest issues of our current democracy – voter turnout and campaign finance – have their origins in the reforms the Progressives championed to bring about fairness in the electoral system.

Finally, the Progressive sensibility taught citizens to think of their votes as their personal property. The Reconstruction Amendments, having expanded the idea of which individuals counted as part of "the people," had yet to change the fundamentally social character of participation: citizens were grouped into organizations and social gatherings with political purposes, not the least of which were political parties. The whole logic of Progressivism distrusted such collective politics. Voters, who once voted in the open as a social act, now entered increasingly complex voting machines that symbolically enforced their separation from friends, neighbors, and organizations as they cast their votes. Among the most publicly oriented activities many Americans engage in takes place in the enforced privacy of a voting machine. The practice of voting changed. Before, it seemed mostly like attending a public event; later, it became more like going shopping: spending one's scarce resource (a vote) on a preferred outcome. In the long history of "the people" in America, it was with the Progressive movement that we shifted decisively from engagement in groups to engagement as individuals.

This outcome is what Robert K. Merton called an "unintended consequence of social action" (Merton 1936). The Progressive reforms certainly did make American democracy fairer, more inclusive, more representative, and more responsive. Without them we would have nothing like the expectations from government we gained in the twentieth century. But new ideas, institutions, and practices bring new constraints as well as new opportunities. The new opportunities of the Progressive era brought along with them constraints that discouraged us from understanding democracy as a collective, social, organized practice.

The end of the Depression and World War II marked yet another new era in democracy. In the United States, Franklin Roosevelt's social policies under the New Deal led to nothing short of a total political realignment of regional and class interest; Ira Katznelson credits it with holding together the country in the face of a tremendous threat in the form of the Depression: "Prosperous and effectively armed by the end of this epoch, the country became democracy's global leader" (Katznelson 2013, 7). The international outrage at the Nazi atrocities in Germany made explicitly racial and ethnic discrimination increasingly difficult to promote. Meanwhile the United States became the superpower anchor of the Western allies in opposition to the Soviet Union and its communist bloc. The logic – although certainly not always the reality – of American foreign policy was promoting democratic government around the world. In the wake of World War II, the emerging global consensus was that peoples had the right to "self-determination," a view that has gone nearly unchallenged as the organizing principle in world politics since then and that implies some form of democracy as the only appropriate mode of government. Dozens of former colonies in Africa, Asia, and Latin America achieved independence in the postwar period.

The American vision of procedural democracy, individual voting, and personal rights became a point of pride. These were, however, severely limited by anxiety over the communist threat. Internationally, American foreign policy was driven more by alliances with countries willing to offer support for American military power than by actual democratic behavior. And at home, people who publicly disagreed were often accused, formally and informally, of being anti-American. These accusations could have enormous effects as government power was used to strip such people of jobs, positions, and freedom, particularly under the provocation of Wisconsin Senator Joseph McCarthy and his House Un-American Activities Committee.

Meanwhile, though, the technical and economic sophistication that had increased steadily since the Progressive era continued to change the practice of democracy. The introduction of radio and recording technologies and increasing literacy helped make the American population into a vast audience, addressed by politicians, commentators, and celebrities alike (Horkheimer and Adorno 2000 [1946]; Adorno 2000; Jenemann 2007). During and immediately after the war, George Gallup and others developed the modern public opinion survey. The survey technique, then as now, uses small, randomly selected samples of people to estimate how the public feels about important issues and elections (Berinsky 2004). This practice is now so prevalent that many Americans think of public opinion as being exactly the same thing as what is measured by such surveys, but that was not always the case. Indeed, in the early years of the survey technique many Americans wrote letters to Gallup, puzzled as to how the pollsters could know how they planned to vote without having talked to them specifically (Igo 2007). Americans had to be taught to conflate the standardized survey with the public opinion it was designed to measure; they did not simply adopt that worldview naturally.

Once more, as with the changes in voting in the Progressive era, the transformation of the American public into a mass audience meant they became more like consumers than producers. Having an opinion before polling was invented meant deciding that an issue was important to have an opinion about, finding an audience for the opinion, and actively expressing that view. It was a difficult, time-consuming, but potentially very rewarding proposition, since relatively few others were able to express *their* opinions. But after public opinion polling became commonplace, the pollster decided what issues were important and provided a ready-made audience through the media. Expressing a view meant making a selection among pre-determined choices from a list. Citizens gained the ability to have their voices better heard, since politicians could not afford to ignore the results of public opinion surveys (Newport 2004). Again, opportunities brought their own constraints.

The Postwar Development of Individualist Citizenship

Three major historical events of the mid-twentieth century helped expand American democracy leading up to 1989. First was the civil rights movement, which had been developing locally for years. In the 1950s, building on this base of long-term organizational strength, it emerged in national media and consciousness (Morris 1986). It made the moral and legal case for ending discrimination on the basis of race across the country, but particularly in the South, where Jim Crow laws were strongest. The civil rights movement was met with great violence and resistance, but was also enormously successful. Indeed, less than two decades after much of the nation first heard of the movement with Rosa Parks' famous refusal to move to the back of the bus and the ensuing Montgomery bus boycott, not only had the legal environment changed to allow full citizenship and participation for African Americans, but widespread public opinion held that racism was wrong (Page and Shapiro 1992, 68–9).

It's important, again, not to overstate the depth of the victories, as African Americans continue to experience more subtle "racism without racists" (Bonilla-Silva 2010), substantial economic and social disadvantages (Conley 2010; Wilson 1997), and outright discrimination (Pager and Quillian 2005). And President Johnson turned out to be right when, after signing the Voting Rights Act, he fretted to aide Bill Moyers that he had "delivered the south to the Republican Party for a long time to come" (Moyers 2004, 167), as white Southerners abandoned the national Democratic Party for its support of African-American voting rights. But from the perspective of democratic cultural development, the movement changed both public opinion and government practice. The movement also introduced an important strain of thinking about democracy and citizenship into American culture. This strain, exemplified by Martin Luther King's "Letter from a Birmingham Jail" (King 1963), emphasizes moral urgency, personal witness, and social movement tactics as central parts of the citizenship repertoire. These ideas infused other major changes of the 1960s and beyond (Blee 2012).

The second crucial development was the movement for women's rights, also known as second-wave feminism. In 1963, journalist and intellectual Betty Friedan published *The Feminine Mystique*, which detailed women's increasing dissatisfaction with their status as housewives. Already prior to that date, women's groups had begun to think about "women's liberation," the idea that women ought to enjoy the same rights and opportunities afforded to men and the same possibilities for multiple roles (Coser 1994). As with the Civil Rights movement, the women's lib movement, as it came to be called, had successes and failures. The most important failure was the movement's ultimate inability to pass the Equal Rights Amendment, which would have amended the US Constitution to require equal rights between women and men (Mansbridge 1986). But the impact of the movement on American culture (Meyer and Whittier 1994), public opinion, and legal developments was dramatic. In a short span of time, the mainstream, obvious principle changed from favoring restricting women to traditionally feminine roles and aspirations (Coontz 1992) to favoring generally equal treatment and evaluation to men (Mayeri et al. 2008).

The third upheaval of the time was the American war in Vietnam. The war began in earnest with the escalation under President Lyndon B. Johnson following the Tonkin Gulf Incident, in which an American ship reported that it had been attacked by Vietnamese forces. Between 1963 and 1972, about 2.1 million

American troops fought in Vietnam, and over 58,000 died or were captured there. The war was intensely controversial inside the United States, often pitting members of families against one another. Finally, in order to recruit enough soldiers, the military relied heavily upon its draft system. That system selected young men randomly to be sent to Vietnam to fight. However, several important avenues existed for avoiding the draft, including being a college student. That, in turn, made social capital crucial as young men with better connections and backgrounds could better manage their educational careers to avoid Vietnam service – and, in many cases, be available to protest at home. The combination of these elements made opposition to the Vietnam War intense, vocal, and very public.

In many ways, these three historical developments – the civil rights movement, the women's lib movement, and the Vietnam War (and opposition to it) – were the foundation for the counterculture and what we think of as "the sixties," even though they all had roots before 1960 and persisted well after 1969. Activists and countercultural movements such as the "hippies" developed a set of ideas about personal liberation that further pushed the idea of "the people" beyond its prior ideals. This all happened in the context of international turmoil as well: the sixties brought riots in Paris and across Europe, student movements throughout the world, and unpopular colonial wars by the European powers as well. The international sense was that things were changing more quickly, and in a more forward-looking way, than at any point in the nearly two centuries since the French Revolution.

The iconic American concept of democracy during this period is embodied in the Port Huron Statement, adopted by the activist group Students for a Democratic Society (SDS) in 1962, which envisioned "a democracy of individual participation, governed by two central aims: that the individual share in those social decisions determining the quality and direction of his life; [and] that society be organized to encourage independence in men and provide the media for their common participation" (Hayden 1962). "Men," the Statement held, "have unrealized potential for self-cultivation, self-direction, self-understanding, and creativity . . . The goal

34

of man and society should be human independence." Similarly important, though, is the so-called Sharon Statement, founding document of the Young Americans for Freedom (YAF), a conservative student group (Klatch 1999). That statement, adopted in 1960, emphasized the superiority of American institutions and policies, *also in the language of individual liberty.* Thus the 1960s generation, marked as it was by deep and severe conflict between the left and the right, endorsed an underlying consensus: that the development, liberty, and autonomy of the individual were the appropriate goal.

Recall just how new this development was. During the Progressive era, reformers endorsing individual rights and liberties had clashed with conservatives, who championed traditions and institutions – certainly not individual self-development or liberty (Lienesch 2007). Similarly, conservative thought at the other key moments of democratic development (the French and American Revolutions and Reconstruction) established concerns about the possible excesses, failures, and dangers of individual liberty and self-determination, not about how best to defend these. So *both* of the documents endorsing democratic advancement in the 1960s (the leftist Port Huron Statement and the right-wing Sharon Statement) saw it as the way to create and reinforce a free, empowered individual, even though the two visions looked to very different political practices and ideals to nurture that individualism. After the 1960s, no more could a serious participant in political debate argue on principle against the *ideals* of individual rights and liberation, of individual equality. To be sure, these ideals were not necessarily practiced, and actors still frequently find ways to justify excluding others, but these justifications are virtually never based on other groups being categorically ineligible or unable to be included. In a very real sense, the strife of the 1960s invented the modern individual and the sense of abstract fair play that has animated most debates since then.

As the conflicts of the 1960s died down, this individual ethos continued and strengthened. The authors of the immensely influential 1985 book *Habits of the Heart* examined the enduring influence of therapeutic individualism that dominated middle-class life of the period: focused nearly exclusively on individual self-actualization and far less on questions of community and belonging (Bellah et al. 1985, 121–3). Many other social movements since then – for example, for gay and lesbian rights or for acceptance of elderly and overweight people – often claim that their object is the "last acceptable prejudice." While this is not literally true for any particular movement, the fact that the phrase has power tells us something about the culture. Since the twin victories of the civil rights and women's lib movements, and the championing of individual liberties of the 1960s, to label a person or view "prejudiced" is to indict that person or view. The implication is that the trend of history is toward an ever-increasing personal freedom (Swidler 1992).

By the 1980s, then, the common ground on which nearly all Americans agreed was "meritocracy." The word was invented in a 1959 satire by Michael D. Young, but was quickly adopted by politicians and commentators. It expresses the general idea that people's status ought to reflect their capabilities and efforts, not their backgrounds. Intense disagreement remained about how best to make this happen, both domestically and abroad, but the principle was essentially unchallenged. Like the other principles of fair play, these ideals are often not actually practiced, and elites have found many ways to maintain their status and pass it on to their children even in the context of ideas and claims about meritocracy (Hayes 2012).

Meanwhile, American foreign policy had been dominated by the Cold War, in which the United States backed countries and movements worldwide that opposed the Soviet Union. In some cases these were relatively democratic, particularly in Europe, where the Western European allies practiced, if anything, more democratic cultural and political systems than did the United States. But elsewhere, the record was far less clear. In Africa, Asia, and Latin America, as well as in the Middle East, the United States backed or assisted many deeply antidemocratic governments, such as South Africa, Iraq, El Salvador, and more. This, in turn, formed a formidable roadblock to democratization in these areas, since movements for democracy were often viewed skeptically and actively opposed and repressed by the American government.

So we return to the pivotal year, 1989, which changed all that. The Soviet prime minister, Mikhail Gorbachev, had begun a process called *glasnost* ("openness") and *perestroika* ("restructuring"), opening the Soviet bloc up to greater communication and cooperation with the West. Popular movements in the Soviet bloc – in Poland, East Germany, and Czechoslovakia in particular – quickly seized on the opportunity, ushering in democratic reforms and eventually the collapse of the Soviet Union and the Soviet bloc across Europe. No longer could third world movements find support from Soviet sources; no longer did the United States support undemocratic states only to contain the Soviets. These changes paved the way for democratic reforms in South Africa, Namibia, Zambia, Yemen, and across the world. Indeed, the revolutions of 1989 represented the most hopeful moment for worldwide democracy in centuries.

Despite the sense that the big struggle was over – scholar Francis Fukuyama famously called 1989 the "end of history" – there remained significant hurdles for democratic development and expansion. Not long after the demise of the Soviet Union, new ethnic tensions in central Europe and Africa raised new international concerns. And tensions in the Middle East, which had long played second fiddle to those of the Cold War, rose to the surface with the Iraqi invasion of Kuwait, the subsequent US-led Gulf War, and ultimately the 2001 terrorist bombings of the World Trade Center in New York and the Pentagon in Virginia. These terrorist attacks, and the wars that followed during the administration of George W. Bush, constituted the main concerns at the world level.

In the wake of the September 11, 2001, terrorist attacks, the American-led wars in Iraq and Afghanistan left both those countries without effective governments. In both cases, the governments prior to 2002 were corrupt, even brutal. The overthrow of those governments had unintended consequences as well, raising fears of power vacuums within which new antidemocratic movements could flourish. A new cadre of American and international experts emerged who tried to engage in "nation-building": establishing the necessary institutions to bring about a democratic and stable society. The experts turned to experiences in Eastern Europe and Africa in the 1990s. They argued for writing effective constitutions and implementing well-designed elections, along with freedom of the press and other civil liberties.

In these cases, along with many of the newly democratized countries that were part of the "Arab Spring" in 2011, democratic institutions did not bring about democratic outcomes. We will have much more to say about this problem – when the organizational trappings of democracy fail to bring about the substantive practices of democracy – but for now the key issue is that democratic *cultures* were absent. Having lived for generations under antidemocratic cultural systems, the people could not feasibly form a public immediately. So the preferences they expressed through elections were not actually the expressions of a public. As Lisa Wedeen (2008) argues for Yemen, democratic cultural practices and democratic institutions are related in a "dialectic" – the existence and development of each fuels and shapes that of the other.

The period since 1989 has seen enormous changes and important developments in domestic democratic practice as well. As recently as 1975, everyone in the United States who watched television around 6:30 in the evening – about 40 percent of all households – watched the same thing: a national news broadcast aimed at explaining the events of the day to a mass audience. By 1985, the introduction of cable and satellite television, as well as local entertainment channels, meant that families could choose among several television options including entertainment, sports, and different kinds of news. With this degree of choice came a *decrease* in political knowledge, probably because people could avoid learning things they considered difficult or not interesting (Prior 2007). Beginning around 1989, these technologies, joined later by internet-based media, were used by increasingly sophisticated media and marketing companies to allow consumers to choose news, information, and entertainment tailored ever more closely to their points of view. The advent of "social media" like Twitter and Facebook, as well as online sources of news and commentary, makes it ever easier for people to pick and choose the ideas they see and pay attention to, a pattern MIT Media Lab scholar Nicholas Negroponte dubbed the "Daily Me" (Negroponte 1995).

One effect of these technological changes has been the ability of politicians to target specific communities of people – certain races, ages, income levels, and areas – in a careful attempt to gain enough votes to win an election. The period after 1989 saw an increasing use of relatively obscure political tactics to manipulate politics by changing the assumptions about time in politics (Perrin et al. 2006) and an increasingly polarized electorate and public conversation. Beginning with the impeachment process of President Bill Clinton in 1998 and the Florida presidential election controversy of 2000, there has been a great emphasis on the political use of technical aspects of democracy (Perrin et al. 2006). This includes voting hours, early voting, absentee voting, efforts to make voting more difficult or more secure, redrawing of congressional districts to favor incumbents and specific parties, and the use of previously rare legislative tactics such as the filibuster and procedural votes on the national "debt ceiling" for partisan ends (Overton 2007). The Supreme Court's ruling in *Citizens United v. Federal Election Commission* and *Shelby County v. Holder* facilitated this process by, respectively, reducing controls on corporate spending in elections and removing federal scrutiny over election processes under the 1964 Voting Rights Act.

After Barack Obama's election in 2008 there was virtually no common ground between the political parties. The Republican Party in particular, led by its "Tea Party" faction, sought to block policy changes it saw as too liberal instead of engaging in compromises (Perrin et al. 2011; Mann and Orenstein 2012). By 2012, much of the public conversation was about polarization and the ways Washington was broken by the intransigence of partisans of both sides, but particularly Republican lawmakers opposed to President Obama (Maxwell and Parent 2012). Along with the Tea Party on the right, left-wing movements have grown as well, including the global phenomenon that began with Occupy Wall Street as well as protests over state governments' conservative turns in Wisconsin, Texas, Indiana, Ohio, and North Carolina. In North Carolina, where I live, a broad coalition of groups protested weekly through the spring of 2013 under the umbrella of "Moral Mondays," involving citizens in protest who had not previously been politically active. This is the new climate a decade into the twenty-first century: media fragmentation and political tools deployed for partisan gain are the big threats to democratic representation, while increased access to information and growing participation in movements and citizenship are its biggest opportunities.

This short and particular history has outlined a set of key turning points in American and world history that have contributed to our modern idea and practice of democracy (Table 1). Throughout the history of American democracy, the central tension between society and the self – the group and the individual – has been resolved using various policy, technological, and institutional mechanisms. It is that tension that provides the driving energy to democratic innovations and that threatens the health of the democratic polity. It is the difference between a group of people and a public, between a collection of people and a collectivity. Leading up to the massive transformations of 1989, each of these historical turning points can be considered a development in what sociologists and philosophers understand as *modernity*: a period of social life characterized by industrial development, scientific and technological progress, alongside poverty and strife, in which our concept of the individual and her relationship with society emerged (Berman 1982; Bauman 2001). At each point in time, publics confront the technologies, institutions, and practices of the time and consider how to use or reconfigure them to respond to the issues of the day. The ways they deploy, change, and create new technologies, institutions, and practices provide the resources for future interactions. That's the best model for thinking about democratic publics at a single point in time. Set that model in motion over time, and those publics use memories of prior experiences and orientations to the future (Mische 2009) to shape their relationships to these practices, technologies, and institutions.

History and Theory of Democracy

Table 1 Key moments in the development of democracy

Time range	Historical development	Scope and conception of citizenship and democracy
500 BC	Athenian democracy	Relatively direct, limited participation; emergence of the term "democracy"
Thirteenth–fourteenth centuries	Emergence of modern democratic practices in Europe (England and Venice)	
Eighteenth century	American and French Revolutions	Modern idea of the citizen, legitimacy of popular sovereignty; invention of "the people" as political subject
Early nineteenth century	Abolitionism	Populist protest as a political vehicle
Late nineteenth century	Reconstruction, women's suffrage movement	Expansion of citizenship rights; expansion of "the people" as inclusive, individualist idea; party patronage and vigorous civic life
Early twentieth century	Progressive era	Rationalization of politics; individual voting; secret ballot; expansion to near-universal suffrage
1930s	New Deal	Expansion of federal power; political reach in protecting people from economic ruin
1950–89	Postwar/Cold War	"Self-determination" as world standard; anti-Soviet focus; civil rights movement
1960s	Social movements	Civil rights, peace, and other movements worldwide expanding individualism, participation, self-expression
1989	Democracy's year	Soviet collapse; fall of the Berlin Wall; democratization in Africa and the Third World; Tiananmen Square protest in China
2001	9/11 and aftermath	New concerns about terrorism; Iraq and Afghanistan wars; Arab Spring

By 1989, modernity was developing into a new form, sometimes called postmodernity. If modernity was characterized by constant innovation in the big institutions of life, in postmodernity *every-thing* can change at the same time: all the parts of the system are moving at once. One symptom of that change was that technologies, institutions, and practices we counted on as having stable meanings and uses during the modern period became instruments of political gamesmanship to be used strategically. This shift brought new challenges and opportunities for democratic publics.

Democracy: A Practitioner's Guide

This historical background provides some insights into how to think about democracy. First and foremost, it's important to recognize that democracy has not always been seen as a good thing. The fact that virtually everyone believes in democracy (or claims to) is less than a century old. The American Founders, egged on by the situation in Europe and their own complaints against the king, evoked the idea of "the people" as the ultimate force for government. But even as the people they imagined was dramatically different from what we now think of as the people, they set up a framework for democratic development that would be reformed and extended over the years to become the way we now think not just about democracy but about all legitimate government.

As a first pass, consider the democracy the Founders envisioned. Private people, living their private lives, would naturally have ideas as to what they wanted government to do and not do. The job of the democratic process was to take that information – what those private individuals wanted – and have it relatively straightforwardly implemented by government. Think of this as a simple ladder – a democratic ladder (figure 3) – by which people's preferences are communicated and represented as government (Perrin and McFarland 2008). Preferences formed at the bottom of the ladder "climb" through information and institutions until they

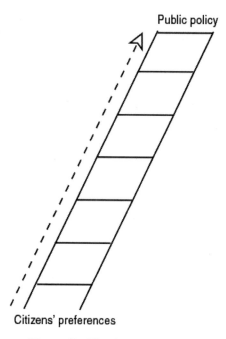

Public policy

Citizens' preferences

Figure 3   The democratic ladder

are successfully represented at the top of the ladder as government policies. As a first conception, the simple democratic ladder works well, and expresses what we basically think democracy ought to be about: government policies that represent the preferences of the people. And there are good reasons to think the simple democratic ladder really does capture some important elements of current American democratic practice.

Starting at the bottom of the ladder, the first question is this: does the public actually *have* ideas and preferences that government can follow? The answer is a cautious, qualified "yes." At least since the end of World War II, there is good evidence that Americans, combined through systems like public opinion polling and elections, have shown remarkably stable preferences on big issues. Indeed, when they have changed their preferences these changes have been well explained through reasonable, rational processes

(Page and Shapiro 1992). Furthermore, although people's views and ideas are certainly constrained by the kinds of information they have access to through media (chapter 5), there have been some important times when public opinion has *not* simply followed messages in the media, which suggests that the public is capable of interpreting information in ways that come from places other than the mass media (Walsh 2004; Perrin 2005).

Another important question to ask is whether and how these preferences are collective. As we saw, the American Founders took for granted an epistemic ideal of democracy: there was a right answer that was best for the people, and democracy was the most likely path to revealing that answer. Few people these days believe in this idea; generally, we think democracy works as a system for managing conflicts between the interests and visions of different groups of people – as Harold Lasswell famously put it, "who gets what, when, how" (Lasswell 1936; Page 1983). That means some people in a modern democracy will lose in any given election or policy decision. Somehow, a democratic culture needs to convince most of these people either that each of these decisions was legitimate even though it wasn't their preference; or that, having lost this time, they may nevertheless win in the future (Walzer 1983). Making people into citizens means making them believe these decisions are not only about them, but about their society more generally, and that in turn *still* depends on institutions that connect individual citizens with publics. Chapter 3 considers these institutions in greater detail.

The last big question for our simple democratic ladder is: how much is the government listening? In the years since the Watergate scandal, Americans' cynicism has grown, and many Americans don't believe the government actually pays attention to the views and wishes of people like themselves (Perrin and Smolek 2009; Hetherington 2005). But research suggests that, in many cases, the government *is* listening, in that important government decisions often reflect public opinion polling on those topics (Manza and Cook 2002; Burstein 2003, 2006). Chapter 4 examines public opinion and government responsiveness to it.

Our discussion of the democratic ladder so far shows a couple of key points to keep in mind. First, democracy, in any form, is *always* representative; there is no such thing as direct democracy. At various times in American history, reformers have sought to create "direct" democracy, where citizens debate (Bryan 2004) or vote directly on matters of importance. Indeed, many states offer the opportunity for voters to put matters directly on ballots, a practice that goes back to the Progressive reforms. And a common claim is that representative democracy is a necessary shortcut: a way to approximate direct democracy in a public that's simply too big to handle direct democracy. This idea reaches back to John Adams, one of the Founding Fathers: "In a large society, inhabiting an extensive country, it is impossible that the whole should assemble, to make laws: The first necessary step then, is, to depute power from the many, to a few of the most wise and good" (Adams 1776). But even a direct democracy would only serve to move the representation up the democratic ladder: in the end, any democratic process must always seek to represent citizens' preferences in policy, and like representation in music, art, and science, those preferences always get changed, shifted, distorted, magnified, and even created through the representation process. This fact doesn't make democracy impossible, or even imperfect – it highlights the fact that we should understand what it means to be represented, what the different options are, and how ways of representing have long-lasting, profound effects on democratic citizenship.

The second key point is that the simple democratic ladder is too simple. People don't just form preferences from private life; they listen to, and learn from, others' practices and past policies (Valelly 1993). Media and institutions don't just carry citizen preferences upwards to government, they also carry ideas and information down the ladder from government back to citizens, and increasingly side-to-side to allow citizens to speak to one another (Perrin and Vaisey 2008; Perrin 2012; Kreiss 2012). A better version of the democratic ladder is the one in figure 4, which lets us recognize that democratic representation is a two-way street: each representation changes not just the policy but the preferences being represented. But even figure 4 is too

Public policy

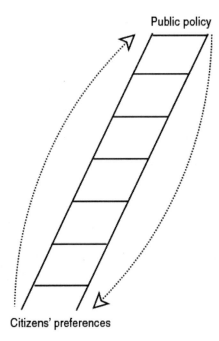

Citizens' preferences

Figure 4   The two-way democratic ladder

simple. There are conflicts and disagreements among segments of the population at the bottom, and differences among agencies and parts of the government and policy apparatus at the top. Some of these conflicts, disagreements, and differences are quite profound. Much of the rest of this book complicates the image in figure 4. In chapter 6 we'll revisit the democratic ladder and add in the information from the rest of the book.

The next several chapters consider each of the elements of the complex democratic ladder shown in figure 4. Chapter 2 considers the individual and small-group elements of democratic citizenship: *what do people need to know, do, and be to be good citizens?* Chapter 3 comes from the other direction, paying attention to the institutions of governance and representation: *what patterns of systems, knowledge, belief, and incentives make society more and less democratic?* We then consider two of the most important institutions that mediate between citizens and governments: public opinion and polling (chapter 4) and the media (chapter 5). Finally, in chapter 6 we consider some of the ways people have argued for reforming democracy and the ways such reforms might affect the democratic culture and performance of the United States and its citizens.

2

Voting, Civil Society, and Citizenship

For democracy to make sense, people need to be able to feel and then act as part of a public – of the *demos* to be represented. This chapter addresses individual-level elements of democratic citizenship: *what people need to know, think, do, and be to act democratically.*

Many studies of political behavior in the United States concentrate on voting as the main outcome and on people's individual characteristics that contribute to voting as the most important elements. The classic *The American Voter*, for example, described people's voting decisions as a "funnel," in which decisions about whether and for whom to vote could be best analyzed by looking at individual characteristics such as race, education, social class, and party identification just before the election (Campbell et al. 1960), a model that was largely successfully reproduced in 2008 (Lewis-Beck et al. 2008). Similarly, Wolfinger and Rosenstone's study, *Who Votes?*, explains voting participation based on individual characteristics of citizens (Wolfinger and Rosenstone 1980). But these approaches assume that the important causes of voting or not voting are about individuals, not the groups or societies they are part of, so they largely ignore the social contexts and patterns of voting decisions (Rolfe 2012).

Several other important strains of research try to identify the ways basic properties of individuals shape their political behaviors. The study of political psychology, for example, locates people's political beliefs in elements of their personalities. Political

48

psychologist Jonathan Haidt argues that the core difference between liberals and conservatives has to do with which core moral values they hold more dear: values of fairness and preventing harm, alongside loyalty, obedience to authority, and purity. "Within Western societies, we consistently find an ideological effect in which religious and cultural conservatives value and rely upon all five foundations, whereas liberals value and rely upon the harm and fairness foundations primarily" (Haidt 2007, 1001). Some scholars have even sought to identify genetic roots for political views, arguing that genetic influences on personality are a fundamental cause of political views (e.g., Verhulst et al. 2012; Hatemi and McDermott 2012; Smith et al. 2012) and participation (Fowler and Dawes 2008).

These approaches, though, tend to ignore the ways similar attitudes or even biological structures might have meant different things at different historical moments or in different cultural contexts. People learn to "package" attitudes into political identities based on their cultural commitments and environments. Again, a sociological angle provides a better way to understand people's attitudes and participation: people are fundamentally social, and they form preferences, attitudes, and decisions through interactions with groups they are part of and those they are not. While individual personalities are likely important elements of political decision making, their influence is filtered through, and ultimately dwarfed by, the social, cultural, institutional, and technical processes that organize democratic citizenship. The key, then, to understanding individuals' political participation is understanding how individuals form and experience their political and *social* environments.

Civil Society and the Public Sphere

The first important element of citizenship practices is the existence of, and participation in, civil society. From developing democracies in Latin America, Africa, and post-communist Europe to Tocqueville's observations about American democratic culture, the idea that people belong to *society*, which is distinct from both the market and the state, is a key feature of vibrant democracy. While governments can and should take steps to help foster civil society, and can certainly do things to quash it, by its very nature civil society is the product of independent action by groups of citizens. Civic engagement requires thinking of oneself as part of a society, recognizing connections with that society and its public, and respecting the legitimacy of divergent views on public matters. While these are not necessarily active tasks, engagement can sometimes require active work such as dissent, voice, and organizing.

In the specific sense, the second element – citizenship – is about the legal connection between a person and her state. But here I treat citizenship more broadly, as the set of obligations people bear toward their polity and the obligations the polity bears toward its members. These require developing a thick *democratic imagination* (Perrin 2006) and paying attention to the connections and disconnections between public discourse and state action. Citizenship is sometimes about *behaviors* like voting and communication with legislators, but is also about *knowledge* and *beliefs*: paying attention to political matters and seeking engagement with them. Research on *attentive publics* (e.g., Arnold 1990) and political knowledge (Delli Carpini and Keeter 1997) demonstrates the importance of simply paying attention as a citizenship task.

Political *behavior* involves citizens enacting their beliefs and knowledge to make claims on public culture and the government. While there is no hard and fast line between kinds of citizenship that are based on communicating and discussing (reading, writing, talking, deliberating) and political behavior, there remains a distinction to be made. Thinking, talking, considering citizens need to vote (or decide carefully not to), visit legislators, write letters to the editor, and so on in order to put ideals into practice.

Voting

Already in the early years of the United States, Tocqueville observed the passion and excitement that surrounded an election in American culture:

> As the election draws near, intrigues intensify, and agitation increases and spreads. The citizens divide into several camps, each behind its candidate. A fever grips the entire nation. The election becomes the daily grist of the public papers, the subject of private conversations, the aim of all activity, the object of all thought, the sole interest of the moment.
>
> Immediately after fortune renders its verdict, of course, this ardor dissipates, calm is restored, and the river, having briefly overflowed its banks, returns peacefully to its bed. But is it not astonishing that such a storm could have arisen? (Tocqueville 2004 [1835], 152–3)

Although this chapter will ultimately consider behavior well beyond voting, let's start with this most common sort of participation. At least since the advent of the secret ballot in the early twentieth century, when voting became largely an individual task, the basic requirement of American citizenship has been deciding for whom (and what) to vote, and taking the time to cast that vote. Voting has become a nearly sacred activity in American life. When I ask my undergraduate students: "What does it mean to be a good citizen?" they almost invariably respond first by saying that good citizenship entails voting. Of course, the picture gets more complicated as we think about who actually votes, who should vote, and what preparations should go into voting. But voting is a ritual Americans use to imagine and reaffirm their connection to a national community they cannot see or actively connect with (Allen 2004). Pundits and analysts alike routinely bemoan the fact that too few Americans vote (Patterson 2002; Valelly 1990). After 50 years of concerns about voter turnout and attempts to increase voting, the extraordinary mobilization by the Barack Obama campaign in 2008 erased all the declines of the previous half-century.

One of the most interesting pieces of evidence of the importance

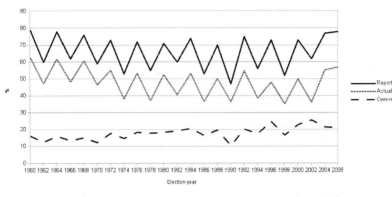

Figure 5   Reported and actual voter turnout, presidential elections,
1960–2012

of voting in our imagination about democracy is how many
people *say* they voted when they didn't actually do so. Between
1960 and 2008, about 17 percent more people reported voting
in presidential elections when they were asked on polls than had
actually voted in the elections (figure 5). Almost as many – 15
percent – misreported voting in non-presidential elections. In
survey research, this is called *social desirability bias*: people tend
to tell pollsters that they do "good" things more, and "bad" things
less, than they actually do. These lies demonstrate that voting
clearly means a lot to Americans.

From one point of view, *not voting* is the rational thing to do.
Voting costs time, energy, transportation, and more, and the
chance that one's own vote will actually change the election's
outcome is extraordinarily small. It makes sense to stay home
(Downs 1957). Deciding in this way is called *instrumental voting*:
deciding whether to vote, and for whom, based on whether the
voter believes her vote could make a difference in the election's
outcome. By some estimates there are around 500,000 elected
officials in the United States (Shelley 1996), which translates into
about a quarter-million elections held each year, on average. Not
a single one has been determined by a one-vote difference. In most
elections that are decided even by hundreds of votes – the 2000
Florida presidential election, for example – there are long legal

battles, recounts, and debates over which votes should count and why, all of which mean that any one person's vote is that much less likely to determine the outcome. For any individual voter looking at any one of those elections, then, the calculation should be clear: there is no good reason to spend the time, energy, attention, and resources to cast a vote that is virtually certain not to make the difference between winning and losing.

And yet 140 million of us do it. We take time away from our responsibilities, travel to a place we might never otherwise go, wait in line (potentially a very long one), and emerge with nothing more than a tiny lapel sticker proclaiming "I Voted" and a feeling of superiority over our non-voting fellow citizens. Clearly, deciding to vote is more than straightforward, individual, rational choice-making based on costs and benefits. People may choose to vote because they hope outcomes will be better for others they care about, not just for themselves (Edlin et al. 2007). And they may care not just about the actual outcome of the election but about what some people call the *mandate*: how many votes their chosen candidate wins or loses by. Since these margins are reported in the media, it may be reasonable for a citizen to vote in order to influence the size of the win (or loss). Many people also feel that voting is a civic duty to activists and soldiers who fought for the right to do so, or that they need to counter the votes cast by others.

All of these are ways in which the individual choice to vote might be expanded by recognizing that voting is never truly individual or isolated. It is never just the educated, emotion-free weighing of issues and the subsequent casting of a ballot. It is a ritual in which lone citizens express personal beliefs that reflect the core of who they are and what they want for their country, balancing strategic behavior with the opportunity to express their inner selves to the world. In contrast to instrumental voting, this is *expressive voting*: voting in order to express oneself, to make a point to the public.

In other words, voting in America has at least two faces: the first, a cold, calculating form of citizenship where what anthropologist Julia Paley calls the "choice-making citizen" (Paley 2001) weighs the costs and benefits of particular policies and votes accordingly; the second, an expression of personal identity and belief. We can't understand who votes, and how, without understanding the two faces of voting that come together in citizens' minds and activities. As productive as the *American Voter* model of studying voting has been, conceiving of voting as decisions made by individual citizens who understand the issues, weigh them, and dispassionately select a candidate has put limits on how scholars have understood voting and how Americans have decided whether, and how, to vote.

Convinced that registration barriers were keeping particularly low-income and African-American citizens from the polls, social scientists Frances Fox Piven and Richard Cloward argued for making registration easier in their influential 1988 book *Why Americans Don't Vote*. In 1993 their campaign paid off with passage of the Motor-Voter Bill, which required states to allow citizens to register to vote when they applied for driver's licenses, substantially reducing the difficulty of registration. The same principle – making voting as easy and convenient as possible – is behind recent trends to allow "no excuses" early voting, "vote by mail," "one-stop voting," and other reforms. Interestingly, most studies have found little evidence that these reforms have succeeded in increasing voter turnout. Indeed, they "may backfire . . . if the symbolic virtue of voting is reinforced by the requirement that one stand in lines and follow arcane procedures, or if citizens are less likely to behave in a public-spirited way if their neighbors are not at the polls to greet (and observe) them" (Rolfe 2012, 2–3). The message citizens get from these reforms may be that voting is only worth doing if it's easy, a message that may ultimately discourage them from making the necessary effort to vote.

Voting in America is among the most cherished ways of expressing political individuality, and in many cases it's the only way citizens actually participate in their political communities. To take part in this ritual, citizens must often decipher complicated ballots in carefully created and guarded isolation. This isolation is not just physical, it's also psychological. We work hard to give citizens the idea that the vote they will cast is *their own*, that the vote says something important about what the voter truly believes and who she is, and that it is among the most important things she can do as a citizen.

Consider the candidates who periodically run for president as independents or nominees of minor parties. In virtually all such cases, the independent candidate stands no real likelihood of winning and is often accused of being a "spoiler" – a candidate who, by virtue of being in the race, distorts the outcome from what it otherwise would be. Voters are regularly implored not to "waste votes" on such candidates, since their votes would be ineffective or even counterproductive.

Yet voters continue to cast ballots for such candidates in substantial numbers, and the 1992 and 2000 elections were probably significantly affected by these votes. In recent elections with a significant third-party candidate on the ballot, 4 million voters (about 4 percent of the total) in 2000 and a striking 20.4 million (nearly 20 percent) in 1992 "wasted" these votes. Even in the closely contested 2004 election, in which there was no serious third-party candidate, more than 1.2 million voters (about 1 percent) voted for a candidate other than George W. Bush and John Kerry. Why?

If we understand a vote as a strategic resource, something like a purchase – exchanging something of symbolic value for one selection among several – it's impossible to figure out why citizens would "throw away" their votes by casting them for a candidate with no possibility of winning. But if we instead consider voting as individuals' opportunity to express their own private, core beliefs, it is priceless.

Consider, too, the controversy over the so-called butterfly ballots in the 2000 Florida presidential election. In heavily Jewish and Democratic Palm Beach County, an unlikely proportion of citizens voted for right-wing candidate Pat Buchanan, whom many Jews considered an anti-Semite, rather than the more likely Al Gore.

In an important analysis, political scientist Henry Brady and colleagues showed that most of that vote was probably due to confusing ballot design – a conclusion shared by Buchanan himself (Wand et al. 2001). Apart from the strategic value of these votes, the idea that the voter's core beliefs might have been (falsely) expressed as a preference for Buchanan was the stuff of anxiety and jokes alike. A spate of humorous bumper stickers and other materials proclaimed "Jews for Buchanan" and "Don't Blame Me, I Voted for Gore . . . I Think". This anxiety persists with reformers' insistence that electronic voting machines leave a "paper trail" – a way, if all else fails, to presumably rescue future elections from technical snafus by linking voters back to their own votes.

In both of these cases, our votes are understood as expressions of who we are, our deepest ideals and values. But this presents a strange paradox. Why should such a thoroughly social behavior, a practice that expresses our core values about how society should be structured, be practiced in enforced privacy? The answer lies not only in the history of voting, but also in the importance of ritual. As political theorist Danielle S. Allen writes (2004), the ritual of voting *simultaneously* allows us to imagine ourselves as members of an abstract national community *and* as effective, thinking, competent individuals.

Rituals like voting are the practices we use to hold society together – to help us, in the words of the anthropologist Benedict Anderson (2006), imagine ourselves as a community (Allen 2004). We carry with us the memories of elections past, refracted through the collective imagination provided by the news media and everyday conversations. Voting connects citizens to these memories, making us a part of them and infusing them with meaning.

Nearly 50 years after *The American Voter*, a team of political scientists analyzed the 2000 version of the National Elections Studies, which the original book had launched (Lewis-Beck et al. 2008). Interviewing thousands of voters in isolation (and also separate from their voting booths and their feelings on voting day), they found that the most important elements of the voting decision remained individual in character: "the basic ensemble of the variables measured in *The American Voter* offers, then and now, a rather complete accounting of US presidential vote choice" (427). That ensemble comprises individual characteristics, membership in specific groups, and attitudes toward specific issues: a suite of measurable elements of individuals that explains voting at that individual level.

It still holds true that if you tell me who you are, what you know, whom you know, and what you believe, chances are good I can tell you (and the world) whether you will vote, and for whom. Wealthy, white, male, and Southern voters are more likely to vote Republican, though those with more education, poorer, and women voters are likely to vote Democratic, and these effects are different in different states (Gelman 2010). Who we are as citizens – our class, race, sex, region of the country, and education – does say a lot about whether we are likely to vote and for whom. Stable political identifications – particularly identification with a political party, the importance of which *The American Voter* first demonstrated and which remains crucial – tell us yet more.

Civil Society

In order to grasp how citizens base their decisions about voting and other matters on the communities they are part of, we need to back up and consider the idea of *civil society*. Civil society is the area of life that isn't governed by economic markets, private family life, or government actions.[1] Each of these areas of life tends to encourage people to act in their own self-interest. In markets, such as when people are employees in the workplace or consumers buying goods, people generally try to get the best deal for themselves, which in turn means they are often in competition with others. In private and family life, people are often motivated by the desire to help those to whom they are closest, again often in competition with others outside their private lives. And in the sphere of government regulation, individual citizens' engagement and that of groups is often subordinated to the bureaucratic work of administration, although government can often foster civil society as well (Skocpol 1996). Of course it is possible, even common, for people to bring ideas about right and wrong and the common good into each of these realms. But that requires work; each of the realms encourages people to think relatively narrowly about their own interests. By contrast, life in civil society tends to encourage people to think outside their own self-interest, to consider the needs of others, of publics, and sometimes even of the common good.

Jürgen Habermas, in his groundbreaking 1962 study *The Structural Transformation of the Public Sphere*, explored the historical origins of civil society in the lively cultural salons and coffeehouses of eighteenth-century Europe. Used to the governing power of royalty, people (and, particularly, the growing middle class or *bourgeoisie*) lacked much opportunity to communicate with one another and think in common. The free spaces provided by the cultural salons offered the opportunity to think about common interests – first literature and art, and eventually political and social matters. It was in these salons that the European public emerged: a social and cultural community outside the boundaries of government, market, and family. Habermas traces the importance of this public in establishing a democratic culture, as people became accustomed to the idea that they could have, debate, and develop opinions and ideas as members of a public. The conditions for producing a public require private institutions too – those coffeehouses were private establishments, and the media, which host many current public spheres, exist in private life as well. As crucial as it is to maintain a public space, such spaces cannot exist without the support and boundaries provided by private, governmental, and economic institutions.

The development of publics through civil society was not limited to Europe or to the specific time period Habermas studied. The general idea – that citizens can come together to deliberate over important matters and, through that process, become a public – is widespread. Wedeen (2008), for example, shows that a similar process takes place in contemporary Yemen, where official political life is constrained by a repressive government. But citizens often gather to discuss literary, artistic, practical, and political matters while chewing qāt, a plant containing a stimulant similar to caffeine. During these qāt chews, Yemeni citizens deliberate over many topics, some substantial portion of which are centered on the "common good" (Wedeen 2008, 118). In the process, Wedeen shows, they come to think of themselves as Yemenis: as members of the Yemeni public.

They promote citizen awareness and produce subjects who critically debate political issues, allowing participants to build an agonistically[2] inclined political world in which disagreements are entertained in common. They are the site for the performance of citizenship, for the critical self-assertion of citizens the existence of whom is made possible through these exercises of deliberation. (Wedeen 2008, 120)

The importance of civil society has been recognized across numerous countries and time periods. During the Cold War, dissidents in Eastern Europe such as Polish journalist Adam Michnik and Czech playwright Václav Havel documented the ways the totalitarian regimes they lived under worked hard to dominate not just the economic and governmental spheres of life but the cultural as well. In his widely discussed essay "The Power of the Powerless," Havel – who would later become president of a democratic Czechoslovakia – writes about the empty symbols that were imposed on the population and that served to undermine the development of an independent public:

The manager of a fruit and vegetable shop places in his window, among the onions and carrots, the slogan: 'Workers of the World, Unite!' Why does he do it? . . . Is he genuinely enthusiastic about the idea of unity among the workers of the world? . . . I think it can safely be assumed that the overwhelming majority of shopkeepers never think about the slogans they put in their windows, nor do they use them to express their real opinions . . . He put them all into the window simply because it has been done that way for years, because everyone does it, and because that is the way it has to be. (Havel 1985: 27)

Like Habermas' evaluation of the development of publics in the eighteenth century, the saturation of culture and the resulting handicap in publics' emergence are not bound to a particular time, place, or culture. Wedeen's study of Syria under the regime of Hafiz al-Asad shows very much the same thing: confronted with symbols of Asad's power everywhere, Syrians found themselves unable to construct an independent public in the constrained civil society that ensued:

Voting, Civil Society, and Citizenship

In Syria, in other words, it is impossible *not* to experience the difference between what social scientists, following Max Weber, might conceive as a charismatic, loyalty-producing regime and its anxiety-inducing simulacrum. There is a shabbiness to Asad's cult, even a cynicism about it. (Wedeen 1999: 3)

The general idea is that governments and cultures can undermine the development of civil society by saturating the culture with meaningless symbols and words; authentic connections between citizens become hard to create (see Schweppenhäuser and Köhne 2011). The ways in which images, ideas, and language affect citizens' perceptions and behaviors will be covered in more detail in chapter 4.

Alexis de Tocqueville, the perceptive French visitor who characterized nineteenth-century American society in his monumental work *Democracy in America*, famously called America a "nation of joiners," recognizing that Americans seemed more likely to join together in volunteer organizations to solve problems than to expect solutions from professional or governmental institutions. In the American context, there is a long tradition of concern that individuals and these authentically independent organizations will be swallowed up by mass society. Political scientist Robert Putnam was widely recognized for his 2000 book *Bowling Alone*, in which he diagnosed twentieth-century Americans as too wrapped up in individual pursuits to sustain the vibrant civil society that Tocqueville had observed and, Putnam claimed, that had sustained American democracy for its first two-plus centuries.

While, to be sure, there have likely been declines in Americans' engagement in organized civic life – from bowling leagues to PTAs and Elks' clubs – Americans still remain more involved in such pursuits, more likely to volunteer, and more involved in non-governmental organizations like religious and civic organizations than citizens of virtually any other country (Paxton 2002). However, these organizations do not always support democratic behavior. Nina Eliasoph showed that many such organizations actually discourage their members from talking about political

60

matters (Eliasoph 1998), and some kinds of organizations are much better than others at supporting rich democratic discussions and, therefore, political imaginations (Perrin 2005, 2006).

Where do Preferences Come From?

The Founders' idea was that preferences were essentially private things. People lived lives that were basically private in character, focused mainly on their economic, religious, and family lives. The needs they had from government were for government to leave them alone and to represent their views and ideas. The sources of those views and ideas were the private lives people led, combined, perhaps, through the voluntary organizations Tocqueville documented.

That idea continues to inform the way many journalists and pundits think about representation to this day. When we think about opinions, we think about them as the property of individual citizens. They can be discovered through various mechanisms, including public opinion polls, various forms of public deliberation, and elections. Americans work hard to maintain this idea – that their views are their own, not the product of the communities they belong to. But there's a lot of evidence to suggest that, in fact, people learn a lot about what they believe, and what they want to believe, by paying attention to others they respect and they think are like them. In fact, people are subject to what sociologist Christian Smith (2003, 10), building on the work of Charles Taylor (1985), calls "second order desires about desires": people don't just want something, they *want* to want it. That's because what people want – whether it's a moral or political preference or just a taste for particular music, food, or art – is a key way people identify themselves as part of communities and publics.

One of the phrases many voters use when asked about their party loyalty is "I vote for the man, not for the party." The idea is clear: an independent thinker, the voter insists that she is not swayed by the package of views and supporters indicated by a candidate's party affiliation. Instead, the voter claims to evaluate the specific policies, character, and personal history of the candidates in order to decide which best suits her preference. This is an appealing idea; if each voter did this, the election would reliably represent the private needs and desires of the majority of the population, and the party structure – which many people see as corrupting authentic preferences – would be unnecessary.

In fact, there are not very many truly independent voters (Keith 1992). Most voters identify themselves as members or registrants of one or the other political party. More importantly, most voters who identify themselves as "independents" or "unaffiliated" lean strongly toward actually voting for candidates affiliated with one or the other party. Their decision to identify themselves as "independent" is about sending a message to the world and to themselves about *what kind of person they are*. It's a curious paradox, and one that shows up in various areas of sociology: people broadcast and defend their individuality as a way of marking their membership in a group. In this case, voters who affirm their independence do so because they are members of a group that values independence.

Imagine that you are a pure citizen of this type, trying to live the twenty-first-century version of the ideal of the independent citizen.[3] You believe you should make up your own mind about whom to vote for. You believe you should know enough about both – or all – candidates to make an informed choice between or among them. And you also need some basis for making that decision. Will it be based on which candidate will be best for you and your family? For your community, your state, your region? For the common good of the whole country? Let's take each of these questions in order.

First is the question of becoming informed enough to make a choice. There are many, many sources of information about political candidates, particularly at the national level, though more local races often have less information available. The first place many citizens think of to go for information is the candidates' internet websites. The first of these sites for presidential candidates appeared during the 1996 election, the web having become a widespread medium in the early 1990s. The 1996 sites were a shadow of what they had become by 2012, less than 20 years later. Candidates in 1996 saw their websites as just a way of getting information out to voters – information that they would otherwise have distributed on paper (Klinenberg and Perrin 2000). Campaigns' use of the web and other internet media has become much more sophisticated since then (Kreiss 2012), and in many ways these mirror other forms of media instead of the relatively calm information sources they were in 1996 (we turn to these changes in chapter 5). But the candidates' websites in their original form are one way that a motivated voter could become informed about the options.

Another source of information is the news media: newspapers, television, and radio, and their online versions. There you could find information that compares the candidates against one another, which might be helpful. After all, just reading each candidate's position papers on all the issues has a number of drawbacks. First, it's tough to know how each candidate will balance the priorities of all the issues: maybe the one who agrees with you more closely on a matter that is important to you doesn't actually plan on doing anything about that matter when she or he is elected! Second, all those position papers are written in a way that makes the candidate who put them out seem more attractive to you: how do you know the flaws in each candidate's argument, the ways in which he or she falls short?[4]

The truth is, it's nearly impossible for most citizens to be fully informed about all the issues that go into a modern political campaign, whether that's a presidential campaign or one further down the ballot. Partially that's because there's just too much information out there to be considered, so any but the most committed of citizens – with the most free time on her hands – would just be stymied by the task of considering it all. But the problem goes beyond mere information overload. Particularly in American politics, where as a practical matter most voters are selecting between two candidates for office,[5] deciding between the candidates means prioritizing which issues, and which positions on those issues, are the most important.

Imagine, for example, that you believe traditional family values are best: the government should encourage people to be married before they have children, to marry people only of the opposite sex, and to reject abortion except in very extreme circumstances. You believe such traditional families are the glue that holds society together, and they should not be undermined by schools teaching children about sexuality or contraception. In general, while perhaps you don't think women's rights should be *restricted*, you probably approve of women staying at home to raise children while their husbands work for pay to support the family.

At the same time, though, you recognize the importance of a strong school system, and you have seen for yourself the difficulties some families have making ends meet. You worry that the widening gap between the rich – who can afford the best for their children – and the middle class means American society is becoming ever less fair. You are, essentially, socially conservative but fiscally progressive. In order to vote for a major candidate you would probably have to choose between these values, because, in general, neither party tends to run candidates with that combination of values. Generally, candidates that are socially conservative also champion fiscally conservative, low-tax, and low-spending agendas, while those that prefer greater social services tend to be socially progressive as well.

In the United States, many citizens are used to thinking with the coalitions of issues that surround the two major parties. In general, the Democratic Party – and its candidates – can be expected to be more favorable to organized labor, gay and lesbian rights, safety-net programs for the poor, abortion rights, and civil rights for minorities. The Democrats also generally oppose military intervention in other countries. By contrast, the Republican Party and candidates prefer limited government involvement in the economy, favoring lower taxes and less assistance for the poor. The Republicans have also traditionally been generally less favorable toward increasing rights for women and minorities, and tend to be more aggressive about foreign military involvement (although presidents from both parties have engaged in warfare). Most attentive American voters in the late twentieth and early twenty-first century would recognize these descriptions, although of course there is significant variation among Republicans and among Democrats. But more importantly, these combinations of positions have changed over time. What we think of as the normal package of beliefs and preferences – being "liberal" or "conservative" – is really the result of the fact that we see the world through the political parties and their coalitions (Perrin et al. 2014).

And these coalitions change over relatively short periods of time. For example, in the wake of the election of Barack Obama as president in 2008, many Americans think of the Republican Party as the one most opposed to deficit spending – that is, to having the federal government borrow money to pay for services it provides. Indeed, polls taken since then consistently show that voters believe Republicans will be better able to "handle" the deficit and debt. Political scientists have gone so far as to say Republicans "own" the issue (for more on issue ownership, see Petrocik et al. 2003). Democrats have cried foul over this image, noting that Republican presidents have presided over far more deficit spending than have Democrats (e.g., Liberal Outposts 2011). More importantly from a historic perspective, though, is the fact that *Democrats* "owned" the issue as recently as the 1988 election. Following Ronald Reagan's second term, Vice-President George Bush was running a campaign touting the prosperity Americans enjoyed during the administration. Journalist Tom Brokaw asked Democratic vice-presidential candidate Lloyd Bentsen about the sense of prosperity, and Bentsen answered: "You know, if you let me write $200 billion worth of hot checks every year, I could give you an illusion of prosperity too."

There are other examples of issue ownership – Democrats, for example, are often assumed to be better able to help poor people, while Republicans are considered strong on national security and defense. These images are relatively durable, even though they do shift at times. The most important thing about them, though, is that they work to help citizens gauge and understand what parties and candidates they tend to agree with because of the mix of issues, ideas, and approaches they stand for.

To be sure, there are plenty of citizens, and groups, whose political ideas don't fit neatly into one or another of the parties. The ideology known as "libertarianism" forms one such group. Libertarians believe, in general, that the activities of government should be strictly limited to its necessary functions: defending the borders and maintaining the rule of law. Thus libertarians usually agree with Democrats on matters of rights. Why should government, they reason, enforce different privileges for people based on their sex, race, or sexual orientation? On the other hand, they generally agree with Republicans on matters of economics such as taxes and government spending, since they see Democrats' support for progressive taxation and programs for the poor as going well beyond government's proper role. Libertarians and others with views that don't fit well with either of the two parties' platforms often find themselves frustrated by how resilient the two-party system is. In the next chapter we'll consider how the American election system reinforces this system and how that might be different with different kinds of political organization.

So political parties are one of the tools citizens can use to make sense of the chaotic political landscape. Indeed, public opinion polling shows that party identification – whether a voter feels like a Democrat, a Republican, or something else – is very durable. People rarely change their identifications, *even when their own political preferences don't agree with those of their party*. To examine why this happens, some of my colleagues and I designed an experiment just before the 2004 presidential election (Prasad et al. 2009a, 2009b). We looked for voters who had voted for George W. Bush, the incumbent Republican president, in 2000, but who also said they disagreed with him on at least one of two important issues in the campaign: the 2002 federal income tax cuts and the relationship between the Iraq War and the terrorist attacks of September 11, 2001. We contacted these voters and asked if we could interview them about their voting plans.

What we found was that, in many cases, these voters were motivated to avoid changing parties. Even though they knew and acknowledged that they disagreed with President Bush on these key matters, many nevertheless planned to vote for him, and were excited to do so. Why? A few did tell us that other issues mattered more: one, for example, disagreed on the tax cuts and the war, but felt that preventing abortion was more important than those issues. But far more people said those issues were very important but came up with new ways of explaining their decisions to stick with President Bush. And in most cases, these reasons focused on two things: the voters' sense of the personal character of President Bush compared with that of John Kerry, his challenger (Prasad et al. 2009b) and the trust that Bush – and Republicans in general – acted honorably and in good faith (Prasad et al. 2009a).

These voters were doing something called *motivated reasoning*. They were psychologically committed to voting for their candidate and their party, even though they disagreed with some of the important positions the candidate represented. The process of coming up with new explanations – rationalizations – for supporting the candidate is motivated reasoning (Kunda 1990; Achen and Bartels 2006). Simply put: when we want to believe something, we often use various ways of searching for and choosing particular information that will let us believe it. Some forms of motivated reasoning are deeply ingrained in people's brain functions (Westen et al. 2006), but personal identity and cultural membership likely play important roles in encouraging people to behave in this way as well.

Motivated reasoning seems very opposed to Americans' common-sense idea of informed citizenship. Our ideal is more like what political scientists call *Bayesian updating*: a fancy term that just means using new information to continuously update a decision. A voter is doing Bayesian updating when she pays attention to what's going on, continuously evaluating whether new ideas, events, or information provide grounds for a new position.

Here's the problem. Bayesian updating is *hard*. It takes an enormous amount of work on the part of a citizen to gather and sort through all that information, and all the more to insure that the information gathered is complete, accurate, and comprehensive. We'll return to systemic problems in the information environment in chapter 5, but even granting that such information is readily available, the cost in time and resources for everyone to do this alone, and for every issue, and then to balance those issues, would be prohibitive. It's not even clear, based on research in psychology, that people *could* do that kind of work if they wanted to. From this angle, motivated reasoning is a reasonable shortcut for voters to use to sift through the enormous amounts of important information.

There are many other tools voters use to take rational short-cuts through the information maze. As discussed above, political parties are powerful ways of combining issues into packages – thereby allowing many, if not most, citizens to decide on the whole package instead of needing to pick through each of the many approaches. To the extent that a citizen believes he is a Republican or a Democrat – or even just that Republicans or Democrats tend to represent him better – he can reliably decide to vote for Republican or Democratic candidates, thereby saving himself a lot of time and trouble! Even if, say, he would prefer the other party's candidates over his own 10 percent of the time, he might still decide that it's not worth his time to make his decisions only 10 percent better. While that's not our image of committed, informed, deliberate citizenship, it's a lot simpler and results in the same decisions most of the time.

Another version of this approach that many Americans find less objectionable than just sticking with political parties is political *heuristics*. A heuristic is just an image or a general rule that someone uses as a shortcut; even if it doesn't result in the best answer to a problem, a heuristic often can result in the most "cost-efficient answer," in that it can give a pretty good answer without too much trouble.

In the case of politics, voters often use heuristics to evaluate candidates and ideas if they don't have all the information, or if it's too difficult to get all that information. A commonly discussed heuristic is the group of issues known as "social issues." Since at least the 1980s, social issues have included views on abortion, with so-called "values voters" opposing abortion rights. In the late twentieth and early twenty-first century, other issues joined these: tolerance for rights for gays and lesbians, research using human embryonic stem cells, among others. These issues are similar in many ways: how people come down on them tends to be determined by their religious and moral views, and they are all areas of behavior and regulation that are not economic. In other words, people usually decide on them based on their moral and religious ideas, not because of ideas about economic rationality or even efficiency. That's not always true; of course a voter could oppose abortion but favor marriage rights for gays and lesbians, in which case this particular heuristic wouldn't work. But for many voters, since these positions tend to go together, knowing that a candidate is appealing to values voters is sufficient.[6] Indeed, there are websites that offer information about how to vote if you are a values voter, making it even easier for a citizen who believes in the whole package to know how to vote without extra work.

Finally, another way of reducing the work necessary to form a position good enough to vote on is to remain part of an *attentive public*. Douglas Arnold (1990) described citizens in attentive publics in order to understand why members of Congress paid attention to the ideas and preferences of citizens in their districts, even when those citizens didn't vote. A citizen can do citizenship work by just watching and waiting: paying attention to what her representative is doing (or not doing) and deciding to get involved if and only if the representative disappoints. This kind of short-cut is most effective for a citizen who cares most about a limited number of issues. For example, a citizen whose only concern is for preserving Social Security may reasonably just watch and wait to see if her representative acts to preserve the program, or if her representative acts to undermine it, before deciding whether even to get involved.

Each of the approaches I've outlined here is a way of reducing the cost of citizenship – whether that cost is in money spent understanding the issues, in time spent on research and interaction, or in energy and mental acuity making complicated decisions. American voters often don't like the idea that they should reduce this cost, even as it's clear that nearly every voter actually does so. The reason we don't like this idea is the particular kind of individualism that is at the heart of American political culture

(Bellah et al. 1985; Swidler 1992; Stephenson 1989). Americans consider their votes as parts of themselves: as sacred rights to be treasured and expended as authentic expressions of our true selves. To vote for a candidate is to offer that candidate "your" vote, and thus your voice of support, even though that voice is certain to be drowned out in the sea of others' votes. The individualist ideal has become the *informed voter*: an individual capable of holding and interpreting all necessary information and coming up with a proper decision.

The rational voter model described at the beginning of this chapter is one reason to be suspicious of the informed-voter ideal in practice, if not in theory. We already learned that it's not really rational even to bother to spend the minimal amount of time and energy required to vote at all, given the minuscule likelihood that your vote will be decisive. Now we learn that to vote *right* is to spend large amounts of time and energy to make sure your vote is faithful and authentic! This is clearly both irrational and impossible.

There's another, more important, reason to be suspicious of the informed-voter ideal. That is the idea that a voter is essentially an individual. As hard as we work to make voting a private affair, though, it remains very fundamentally a collective, social behavior – indeed, among the most publicly important behaviors many Americans engage in. Danielle S. Allen, writing about the importance of voting in the wake of the civil rights movement, explains:

> . . . democratic people *need* metaphors to make "the people," the body of which they are a part, conceivable to themselves . . . Where, what, and who is this "the people"? And how does it act? . . . Voting does not merely legitimate democratic politics but also provides a practical solution to that imaginative dilemma . . . In short, citizens can explain their role in democracy only by expending significant conceptual and imaginative labor to make themselves part of an invisible whole. (Allen 2004: 16–17)

I suggested in the first chapter that we should understand citizenship as the practices involved in making and participating in *publics*. From this point of view, the right question is not whether a voter is fully informed about all the issues, but rather *what public her vote will put her in*. Values voters constitute one such public; others might be educated liberals, or business conservatives, or civil libertarians. Publics can overlap one another (you don't always have to choose to be one or another), and the boundaries can be fuzzy. But if we stop thinking about voting as putting one small piece of oneself into the voting booth, and instead think about expressing one's choice of public, the decision to vote becomes both more social *and* more rational.

This is one of the key sociological points I want to make in this book. Voting is a citizenship *practice* based on a social *technology* and an *institutional configuration*. It is not just an isolated behavior. Practices are patterned behaviors that link individuals to societies – in this case, individuals to *publics* – and, in the process, help create, shape, reinforce, and define those publics. Recall from the last chapter that the *demos* being represented in democracy is more like a public than like "people," a collectivity more than a collection. Because of this fact, we need to understand what seem like micro, individual decisions like voting as entirely, completely, fundamentally *social* behaviors. Deciding whether to vote, and for whom to vote, and even *how* to vote (since there are many ways to vote such as in-person early voting, absentee ballot, etc.), are acts that trigger belonging to a social group.

The rules, practices, shared understandings, and structures of these decisions matter a lot, and we'll get to these in the next chapter. For now, think about this exciting paradox: the most common practice Americans do to engage in, and signal their membership in, a collective public is one that is intensely private. To prepare to engage in the most public of activities many citizens engage in, a voter enters an isolated area, walls off connections with others, and expresses her will in enforced isolation and privacy. Even more modern machines like the ones we use today all feature physical barriers to separate citizens from one another. Imagine how voting might have been different in the nineteenth century, when people would have to signal their voting intentions by taking a ballot from a party official before depositing it in the ballot box. Or imagine how things might be different if individual voting were held in a way more like voting in Congress: out in the open, so everyone can see how everyone else voted. I'll consider more about these ideas in chapters 3 and 6.

In 1990 I traveled to East Germany – Berlin, Dresden, and the coal-mining town of Cottbus – to observe the lead-up to the first free elections in that country following the fall of the Berlin Wall and the collapse of the Soviet bloc. Under the communist government during the Cold War, East Germans had been taught to be at once safe and terrified: terrified of the secret police ("Stasi") and the possibility that they would be turned in by a friend, a neighbor, even a family member; but safe in that their jobs and financial security were not really at risk. The 1990 elections changed all that, bringing Western-style democratic participation, political parties, and elections, along with the collapse of the economic security system citizens had known. East Germans voted overwhelmingly for unification with West Germany, which took place the following year, and in doing so they were asked – in a sense, they asked themselves – to reimagine themselves as members of a unified German public.

I observed another election a year later, in some ways similar, in others quite different. This one was in Zambia, and it was the first free election in that country since independence from Britain in 1964. As in East Germany, the very fact that there was an election was an enormous feat. I watched as a man cast the first vote of his life after standing hours in line; he had the weight of the world on his shoulders as he imagined himself as part of a new, democratic, Zambian public. Hundreds of locked boxes of ballots were trucked to the capital, Lusaka, where they were dumped on tables and counted by hand as hundreds of international observers watched.

It's not just in foreign countries that the act of casting a vote is endowed with nearly sacred status. The most successful and most popular social movement in US history – the civil rights movement – made the right to vote a central symbol of empowerment and success. Thousands of African-American citizens risked arrest and bodily harm in order to be allowed to cast their votes, even though they knew that no one of those votes would make a difference in the outcome. Perhaps the most important piece of legislation to emerge from that movement was the Voting Rights Act of 1964, which solidified the right to vote and insured that the federal government would guarantee representation for black voters in Southern states. It is here, at the voting place, that each individual experiences her connection with the public of which she is part, and it is here that all the public commitments and private concerns combine into the chance to express publicness. How ironic, and how important, that the symbolic technologies and practices of voting – the signals sent by how we vote and what we're told to pay attention to – all signal that our concerns should be private as we engage in our public commitments.

The 2012 election season in the United States saw an open and frank debate about precisely this question of publicness. Among the most contentious issues behind the scenes was the series of state laws passed, generally by Republican legislatures, to increase the requirements for voting. Most commonly, these were "Voter ID" laws, requiring citizens to show a valid state identification card in order to vote. The laws were promoted and passed despite objections that there was virtually no evidence of people actually voting when they were not allowed to do so, and that substantial numbers of citizens lacked the necessary identification cards to be allowed to vote under the new regulations. Supporters of the laws argued that the vote was sacred and that even a few fraudulent votes threatened the purity of the election; opponents, too, argued that the sanctity of the vote meant that even a few legitimate voters turned away for bureaucratic reasons would taint the vote.

These controversies and practices demonstrate that the public is a fragile collectivity that commands respect. The practices that connect individuals and publics are important not because any one of them makes any difference to the outcome, but because they constitute the cultural connection between citizens and their communities. Consider another example from the 2012 election: key themes of the convention speeches of the two presidential candidates, Mitt Romney and Barack Obama. At his convention in Tampa, Romney said "President Obama promised to begin

73

to slow the rise of the oceans and heal the planet. MY promise
. . . is to help you and your family" (Romney 2012). In contrast,
consider Obama's speech in Charlotte:

> We, the people, recognize that we have responsibilities as well as
> rights; that our destinies are bound together; that a freedom which
> asks only, what's in it for me, a freedom without a commitment
> to others, a freedom without love or charity or duty or patriotism,
> is unworthy of our founding ideals, and those who died in their
> defense.
>
> As citizens, we understand that America is not about what can be
> done for us. It's about what can be done by us, together, through the
> hard and frustrating but necessary work of self-government. That's
> what we believe. (Obama 2012a)

These are differences in rhetoric, not necessarily matching
differences in policy positions. Mitt Romney promised
environmental protection and Obama promised help to individual
struggling families. But the difference in language, symbolism,
and emphasis is stark and important. It demonstrates the different
conceptions of the public present in the two candidates' governing
philosophies. For Romney, the public is a collection of individuals
and their families, and their priorities are those private concerns.
For Obama, the public is a collectivity to which individuals and
families are connected through rights and obligations, benefits and
costs. Each candidate did the country a service by offering such a
clear choice between visions of the democratic public and the role
of government in that public.

In the early twentieth century, the great French sociologist Emile
Durkheim noted a strange paradox in how society was modern-
izing. In general, he pointed out, societies became less mystical
and less religious as they modernized. People became more self-
reliant, more economically productive, more individualistic, and
less community-oriented. In older societies individuals were connected to their communities through "mechanical solidarity":
because people were similar to one another and shared a common
consciousness of religious belief. In modern societies, by contrast,
individuals were connected through their differences with one

another, because those differences complemented one another: a mechanism called "organic." How ironic, then, that:

> There is indeed one area in which the common consciousness has grown stronger, becoming more clearly delineated . . . : in its view of the individual. As all the other beliefs and practices assume less and less religious a character, the individual becomes the object of a sort of religion. We carry on the worship of the dignity of the human person, which, like all strong acts of worship, has already acquired its superstitions . . . It is indeed a common faith . . . It is indeed from society that it draws all this strength, but it is not to society that it binds us: it is to ourselves. (Durkheim 1984, 122)

The common religion of modern society, then, is individualism, and just as with other forms of religion, it requires rituals and beliefs to maintain its sacredness (Durkheim 1995, 44; Fields 1995, xxxiv). In the context of the twentieth- and twenty-first-century United States, these rituals and beliefs surround individuals' voice: their ability to speak in, and thereby constitute, publics (Bellah et al. 1985) by "enacting efficacious citizenship" (Jepperson and Swidler 1994).

Of course, voice – and efficacious citizenship – go well beyond voting into other forms of political involvement (Rosenau 1974). Citizens can circulate and sign petitions; answer public opinion pollsters; organize, join, and participate in organizations; send letters to representatives and to the editor (Perrin and Vaisey 2008); read and post blogs (Lawrence et al. 2010); read and post in social media such as Facebook and Twitter (Kreiss 2012); protest, run for office, and more. Each of these is an opportunity for voice: a way that citizens can make their ideas, preferences, and concerns known. Furthermore, just paying attention to what's going on, listening, and talking to others are important kinds of citizenship activity (Perrin 2006; Eliasoph 1998).

Each of these practices is patterned, in terms of both what people do and what it means. In California – whose initiative process is so heavily used that petitions are widespread – voters know what a petition is, how to sign one, and even how to avoid people asking for their signatures (DeBow and Syer 1997). Since at least the middle of the twentieth century, people have known what public opinion polls are and have understood what it means to respond to them and to read their results (Igo 2007). These forms of participation form our current *repertoire* of citizenship. Charles Tilly, in his pioneering study of political repertoires in history, points out that the primary form of political protest at another historical moment – eighteenth-century England – was the food riot. Working-class people would gather and protest the price and availability of basic food staples, *even though these were not really their primary complaints!* Tilly surmised that the historical, cultural environment of a particular time and place provide a specific set of ways people can get involved in political life; these modes of action are most likely to be used, even if they don't really match the grievances of the citizens using them or the demands they are pursuing (Tilly 1993). Ann Swidler expanded the idea of repertoires, showing that people use familiar ways of thinking and talking about important matters even when those ideas don't match the realities of the situations they're talking about (Swidler 2001). This is not to say that every political activity is already determined by its group context; in fact, citizenship is a creative practice in which people combine their capabilities, their repertoires, and their concerns to match the problem they seek to approach. But like other forms of creativity, it is patterned by what came before. People are much more likely to combine or slightly modify elements from a repertoire than they are to invent new ones altogether.

The job of any citizen in the context of a rich list of possible ways of getting involved, a mass public that's hard to imagine, and some degree of interest in speaking her mind is to assemble the right tools to exercise voice. In a study I did in 2000 (published as Perrin 2005, 2006), I asked groups of people to talk about how they would approach four different political scenarios: one about a corrupt senator, one about airport noise, one about racial profiling, and one about a polluting local factory. In many cases, people argued against doing anything at all, either because they were too busy, or because they didn't care about the matter, or because they felt they could have little effect on the situation. But in many cases, they did want to do *something*. Regardless, what kind of public they were speaking in – that is, what kinds of people they were with – strongly affected what they said. People speaking in church groups – Catholic and Protestant – emphasized voice in its purest form. They wanted mostly to say what they believed was right. By contrast, those in business and union groups focused on making a difference: on tactics they thought would influence the outcomes. And those in sports groups worked hard to argue against involvement at all.

Taken together, the repertoire of political actions and the cultural value of participation through voting and other methods mean that citizens' political activities are driven largely through their sense of what kind of person they believe they are and want to be and what groups they join and participate in. This is true of many other forms of behaviors, well beyond politics and citizenship. Identity, as one team of scholars explains it, means "the psychological structure or system that organizes diverse schemas about the self and its relations to others" (Johnson-Hanks et al. 2011, 14). In other words: people observe a complicated world of schemas (ways of organizing or categorizing information), groups, and behaviors, and try to match their own behaviors to the kind of person they believe they are or want to be. Some people are activists at heart: they behave as activists, writing letters, joining organizations, and marching in the streets. Others are cynics and "inside dopesters" (Riesman et al. 1961), seeing themselves as above the fray and paying attention mostly to which candidate is likely to win or lose. Still others identify themselves with a particular party or way of thinking, and others (proudly or not) as altogether politically disaffected. In just the same way that voting is as much about signaling the voter's connection to the public as about influencing an election outcome, each decision a citizen makes about participation in citizenship activities (including *not* to participate in them) is not just an individual act but a statement about what kind of person – and what kind of citizen – she is.

Americans have long had an uneasy relationship with the idea that their activities are so social, so bound to community. On the one hand, as Tocquville famously observed, Americans are culturally a "nation of joiners," predisposed to get together in groups to address concerns both local and national (Tocqueville 2004 [1835]). But that same culture values the individual as a choice-making citizen: a person who decides for himself, not because of group connections. For a study of people who write letters to the editor (Perrin 2012), I interviewed several editors who select such letters for publication. Among their most common complaints was that people write letters as part of groups: because they are urged to do so by group leadership, or because they get together with other group members and write together. For these editors, the fact that letters come from organized groups makes them somehow less authentic; their imagination of the true, authentic citizen is one who develops ideas *on her own*, without the "outside" influence of an organization or social environment. But political ideas are likely to be better thought out, more thoughtful, perhaps even more important, when they're shared with other citizens, as in a group or organization! The vision of authentic citizenship the editors' practice implied – and, because they choose which letters get printed, *created* – was just as Durkheim envisioned: an "eminently social" (Fields 1995) construction of a social value for autonomous, individual voice.

One important result of the fact that citizenship is so thoroughly about social identity is that there are significant, persistent, and meaningful inequalities between groups of people in terms of their engagement in citizenship and, therefore, their voice. People with less education, members of minority groups, and those with lower income are consistently less likely to vote (Wolfinger and Rosenstone 1980). People are more likely to vote if they are asked to do so by a friend or campaign worker – that is, if they are brought into the social fabric of the campaign (Rosenstone and Hansen 1993). The problem is that people who are contacted in this way are also more likely to be those who are more educated, have higher incomes, and are not members of racial and ethnic minorities. So the ability to mobilize voters through group work ends up maintaining or even increasing the social inequalities that define voting patterns in the United States.

Education works similarly, at least for some forms of

citizenship activities. In an important study, Nie et al. (1996) found that increasing education for everyone increased voting – a promising idea, since it suggests that we could increase thoughtful participation by providing more education. But other forms of citizenship – joining groups, running for office, and other forms of high-involvement citizenship – were based on *relative* education, which means that as more people gained more education, the level of education that gave rise to those kinds of citizenship rose too. So increasing education might have increased voting, but it didn't serve to increase citizens' voice in the other kinds of political engagement. Systematic inequality in political voice means that the ideas and views that get represented up the democratic ladder don't really match the ideas and views of the whole population at the bottom of the ladder. Instead, the views that are represented are weighted toward those kinds of people who can and choose to exercise voice. Thus, the cultural patterns of citizenship activity – the different ways individuals and groups choose to engage with publics – matter in terms of who, and what, is represented in democracy.

Citizenship as an Eminently Social Thing

I've argued here that citizenship is, to paraphrase Durkheim, an eminently social thing: even when it's done individually, it expresses and builds a connection with a public. The public, in turn, is formed and shaped by the collective interactions of citizens engaging in strategic, expressive, voice-based citizenship. To close the chapter, we return to the question of what people need to know, do, and be in order to be good citizens.

First, although we have a long history of valuing the informed citizen, it is virtually impossible for most citizens to actually practice that value. The scope of things to know and positions to evaluate is simply too vast for citizens reasonably to appropriate them all. The good news is that citizens need not know quite so much in order to still practice good citizenship: some common shortcuts help citizens manage the fire-hose of information.

Because of heuristics and group membership – and the fact that citizenship is fundamentally about joining and forming publics – citizens can count on signals from media, leaders, parties, organizations, and their own social networks to substitute for detailed, technical knowledge. Of course there are dangers in this, with biased media, skewed social networks, and more. But if citizens know *whom* they trust and what *values* they hold dearest, they can be fairly accurate in evaluating what they hear, see, and think.

Second, citizens need to exercise voice through whatever combination of practices appeals to their sense of civic selfhood. Good citizens are those who energetically practice public life, interacting with other citizens to consider and promote ideas of the common good, values, and beliefs. So what citizens need to *do* is pay attention to the kind of public their actions are helping form and seek to use their actions to advance the kind of public they consider important.

Finally, what do citizens need to *be* in order to be good citizens? They need to be eminently social, cognizant and appreciative of the collective publics of which they are part. They need to be information processors, yes, but also values processors, paying attention to their role in the growing, changing nature of their publics. All of these are best fostered by what citizens need to *have* to be good citizens: an active public life, honest and frank discussion around them, and plentiful opportunities and forums for exercising voice and listening to the voices of others.

3

Deliberation, Representation, and Legislation

In 2001, I wrote an op-ed in my local paper opposing the creation of a free-trade zone in North and South America. In it, I emphasized that the proposed zone was antidemocratic because it removed important decisions about social policy – worker protections and environmental issues, for example – from public discussion (Perrin 2001). In response, an economist wrote a letter to the editor claiming that the legislation could not be antidemocratic because "every treaty must be ratified by the Congress" (Grennes 2001). Whatever the merits of the free-trade zone, this dispute was about what makes a decision democratic. My contention is that a decision is democratic if it offers authentic representation of the public's preferences and concerns. By contrast, Professor Grennes emphasized the democratic *institution* (the Congress) as the standard for evaluating how democratic a decision is. In this chapter I provide a system for understanding democratic decisions as those that represent the public's interest faithfully.

Deliberation and the Public Sphere

If citizens' behavior is at the bottom of the democratic ladder, social and institutional systems are the means by which their behaviors turn into representation as we move up that ladder. Like elements of micropolitics, these more macropolitical concerns work in both directions: funneling citizen preferences into institutional outcomes while distributing these institutional outcomes back out to attentive and active citizens.

Citizens don't (usually) just naturally deliberate. Rather, they do so when forums and opportunities exist to shape and nurture that deliberation. Because opinion is fundamentally a social phenomenon – public in its very essence – institutions like forums, newspapers, town meetings, and other spaces foster political expression (Perrin and Vaisey 2008; Perrin and McFarland 2011; Ferree et al. 2002). Organizations, groups, and movements provide similar "free spaces" that evoke citizens' democratic imaginations (Polletta and Kretschmer 1999). Deliberation is a function not just of individual citizens' desires to express themselves, but also of the opportunities for that expression to be voiced and heard.

The structure of social and governmental institutions strongly affects the way democracies behave. Consider the difference between voting in a proportional-representation system like those in much of Western Europe and voting in a geographically representative system as in the United States. Both systems are democratic; each depends enormously on how the system is set up. In much of Western Europe, representation favors abstract ideas and policy proposals; people are represented through groups or parties, not (necessarily) based on their place of residence. By contrast, in the United States, the fact that we vote for individual candidates who must win a plurality of votes in a geographic area means that candidates emphasize specific coalitions and personal leadership qualities.

Once electoral systems have produced legislative bodies, there are also complex systems by which those bodies produce legislation. Most policy is the result of legislation (although executive and judicial decisions exercise important power, checks, and balances as well). Thus the legislative system – the structure and rules, but also the traditions and cultures – forms a key link in the democratic polity. It forms the final rung on the democratic ladder that began with the first section of chapter 2, connecting micropolitical preferences to legislative outcomes and those outcomes back to individuals' ideas and beliefs.

Deliberative Forums, Opportunities, and Threats

In the previous chapter, we considered what people need to know, do, and be in order to practice good citizenship. Perhaps the single most important message is that they have to be part of publics; even the most individual acts of citizenship are fundamentally social in character. The first step in the representation process is citizens learning, choosing, and expressing their ideas and preferences through democratic preferences. (We'll eventually get to the fact that ideas, preferences, and information flow *down* the ladder as well as up.)

The next step up the ladder contains the practices in which citizens communicate with one another and with leaders and experts. This is sometimes called the *public sphere*, following the work of Jürgen Habermas. The modern public sphere – which emerged in the European artistic salons of the eighteenth century – is the social realm in which people express their views and positions, listen to the views and positions of others, and potentially change their own ideas based on what they hear from others. Habermas points out that, in these early public spheres, people discussed not just immediate matters of policy but abstract questions of taste, art, and literature. They thereby constituted publics that, eventually, became interested in and available to comment on political matters as well.

In explaining the ideal characteristics of public spheres, Habermas emphasized their openness, rationality, and reason-exchanging nature. Here, citizens would be able to voice their views in a rational, dispassionate way; listen to other citizens doing the same; and arrive at a mutual decision through rational discussion on the matter at hand. This is an appealing idea to many Americans, because it encompasses our ideals of allowing every citizen to have a voice and of embracing the best available solutions to every problem, no matter where those solutions come from. If every citizen could consider her ideas; develop them well; express them in a public forum; listen to the ideas of every other citizen; and reach an agreement with every other citizen about the right course to take, that would come awfully close to true, transparent democracy. The ideas that reached the top of the democratic ladder would be the best and most generally appealing ones among all those that had started out at the bottom.

While it may seem Pollyannaish to some, this image of the public sphere has long been popular in American political culture. When I held focus groups asking citizens what they would do about several important issues, one of the first questions they raised was about *voice*: could they make their concerns and preferences heard? And if so, how? Among the most popular actions they considered was writing letters to the newspaper editor: an action that allows them to express ideas to an anonymous public (Perrin and Vaisey 2008; Perrin 2012). A 2012 commercial for the cable news channel MSNBC features former Carter administration figure Chris Matthews explaining why people should vote: "I want to matter. They don't want you to matter." Although Matthews' point was partisan (accusing the Republican party of not wanting the viewer to matter), his emphasis on the importance of citizens' voice in public is evidence of how powerful that principle is for American viewers in general. Even though we don't have a perfect public sphere, many Americans believe implicitly that the public sphere Habermas prescribed is the highest goal of democracy.

Consider perhaps the most "American" of painters, Norman Rockwell. In his painting *Town Meeting*, he explores the idea of voice and its centrality to our imagination of democratic citizenship. An apparently working-class man, dressed in an open, blue collar and jacket, is standing at a rail at a town meeting. He is disheveled but determined; respectful yet confident. Hat in hand (literally), he looks up, grasping the rail while a cadre of more respectable-looking folk, sitting down, gaze up at him as he prepares to make a point. The speaker's mouth, along with those of everyone else portrayed in the painting, is closed, presumably in deference to an authority located outside the painting: an interesting choice given that the painting is, in a sense, about voice. Later, *Town Meeting* formed the basis for Rockwell's more famous painting, *Freedom of Speech*, part of his "Four Freedoms" series. There the speaker appears more defiant, his mouth is now open slightly, and he and the audience have gained copies of the town's

"Annual Report," which presumably provides the background for the town meeting discussion. Susan Herbst (2004) shows the many ways Rockwell expressed democratic impulses in much of his work. These two paintings in particular illustrate the ideals of voice in the American context: individual expression, confidence, and equality of opportunity to make one's voice heard.

The ideal of direct democracy – or, as political scientist Frank Bryan (2004) described New England town meetings, "real democracy" – is very attractive. In fact, many Americans assume, as Bryan does, that town meetings where citizens deliberate directly and emerge with their own decisions are the essence of true democracy. It follows that representative democracy is "second best": we are forced to make do with it because our country (and just about every other country) is too big to make direct democracy possible. Thus, the story goes, we "outsource" decision making to professional representatives whom we trust to implement our interests and ideals because the job is just too enormous to do ourselves. This same impulse toward "direct" democracy is behind the use of ballot questions and behind proposals for "electronic town halls" and the like. There are two problems with that idea. First, even "direct" democracy is, by necessity, representative; second, never in the history of the United States (or other democracies) has there been a public sphere that actually looks like the open, reasonable, thoughtful, and deliberative space imagined by Habermas and others. Even the storied New England town meeting immortalized by Rockwell does not overcome the inequalities and prejudices citizens hold (Mansbridge 1980, 132–3).

What does it mean to say that direct democracy is also representative? Return to the democratic ladder at its most basic: people have preferences at the bottom, and when the ladder is working well, those preferences become policy as governments do what the people want, or don't do what they don't want. But as we saw in the first two chapters, people are never unanimous in their preferences, and often they are not even clear. Furthermore, policy isn't just preferences, it involves setting in place practices and institutional patterns that take those preferences and make them happen (Miller 2009, 35–58). Something has to be *done*, actively, to make preferences into a general will, and to make that general will into actual policies. The first of these tasks is carried out by public opinion and deliberation (culture); the second by legislation and policy making (institutions), often with public input. Neither is transparent. So even when the democratic ladder works well, it always contains active processes of representation, no matter what particular systems do the representing.

Consider, for example, the proposal from presidential candidate H. Ross Perot that many matters of public importance should be put to popular vote in an electronic town hall (Kelly 1992; Schwartz 1994). Perot proposed that television stations broadcast a national conversation and allow citizens to debate and ultimately vote on important issues, most prominently government tax and debt policies. "If we ever put the people back in charge of this country and make sure they understand the issues, you'll see the White House and Congress, like a ballet, pirouetting around the stage getting it done in unison," Perot declared in his signature Texas accent. But the electronic town hall would require someone to set the agenda; to decide who speaks, when, and on behalf of whom; and to decide what choices will be offered to citizens sitting at home and reporting their views by telephone. As Monique Girard and David Stark (2007) put it in their study of deliberation about rebuilding New York after the 9/11 terrorist attacks: "publics [are] distinctive combinations of social networks, protocols, and technologies. There is no public, no public assembly, without protocols and technologies – even if these are as simple as chairs around a table and everyday conventions of conversational turn taking" (151). There is literally no such thing as direct democracy unmediated by any representation or organizational process.

The other error in Americans' ideal of a deliberative public sphere is that no such thing has ever existed (Schudson 1992a). Town meetings included some citizens and excluded others. Even among those allowed into the room, some people carry more credibility than others, both for good reasons (such as their experience or expertise) and for bad (prejudices brought in from other parts of life; see Ridgeway and Bourg 2004). The amount of time it takes for a group to arrive at a consensus, even on small matters, can be very large; different people have different amounts of time available based on work, family, and other obligations. Finally, people's views are never strictly calm and rational; emotions, identifications, psychological states, and ideological commitments are genuine facets of citizens' lives and therefore of their political views. Requiring pure rationality and calm reason giving would certainly mean excluding a very large number of citizens' views. As Danielle Allen writes: "Public discussion that wishes to address problems of distrust, and generate reciprocity, must not banish the problem of interest, but tackle it directly . . . [If] speakers . . . enter the deliberative forum already mutually well-minded toward one another . . . the battle to achieve a reasonable policy outcome is already 75 percent won" (2004, 56). Calm, rational, deliberative direct democracy is clearly impossible, even though many Americans consider it an ideal. And even if it were possible, it's not fair to limit citizens to particular kinds of reasons. If people are genuinely angry, or happy, or fearful, those sources of opinions should be respected by any public discussion.

One alternative is to create deliberative places where citizens can come close to their ideals of direct democracy. Political scientists John Gastil and James Fishkin have organized several major experiments in this direction, bringing together ordinary citizens for intensive deliberations over current issues and elections (see Gastil 2000; Fishkin and Luskin 2005). For these exercises, citizens are gathered at a central place and often offered some sort of incentive to participate (a small amount of money, for example). They are asked to answer a questionnaire to record what they think beforehand; then the group deliberates about the issue. Finally, another questionnaire is taken to assess how people's views have changed (or not). By and large, these experiments are quite successful. Citizens in the deliberative settings take seriously their roles and deliberate earnestly and thoughtfully; the attitudes they report after the discussions show that they have listened to and considered the opinions of the others in the room. Although there are serious objections to some of the claims made (e.g., Dryzek 2005) the overall success of the deliberative model has led to its use in many different countries and contexts (Fishkin 2009). Governments across the world, including British Columbia, Chicago, and Porto Alegre, Brazil, have used the model for big decisions affecting large parts of the population. An entire industry has developed to help local governments, corporations, and other organizations use deliberation as a way of providing legitimacy to decisions they need to make (Lee 2012).

In an influential book, Bruce Ackerman and James Fishkin recommend creating a two-day national holiday, Deliberation Day (Ackerman and Fishkin 2004). This would implement deliberative forums nationwide on a given day, thereby facilitating a national conversation. "Everything else would change," they predict.

> The candidates, the media, the activists, the interest groups, the spin doctors, the advertisers, the pollsters, the fund raisers, the lobbyists, and the political parties. All would have no choice but to adapt to a more attentive and informed public. When the election arrived, the people would speak with a better chance of knowing what they wanted and which candidates were more likely to pursue the popular mandate. (3)

There are many attractive things about this idea. Giving the idea of a national conversation the legitimacy of a national holiday might encourage more citizens to pay attention to citizenship, and it might produce better outcomes as well. It might even be feasible, given enough national energy and funding, although the effort and costs involved would be very large indeed. But similar concerns to those surrounding Perot's electronic town hall arise. Who decides which of the many issues of the day will be discussed on deliberation day? And perhaps most importantly: what if ideas are motivated by group membership or solidarity? By emotion, hatred, prejudice, or misinformation? All these would interfere with the deliberative ideal Ackerman and Fishkin present; and all, or some combination, are very likely given what we know about people's political and social natures.

These efforts to create forums where citizens can deliberate and decide on important issues face a central problem. If they enforce rules about what the deliberation will look like, they can make the conversation rewarding, thoughtful, communicative, and even productive – at the risk of making it all but irrelevant to real-world decision making. But if they leave the boundaries open, the terms of discussion loose, and the rules lax, the conversation often ends up sounding more like messy noise than focused problem solving, but it more faithfully represents the genuine character of citizens' thought. Legal scholar Cass Sunstein explains: when people join deliberative groups and come in with ideas about the questions they'll deliberate about, the effect of the group is often to reinforce their existing preferences. In talking about them and defending them against others, they come to believe their pre-existing ideas more strongly. Bringing together a group of citizens who already believe different things – whether because of their individual ideas or because of groups they are part of – often results in a group "going to extremes" (Sunstein 2000), ending up *more* starkly divided after their conversation than they were before. There's nothing inherently wrong with these genuine divisions, but in order to be made into public policy there needs to be some process of reconciling them, however temporarily.

A similar pattern to that of these small group conversations emerges in the national conversation. Consider the 2012 American presidential election, which featured Republican Mitt Romney challenging Democratic incumbent Barack Obama. To the great disappointment of his liberal base, Obama had spent much of his first term trying hard to compromise with conservatives in Congress: through offering tax cuts, a compromise on the procedural question of the federal "debt ceiling," even through a conciliatory approach to the signature policy proposal of his 2008 campaign, health care reform.[1] Indeed, his approach was so conciliatory that one prominent congressman, Gary Ackerman (D-NY), referred to his negotiating style as "bargain[ing] at a strip poker table, and the president showed up half-naked" (Munro 2011). And conservative commentator Will Saletan identified him as a "moderate Republican" in historical terms (Saletan 2012). Meanwhile, Romney had governed Massachusetts as a moderate, and was referred to during his term as one of a handful of Republican governors who avoided hard-core partisanship in favor of pragmatism. But in the context of a national election campaign, both men were portrayed as – and Romney, at least, ran as – ideologically committed, dogmatic, and extreme. This is not *only* because of the tendency of groups to go to extremes in conversation, but the pattern reproduces itself at that level too.

Because groups go to extremes, and because people who are committed to an issue tend to be the same ones who talk about it, we face another paradox. People who participate in politics are, in general, partisans: they care about an issue, a candidate, a political philosophy. They enter politics to promote these things: to defend them against other alternatives and to make their voices heard. These are precisely the kinds of mental preparations that make someone a good activist. However, they are not particularly good traits for someone entering a deliberation, where compromise, listening, and calm dialogue are called for. This is one reason why two values of democracy – participation and deliberation – are often at odds. People who participate are rarely patient with deliberation; those who take the time and attention to deliberate often lack the passion and clarity of conviction necessary to participate. Diana Mutz, the political scientist who discovered and best describes this contradiction, suggests that we may need to choose one or the other, as deliberation and participation may simply be incompatible (Mutz 2006). Ben Berger, following up on this idea, suggests that we should be less concerned with getting citizens very involved in politics than with getting them slightly involved, just enough to lend their voices (Berger 2011).

Since we are interested in making democracy more representative – in moving the hopes and dreams of citizens up the democratic ladder into the realm of public policy – it makes most sense to avoid imposing extra rules on public communication and, instead, to find the best ways for people to speak, listen, debate, and decide, even if these are prone to producing polarized debate. In fact, to the extent that people actually feel angry, helpless, sad, upset, or otherwise emotionally invested in politics, these ought to be characteristics of the debate they engage in. It's for this very reason that Michael Schudson insists that conversation is not "the soul of democracy": conversations are calm and friendly, while democracy needs conflict and passion (Schudson 1997). Political theorist Chantal Mouffe calls this *agonism*: the idea that politics is best served when people disagree vehemently, faithfully bringing the reality of social conflict into the realm of politics (Mouffe 2005, 3). No less a political figure than Barack Obama expressed this idea in his 2012 victory speech:

> Democracy in a nation of 300 million can be noisy and messy and complicated. We have our own opinions. Each of us has deeply held beliefs. And when we go through tough times, when we make big decisions as a country, it necessarily stirs passions, stirs up controversy.
>
> That won't change after tonight, and it shouldn't. These arguments we have are a mark of our liberty. We can never forget that as we speak people in distant nations are risking their lives right now just for a chance to argue about the issues that matter, the chance to cast their ballots like we did today. (Obama 2012b)

In this view, democracy is not a system of coming to consensus or agreement, but a system of managing and airing social conflict so that social order does not disintegrate into chaos. The sociologist Lewis Coser suggested in his landmark book *The Functions of Social Conflict* (Coser 1954) that social conflict helps societies stay together by providing a kind of escape valve. Societies that experience and even tolerate internal conflict are ultimately stronger than those that deny or reject such conflict. The agonistic view of democracy – which I believe is the best way to understand democracy in modern societies – holds similarly that democracies that seek to squelch conflict are likely to end up illegitimate, with their publics feeling unrepresented and without a voice. "One of the main tasks for democratic politics consists in defusing the potential antagonism [fundamental divisions between groups] that exists in social relations ... Conflict, in order to be accepted as legitimate, needs to take a form that does not destroy the political association" (Mouffe 2005, 19–20). The task of a public sphere, in my view, is hosting these competing, antagonistic voices while preventing the antagonism from becoming destructive.

One additional advantage of thinking about the public sphere not only as a place constituted by rules and ideals but also as a set of practices that express and carry out social conflicts is that we can understand citizens' involvement in public spheres as accomplishing both *participation* and *deliberation*. Recall that citizens who deliberate are less likely to be active participants in other areas of political life, probably because deliberation makes them less sure of the merit of their own ideals. If political talk could be one kind of political action (Perrin 2006; Eliasoph 1996, 1998), we might be able to avoid that dilemma. But that means abandoning the idea that political talk should follow a restrictive set of deliberative rules, and instead looking at how political talk can be an avenue for providing citizens with *voice* in public.

What do we mean by "voice?" In 1970, the economist Albert O. Hirschmann coined the concept of voice as one approach individuals could take toward institutions in decline: they could seek to offer feedback to those institutions, whether they are companies, organizations, or even countries. This is an alternative to people's simply leaving when they are dissatisfied (which is particularly difficult when it's a *country* in decline) or suffering silently. In the realm of politics, voice is the ability of citizens to be heard: to express their concerns, views, and preferences in publics. Voice is the focus of virtually all political engagement: people use attention, resources, and ideas to try to express their concerns, preferences, and views (Verba et al. 1995). People may exercise voice whether or not their preferences are implemented as policy; what's important is that they try to speak, and secondarily that someone is listening (Dobson 2012). And because people learn from their past experiences, it's important too that their voice is successfully represented, at least some of the time.

When I did my research on political microcultures (Perrin 2005, 2006), citizens in the focus groups I convened to discuss hypothetical controversial situations reiterated that the most important standard for democracy was that people could speak. They didn't have particular rules about how that should happen, but overall they expressed a common-sense idea of political engagement: people should be able to speak when they wanted to, and others should listen. That vision should be understood as a minimal condition for public spheres:

- people can speak, based on whatever ideas, preferences, feelings, and loyalties they hold;
- people should listen, even if they disagree; and
- interactions should avoid name-calling and other forms of argument based on *who the person is* instead of *what the person is saying.*

These elements – an agonistic yet civil clamor of disagreeing, emotional, passionate, and committed voices about the public – form a pragmatic theory of the public sphere. They are not so much rules for individuals' behavior, or conditions for admission to the public sphere. Instead, they are principles for use in evaluating the health and success of public spheres as they actually exist. To what extent do these standards characterize American citizens' current experience of voice?

Access to Disagreement: Segregated Political Networks

In order for political talk to achieve these ideals, one crucial element is *access to disagreement*: citizens need to be able to hear one another talking in order to listen to and evaluate those voices. In Rockwell's town halls, citizens faced one another in the same room, offering disagreements as they spoke face to face (Bryan 2004). As the mass media grew over the course of the twentieth century, access to information became more a function of the media, and citizens turned to television news and newspapers to form their political communities. By the 1970s, many Americans – over a third of households on any given night – tuned in to one of a few prime-time television news broadcasts that provided everyone with pretty much the same information and ideas. Even when people disagreed – as they certainly did, and sometimes very vocally – those disagreements were based on a common core of ideas and information because the entire nation had that base.

The evolution of information technology since that point has been remarkable. In the 1980s, cable and satellite television dramatically increased people's access to different television channels. No longer was everyone who watched TV watching the news; and no longer was everyone watching the same basic news information. Offered the choice of evening television programming, many people chose entertainment over news. And television news channels responded, offering particular audiences news tailored to their political preferences (Prior 2007).

The most important change in the mass media environment was the creation of Fox News Channel (FNC) in 1996. By 2000 its availability was widespread, albeit idiosyncratic (DellaVigna and Kaplan 2007). FNC was founded specifically to combat what its founders considered the liberal bias of existing mass media news.[2] Although the network's slogans ("Fair and Balanced," "We Report, You Decide") imply that its approach will be akin to traditional media principles about objectivity (see Starr 2004; Schudson 2002, 2003), in fact, from the beginning, its mission was providing a decidedly conservative angle on the news for viewers who identified themselves as conservatives and wanted information that fit with that worldview. By 2002, FNC was the most-watched cable news channel, eclipsing industry pioneer CNN. And in the mid-2000s, cable channel MSNBC responded by refashioning to provide a liberal alternative to FNC. Whether you watch FNC or MSNBC, though, the most important effect of these changes is that audiences select themselves: people are able to avoid the emotionally difficult, but democratically essential, likelihood that they will have to confront ideas they disagree with.

While today individual stations affect specific audiences, the same trend characterized entire forms of communication earlier in history as well. The radio, declared theorists Max Horkheimer and Theodor Adorno, was "democratic" while the telephone was "liberal." They meant that the very form of the technology – the radio creating a mass audience, the telephone an individual communication outside the public – shaped the kinds of political ideas that could be imagined and discussed in these media (Horkheimer and Adorno 1969). Observers bemoaned the rise of the telephone as undermining social engagement and public life – worries that, in one sense, turned out to be very true, but in another clearly did not, as social life certainly did not die in the wake of the telephone's introduction (Fischer 1992).

The rise of the internet as a form of communication is similar to the telephone's rise in a prior era. It means citizens have access to a vast array of information – but that they are rarely exposed to information they don't seek out. As we have seen above, this phenomenon is what Negroponte dubbed "The Daily Me": information so tailored that learning a new idea, approach, or point of view is very unlikely (Negroponte 1995). People select internet sites and blogs that they expect to agree with, and that present information for their point of view (Lawrence et al. 2010; Veenstra et al. 2008). This phenomenon has been criticized as *epistemic closure* (Sanchez 2010; Cohen 2010). The advent of mobile technologies and social networking sites like Facebook and Twitter follows very much the same trend: plenty of information and ideas, but so thoroughly segregated that readers are far more likely to encounter information they agree with than information that challenges their worldview. Taking this concept even further, the Microsoft search site bing.com unveiled an election-themed search engine in 2012, complete with a "Unique left to right news selector [that] lets people filter the news the way they like it, including from the right, left or center perspective. Just click on a box and see the news of the day filtered accordingly" (Bing Team 2012). Journalist Bill Bishop showed that even in the most basic of decisions – where to live – Americans have sorted themselves so that they tend to live in communities, neighborhoods, and even counties that are segregated by lifestyle and therefore by political views. Selection into these communities with other "people like me," in social class but also styles of consumption and worldview, makes people more comfortable and probably happier, but diminishes the democratic potential of the public as there are simply fewer connections to provide new, fresh ideas and information (Bishop 2008).

Political science research has established that most Americans actually *do* know someone they disagree with politically (Huckfeldt et al. 2004; Huckfeldt 2007), but rarely take the opportunity to converse with them about those matters of disagreement. And people whose networks are closer-knit are also less likely to reason well about political matters (Erisen and Erisen 2012). People are most likely to encounter disagreement online when they are talking about something other than politics. For example, hobby and leisure groups may include people with very different political views (Wojcieszak and Mutz 2009), but once again the central question is open: do people use these ties to engage about disagreeing ideas, or do they shy away from such uncomfortable conversations in the interest of politeness, amity, or even civility?

In order to speak to contemporary publics, citizens often turn to *mediated public spheres*. These are technologically constituted spaces where citizens can "speak" and expect others to hear. Perhaps the oldest of these is the letters-to-the-editor column found in virtually every American newspaper, and which has existed in one form or another since colonial times, and in its current form since at least the middle of the nineteenth century (Nord 2001; Mott 1941). But in the past half-century several new forms of mediated public spheres have emerged. These include radio talk shows, call-in television shows, electronic comment boards beginning with early bulletin-board systems (BBSes) and continuing through current blogs and commenting engines, and contemporary social media such as Twitter and Facebook. These forums are importantly different from one another, but they all share some important characteristics.

First, mediated public spheres are generally *asynchronous*. Thinking back to Rockwell's ideal of speaking in a town meeting, the speaker there can tell nearly instantly what his audience thinks through their facial expressions, sounds, and responses. In a mediated public sphere, that is not the case. Instead, each speaker[3] sends her message out "into the air" (Peters 1999), and her intended audience may or may not pay attention and respond. Some mediated public spheres offer relatively quick responses, as on radio talk shows when another caller, or the host, may respond within minutes. Others, such as letters to the editor, take much longer and often never offer that sort of feedback. Technological advances are reducing the time between sending a message and receiving an answer, but they do not change the fact that the response is separate in time and space from the original message.

Second, mediated public spheres are *poorly bounded*. Again, thinking about the town meeting, the audience is gathered in the room with the speaker. In a mediated public sphere, the public is created by being addressed through the technological medium (Warner 1992, 2002). A person calling into a talk show, writing a letter to the editor, or participating in an online conversation can rarely actually see or even imagine the entire potential audience for his message. Since we know that, in face-to-face interactions, people seek to adjust their style and arguments to the others in the room (Eliasoph and Lichterman 2002; Perrin 2005), when people enter mediated public spheres they need to find other ways of estimating what audiences will react well to. In other words, they have to estimate the contours of a public they have never seen and can never see. This is a tacit limit on the free-for-all danger of agonism: norms of politeness keep people from extremism face to face, though that is often not the case in anonymous, online forums.

There are two ways speakers may try to estimate the form and content that will be convincing to this public. One way is to pay close attention to what's been in the public sphere before. Letter writers often read the letters column as well (Perrin 2012); talk show callers listen to the show they're calling as well as to other shows (Bobbitt 2010; Herbst 1995); online posters likely pay attention to other online postings. However, evidence from my study of letters to the editor suggests that in many cases writers are either not particularly good at figuring out what successful letters to the editor are like, or don't care and prefer to express themselves in their own way even if that makes the likelihood of publication remote. The other way people can try to be convincing is to figure out what would be convincing to the public they *can* see and interact with: their friends, family, neighbors, and co-workers. They use their social connections as sources of information about what's convincing.

The problem with this method is that most people's social networks don't do a very good job of representing the general public. Partially because of *homophily* – the fact that people tend to connect with others who are like them (McPherson et al. 2001) – and partially because people prefer to discuss important matters with people they agree with, these estimations are subject to *pluralistic ignorance* (Taylor 1982; Breed and Ktsanes 1961). Pluralistic ignorance is the error of assuming everyone else is like the people one knows personally. For example, a voter might exclaim: "how could Mitt Romney have lost? Everyone I know voted for him," even implying that there must have been voter fraud. But the far more likely reason is that Americans' social networks are divided, leading to pluralistic ignorance. Romney voters mostly talk to other Romney voters, Obama voters to other Obama voters. This also explains "epistemic closure" (Sanchez 2010), in which people rarely encounter opposing viewpoints during everyday conversation and news discussions.

The problems with segregated political networks begin with the simple fact that people without access to a range of information and ideas can't make as good decisions, but the problems don't end there. Media sources don't just shape the views of their audiences; they're also shaped by their audiences' shifting expectations of the media. In an environment of vast media choice, media outlets are increasingly tuned to providing what their customers want – and what they want is increasingly news, information, and ideas that reinforce what they already think. In our study of white conservatives in the 2004 presidential election (Prasad et al. 2009a), we asked people what media sources they preferred. One Republican voter told us: "I watch Fox News because it's more objective, more conservative." We pressed him: which was it, more objective or more conservative? He ultimately agreed that he watched Fox because it was more conservative – he understood that he was giving up some degree of objective news coverage in order to get a point of view he expected to agree with.

In response to some of these dynamics, there have been many calls for increasing civility in public discourse. President Obama famously implored politicians and citizens to "disagree without being disagreeable," and many commentators seem to agree that incivility mars our political landscape. The new incivility includes violent imagery, extreme comparisons, and a cluster of claims about race, immigration, and President Obama's personal background. Each of these serves as a way to undermine the legitimacy of citizens and leaders in the public sphere by emphasizing who is speaking instead of engaging with what is being spoken. These examples are from the right, but the left, too, merges criticism of the *speaker* with that of the *speech*. The main such strategy on the left is impugning the motives and character of large funders, which I believe is a far worse approach than arguing with the substance of what is being said or done with those funders' money.

What some scholars have termed the "Outrage Industry" (Sobieraj and Berry 2011) – intensely partisan television and talk radio – is a hotbed of this kind of incivility, and is far more prevalent on the right wing than the left. Radio host Glenn Beck said that President Obama "will find a gay, handicapped, black woman, who's an immigrant" to be the Supreme Court nominee to replace Justice Stevens. "She could be the devil, she can say, 'I hate America, I want to destroy America.'" There is, in fact, no chance that President Obama would consider nominating someone to the Supreme Court who says she hates America; or that any of those demographics would actually be a defense if she had said she wanted to destroy America. Beck, of course, knows this, but makes the comment anyway in order to pander to the biases of his listeners.

There are also examples on the left that invoke this sort of personalization. Consider, for example, hosts Mike Malloy or Keith Olbermann, who feature similar styles, such as Olbermann's famous "Worst Person in the World" segment, which specifically impugned the person, not the idea. These examples substitute attacks on the character of opponents for considered argument of any sort. They make opponents into villains to be destroyed, not opponents to be debated or listened to.

But I have two concerns that civility may be over-prioritized. First, focusing too much on civility can keep us from saying what we believe is right because we don't want to offend others. And second, all too often the accusation of incivility is used as a way of silencing people instead of listening to and considering their points. Incivility may even be a "weapon of the weak," one of the relatively few resources the less powerful have at their disposal to voice disapproval of the status quo. Norms of civility and truthfulness are very important, and of course non-violence is a must, but it's also important that genuine and frank concerns be able to be aired.

Why people engage in political reasoning is very important to *how* they reason and what conclusions they reach. There are many reasons people may be motivated to reason politically, including to match their friends', neighbors', etc., views, or even to oppose those views if they prefer; to avoid cognitive dissonance, that is, to avoid the discomfort that comes with holding beliefs that contradict one another; to confirm their existing biases; to expand their minds (a pro-intellectual state of mind); or to be true and accurate. Depending in part on the motivation, the emotional state people are in when they are thinking politically makes a big difference in what they think. Probably the most important facet of that emotional state is "hot" vs. "cold" cognition. In hot cognition, people are emotionally aroused and likely to reason more automatically; maybe even subconsciously. In cool cognition, they tend to be careful and analytic. It's tempting to just say that cool cognition is better and leave it at that, but many of the ways we expect citizens to express themselves are quick and automatic. In fact, most people's everyday political thinking is probably more hot than cold (Redlawsk 2002).

Is civility, then, really the right primary value? As Danielle Allen (2004) has pointed out, if we require civility and openness as the tickets to admission to deliberation, we've avoided doing most of the work involved. I'd suggest, instead, that civility and incivility are tools people use for engaging in political conversations (see Herbst 2010 for an extended discussion of this idea). While civility is a good thing, it's far more important for people to be *frank*: to be able to express, fully and passionately, their ideas and preferences. In another context, Bickford's (2001) article, "Anti-Anti-Identity Politics," taking off from Clifford Geertz's classic "Anti-Anti-Relativism" (Geertz 1984), argues that even if identity politics is imperfect, the opposition to identity politics is worse.

Similarly, I advocate an "anti-anti-incivility" position. Even if incivility is bad, the opposition to incivility tends to silence people who ought to be allowed to speak and be heard.

Alongside civility, the other standard that's been receiving much play recently is sheer truthfulness. Over the past few decades it has become commonplace for candidates, campaigners, and citizens to accuse those they disagree with of lying. A favorite expression in these debates is the late Senator Daniel Patrick Moynihan's quip: "Everyone is entitled to his own opinion, but not to his own *facts.*" To be sure, candidates and politicians do have a tendency to stretch the truth, so an understanding of the claims they are making and whether these claims are in fact true is very important. The role of the fact-checkers is therefore absolutely crucial – as long as it's not the primary focus of coverage. Fact-checking has an unintended consequence when it takes over the coverage. Citizens consuming the media don't just learn the answers, they also learn what questions are worth asking. The obsession with fact-checking teaches citizens that the important thing to pay attention to is truth vs. falsehood, not the matters of moral difference and emphasis that should be at the heart of any major political decision.

In the 2012 presidential campaign, news organizations raced to be first with fact-checking stories after each of the presidential debates, and partisan voters circulated these stories like ammunition in their favor. During one of the debates, the moderator (CNN's Candy Crowley) corrected Romney's account of Obama's portrayal of the attack on a US consulate in Benghazi, Libya. Her decision to intervene with factual information did not shut down the public conversation; rather, Rep. Jason Chaffetz (R-Utah) accused her of going beyond her proper role: "When you have two candidates disagreeing, it's not the role of the moderator to say, 'Mr. President, you're right' or 'Gov. Romney, you're right,'" he said later on CNN (Cohn 2012).

In a similar vein, late in the election season Republican commentators and pollsters offered many predictions that Romney would win despite widespread polling showing a small but consistent lead for Obama nationally and in most of the "swing states." Commentators insisted that Romney held enough of a lead with "independent" voters, or that greater enthusiasm among his voters would prove the polls wrong and push the election his way. Of course, they turned out to be incorrect, and perhaps the most famous analyst after the election became Nate Silver, the self-styled statistics geek who writes the fivethirtyeight.com website. The site pulls in polling data from many different polling firms and uses a sophisticated model to evaluate the likelihood of victory for each candidate. After Silver "called" every race correctly, he was hailed as providing a victory for numbers and science, facts over ideological preferences. To some extent, that is correct: Silver's scientific approach did produce more accurate results than the ideologically tinged preferences of the commentators. But to emphasize the victory for facts is to avoid the reasons behind those facts. Obama won the election because he convinced a majority of voters – nationally and in important states – that his vision and his governing style were better than those offered by Romney. That conviction is not a matter of fact but one of value and opinion. It's important to keep sight of the fact that political decisions are, in the final analysis, about morality, judgment, and preference, not about facts and truthfulness.

Like civility, truthfulness is obviously important, even central, for an adequate public sphere. But two fully truthful candidates who agree entirely on the facts will still disagree on the right decisions to make for the future. And like my suggestion of an "anti-anti-incivility" position above, I think an "anti-obsessive-fact-checking" position makes sense. That's because citizens learn by listening to and reading these claims. They learn that truthfulness is the only important criterion on which to judge political candidates and positions. Concentrating on civility (civil–uncivil) and truthfulness (true–false) is in danger of crowding out talk of fairness and morality. Of course people can think in both ways at the same time, but the cultural lessons learned are to avoid talk of values and fairness in favor of the more technical questions of civility and truthfulness.

A successful public sphere would make room for all these voices: calm and agitated, emotional and logical, civil and uncivil, as long as they are frank and honest. It would make sure the cultural environment is not saturated: people need to be able to make new connections, new ideas, and creative approaches to citizenship (Perrin 2006). Indeed, it would make room for anger, dismissal, refusal to listen to others, even disruption when they are the authentic expressions of people's frank feelings, ideals, and preferences. Some matters evoke that level of emotion and commitment, and we should respect that. The set of standards for this public sphere is simultaneously lower and higher than the traditional deliberative rules others have offered. The standard is lower because I don't think we should require the level of respectfulness and rational argument that deliberative democrats often propose. But it's higher because this public conversation is cacophonous. It's noisy, messy, and conflictual. But that's fine. In fact, it's important, because that's a public that is faithful to the reality of social conflict over matters of interest, morality, and focus. This vision of public deliberation is a cultural environment for successful citizenship: multiple sources of ideas, preferences, and approaches, multiple forums for communicating and thinking together, and representative systems for transmitting the output of public deliberation into the process of policy making. It is to that representative system that we turn next.

Electoral Systems and Practices

Once people have formed ideas and preferences and communicated these with one another to form a public, we need tools for taking those public preferences "up the ladder" to be represented in political offices and public policy. Like every other step of the democratic ladder, election systems pass information both up and down. They are intended to pass information up, from public opinion to government. But they also teach citizens what representation is like – citizens think with the examples they see in electoral systems and, often, come to see the principles of democracy as being the same as the practices of elections (see, e.g., Skocpol and Fiorina 1999; Perrin 1995). As discussed in chapter

1, the introduction of the secret ballot in the United States was a relatively recent innovation, well after the democratic "habits of the heart" were formed in American culture (Tocqueville 2004 [1835]). For much of American history, the secret ballot was not the obvious technique it has become today. Most Americans now consider it utterly indispensable – part and parcel of the self-evident practice of democracy.

In the broadest sense, electoral systems are structures that citizens trust to manage the aggregation of public opinion across differences of time and space. These systems take the fluid, messy, even contradictory realities of what publics think and make these into the temporarily fixed award of an office to a candidate. Like any technology, electoral systems contain errors. They foreclose some actions and ideas while encouraging and enabling others. The question to ask is: which such actions do they constrain and enable, and to what effect? This is a very complicated idea, full of moving parts, so let me pull it apart piece by piece.

First, electoral systems are structures. That means they are practices written down in law, described technically, and that endure across long periods of time. While people can, and do, debate the details of the structures, at any given moment those structures are generally set. Voters do not head to the polls wondering how their votes are supposed to be counted (although they may come with anxiety as to whether those rules will be followed, a distinct concern). Candidates for office agree to a set of rules that are very likely to be followed, again with the exception of system failures that are relatively rare in industrialized democracies.

Electoral systems are also about trust. Recall that voting is a ritual behavior, one that teaches voters that they are part of a larger public and helps them to imagine their status as part of that public. Voters must trust that their votes will be counted and that the system will be followed. There are various methods available for verifying this trust, from exit polls (Wand et al. 2001) to international observers, a common fixture at elections outside the United States but relatively rare here (Mackenzie 2012). But everyone involved must believe that, in general, the results of the election will represent the way the majority of voters cast their votes.

The job of this structure is to aggregate public opinion. Although publics are collectivities incorporating groups of individuals, it is those individuals who actually cast votes. The work of aggregation involves counting all those individual votes and constructing out of them a single, proportional answer. This is generally expressed as the total number of votes cast for each of the options, with the shares also expressed as percentages.

The final element – aggregation *across space and time* – makes that aggregation process even less straightforward than it seems. In the United States, elections are strictly scheduled: the Tuesday after the first Monday in November is when presidential and congressional elections are held, although other dates are used for local, state, and primary elections across the country. That date is the *electoral moment* (Geddis 2003):[4] it is the point at which the public's opinion is captured and assumed to be binding until the next election. Of course, election day is not a moment but a whole day, and with recent reforms allowing early voting it can even last a month or more (Gronke et al. 2007). But the aggregation is treated as a single moment; no accommodation is made for opinions that may form or change while the polls are open. Representation is virtually all by geographic unit: citizens' representatives to state and federal governments are chosen to represent the area they live in, such as their congressional district or state. So the function of each election is to take the ever-changing, even mysterious, character of public opinion as it exists among people and nail it down for a specific space over a specific period of time.

The idea of representing people based on where they live, and doing so over a specific, defined amount of time, is so ingrained in Americans' ideas of democracy that we often have trouble thinking outside that scheme. But other countries provide examples of other ways of organizing representation. One key example is parliamentary democracy, which is practiced in many countries including France, Germany, Israel, New Zealand, and many more. In this system, citizens cast votes for parties, not for individual candidates. Each party gets a number of seats in the parliament based on the proportion of votes it received in the election. The parliament is then responsible for electing a national leader, often called the prime minister. Thus citizens are represented based not on where they live but on what party they voted for. People particularly concerned about the environment, for example, may choose the Green Party, as many did in Germany in the 1980s. Of course, people who have specifically regional allegiances may vote for a regionally focused party, such as Italy's Northern League, which focuses on the northern section of the country.

Parliamentary systems often provide more fine-grained representation, since groups and interests don't need to form a majority in any one area in order to be represented in Parliament. For example, compare the Green Party's fortunes in Germany to those in the United States. The Greens formed in Germany in 1980 as an alternative to the traditional division between the conservative Christian Democrats and the progressive Social Democrats (there were several smaller parties as well). By 1983 the Greens had already achieved representation in the German Parliament, and in 1998 they became part of the country's coalition government (Poguntke 1993). By contrast, the US Green Party began activities only four years later, in 1984, and by November, 2012, the only elected officials were at the local level – no state, federal, or congressional officials. While some of the difference may be due to the political views of the two populations, Green popularity in the United States would likely be sufficient to elect at least one representative in a parliamentary system.

This is not just a hypothetical concern; there are many ways in which Americans who live in different places but think similarly might find themselves better represented under a parliamentary system. As political theorist Michael Walzer points out, one group is persistently underrepresented in American politics: African Americans (Walzer 1983). The Voting Rights Act of 1964 sought to remedy that situation by requiring that formerly segregated states have congressional districts that provide sufficient African-American populations to represent this group adequately. But as successful as the Act has been, it has led to persistent disputes over district boundaries and requires that districting commissions consider race over and above other kinds of identities.

Legal scholar Lani Guinier suggested a variation on parliamentary elections – proportional representation – which would allow people to vote within states based on their interests and concerns instead of just their places of residence (Guinier 1994). Thus African Americans *could* decide to vote as a bloc – a public – in order to gain representation as African Americans. Or people could decide to vote based on other identities: social class, religion, views of the common good. The idea highlights two important strengths of the parliamentary system. First, and most important, it is very flexible in terms of allowing people to decide what publics are most important to them instead of imposing a geographically based public upon people. Second, it removes some of the personality conflict from elections since citizens vote for parties – basically, for bundles of policy positions – instead of for candidates.

There is no perfect system, though, and there are important weaknesses to the parliamentary approach as well. The most important weakness is instability. Countries like Israel and Italy have experienced many changes in power over time, as different parties in parliament jockey for power and try to pursue their own positions in a complicated system. Neither citizens nor businesses nor international contacts can be sure of the country's direction. This could be called an excess of democracy – too much agonism! – and it certainly weighs on the countries' citizens and impedes their routine functioning. Another issue is that less populated places – such as rural areas – are likely to be poorly represented in these systems. The geography-based approach guarantees that rural areas get at least some representation, while a proportional representation system would likely draw most of its representation to the places with the most people: the urban areas.

There are other proposals for implementing proportional representation in local, state, and even national contexts. One popular option is instant runoff voting (IRV). In many areas, when a multi-candidate race results in no clear majority, a new election is held between the two top vote-getters. This is called a runoff election. IRV skips the second step by allowing voters to provide a rank-ordered list of candidates, starting with their first choice and then working down to their last. In addition to reducing the cost of the election itself, this also allows people to vote for their preferred candidate even if they expect her to lose, since their vote will not be discounted for doing so. A similar method called single transferrable vote (STV), for multi-office elections, is used in a few places including the Cambridge, Massachusetts municipal elections. In chapter 6 we'll return to questions about electoral reforms and how they might work.

It's important to recognize that American political design was *intended* to provide only limited democratic input to government. Founding Father James Madison, for example, feared the excesses of democratic fervor that might take over. So the stability provided by the geographic, fixed-time system was one of the key benefits the Founders sought. But as democratic culture grew, particularly during the Progressive era, leaders designed more tools to give the people more input into governmental functioning. These tools include popular referenda (ballot questions), in which people are allowed to vote directly on a particular question; recall petitions, in which governors and other public officials may be removed from office by a popular vote; and more. These joined other relatively extreme measures that are older, such as impeachment of the president (which is a Constitutional measure) and the filibuster in the Senate, which allows a minority bloc to keep legislation from passing. The original filibuster rule required that a Senator take the floor of the Senate and continue speaking to preclude the vote from happening; since 1975 all that has been required is that a Senator affirm that he *intends* to block the legislation.

Until the 1990s, most of these procedures were relatively rarely used, and (with the exception of ballot measures, which were already very common in some states) considered last-resort options for dire times. But an important reality of social life is that, just as users search for and use tools, those same tools can lead their users in particular directions ("when all you have is a hammer, everything looks like a nail"). Faced with the opportunity to use the impeachment process for short-term political gain, Republicans in Congress impeached President Clinton for perjury following a sexual affair with White House intern Monica Lewinsky. Public opinion largely considered the charges not worthy of impeachment, but the proceedings continued as a national event (Sarfatti-Larson and Wagner-Pacifici 2001). Generally, although there is dispute as to whether the impeachment was justified (Posner 1999), most analysts agree that it was a "partisan impeachment"; the main impetus for pursuing the impeachment was Republicans' partisan desire to reduce Clinton's power and to position themselves for the upcoming 2000 election (see, e.g., Quirk 2000). The "cumbersome and antiquated" impeachment process was so unpopular that it "defanged" impeachment (Gerhardt 2001), making it at once commonplace and less extraordinary and, therefore, potentially less useful as a last resort than it had been before.

The Clinton impeachment was the first of several new uses of existing laws for political gain (Perrin et al. 2006). In California, the voter recall procedure was used to recall Governor Gray Davis, not because of extraordinary wrongdoing but because of policy disagreements – a process that involved many of the same people as the Clinton impeachment and that, similarly, constituted adapting a procedure intended for extraordinary purposes to make it useful in partisan proceedings. In Texas and later Wisconsin, Democratic lawmakers left their respective states to avoid being compelled to vote on legislation they expected to lose on. And inside Washington, the use of the filibuster technique in the Senate – originally "generally reserved for issues of great national importance, employed by one or more senators who were passionate enough about something that they would bring the entire body to a halt" (Ornstein 2008) – skyrocketed during the 110th Congress, in which Republican senators used the technique to block Obama administration measures. Each of these cases is an example of routinizing an extraordinary tool: since the 1990s, at least, there has been an "increasing tendency of politicians (and their allies) to use media revelations, congressional investigations, and judicial proceedings to defeat their opposition" (Gerhardt 2001, 60). In many, though not all, of the cases, the tools allow actors to short-circuit the normal expectations of time and place of representation: that is, to change the meaning of the electoral moment. In their original intent, they are checks and balances that can prevent the misuse of power, but when they are reinterpreted as ordinary tools of political life they interfere with the dynamics of democratic representation.

Considering several of these cases, my colleagues and I identified a set of "time frames": different ideas and language about time in politics that individuals, media, and political actors deployed to try to take political advantage of the fixed time and space of American representation (Perrin et al. 2006). Grassroots activists, too, often try to express their views "between elections" (Rosenau 1974) in part by bringing up the fixed time and space of representation. For example, a demonstrator at the 2011 Occupy Wall Street protests in New York carried a sign, widely distributed online: "This is not the world our parents wanted for us & not the 1 we want 4 our kids." Similarly, a Tea Party movement protestor carried a sign: "I want an America that my dad remembers." The signs explicitly link to ideas about how parents and children envision the world and the hopes and expectations that link the politics of generations.

In a similar case, demonstrators protested Wisconsin governor Scott Walker's 2011 legislation stripping collective bargaining rights from public employees. One sign read, simply: "I voted for Walker and I'm sorry!" The demonstrator is symbolically revoking her endorsement of the governor, even though there is no legal mechanism for her to do so. Later that year Walker was subjected to a rare recall vote, another example of the use of extraordinary tools, which allowed the voter to cast a new vote, but that is different from revoking the vote she had already cast. Democratic senators left Wisconsin to avoid being forced to cast votes in a losing effort, prompting Republicans to criticize them for neglecting their responsibility to represent their constituencies. Another sign, responding directly to that criticism, read: "Don't tell me that the Democratic senators are not doing their job by not being here, they are doing *exactly* what I *elected* them to do." Here the sign explicitly explains what the writer expects of representation and argues that the departure is faithful representation.

Electoral Reform, Turnout, and the Value of the Vote

All these questions about the environment for public participation – deliberation, electoral systems, the electoral moment – raise the question of what reforms might increase the likelihood of people actually voting. Recall sociologists Frances Fox Piven and Richard A. Cloward's claim that the burden of having to register to vote was reducing turnout in the United States (Piven and Cloward 1988). Their case built on important research by Powell (1986) and echoed later by Patterson (2002, 130) showing that American structural roadblocks to voting constitute an important part of the reason Americans don't vote as reliably as citizens of other democracies. Piven and Cloward proposed what became the Motor-Voter law. Motor-Voter requires states to allow people to register to vote when they apply for driver's licenses – thereby reducing the number of separate visits they must make. But as it turned out, Motor-Voter increased the number of people who *registered* to vote, but didn't increase actual voter *turnout* (Brown and Wedeking 2006). In recent decades, many states have also implemented reforms to allow citizens to vote early – sometimes as much as six weeks prior to election day – in the hopes that easier access to the polls will increase turnout. These reforms, too, have mostly failed to increase the proportion of citizens who vote (Burden et al. 2012; Gronke et al. 2007). Meanwhile, the 2008 presidential election – pitting Barack Obama against John McCain – featured the highest voter turnout since at least 1960. Turnout fell somewhat in 2012 from those levels but remained well above 50 percent. These increases may come in part from reforms making it easier to vote, but are probably mostly the result of greater citizen attention to politics.

The bottom line is that most efforts to make voting easier and therefore increase participation have been marginally successful but have not caused dramatic shifts. This implies that the main barrier to voting is probably not really structural but cultural. Most citizens inspired to participate will, in general, do so. Those not inspired to participate will not, even if barriers to their voting are lowered, assuming the voting process is mostly fair: a necessary baseline but far from sufficient.

In the wake of the 2000 presidential election in Florida – in which the final national outcome was decided by only 537 votes – attention returned to voting procedures and how they might change election outcomes, particularly when the elections were as close as that one. In particular, Republican legislators began a series of laws making voting harder through means such as requiring official identification before voting, registering well before the election, and even "purging" voters from registration rolls for various reasons (Overton 2007). As there was virtually no evidence of votes being cast illegally, the motivation for these laws was probably to increase the difficulty of voting, thereby tipping the scales toward voters with more resources – and therefore more likely to vote Republican. Indeed, many of the laws were targeted to fall particularly on Democratic-leaning constituencies, and Pennsylvania House Republican Majority Leader Mike Turzai said as much: "Voter ID, which is gonna allow Governor Romney to win the state of Pennsylvania, done" (Reilly 2012).

In fact, though, Obama won Pennsylvania, and other states where voter suppression techniques were implemented saw mostly very long lines as citizens who wanted to vote sought to make sure they could do so. The importance of such measures, then, is mostly symbolic, not structural. They serve to convey messages to citizens about what votes are worth, and about the ritual practices we considered in chapter 2. Ironically, then, if anything voter suppression techniques in 2012 may have *increased* citizens' interest in voting.

What Does It Mean to Represent?

Chapter 2 closed with the idea that citizens' ideas need to be considered, voiced, and practiced in order to be represented in democracy. This chapter added the idea that there are systems that take those ideas and make them public and represent them higher up the democratic ladder. Through deliberation, conversation, argument, protest, and participation, citizens can listen to others and make their views known. Ideally, these systems take that public opinion and translate it into policy outcomes. In the next two chapters, we consider whether they in fact do so: to what extent public opinion is reflected in the media and in governmental actions.

4

Public Opinion, Policy Responsiveness, and Feedback

In the first three chapters, we examined the historical, individual, and system-level pieces of the democratic ladder. Ideas and preferences that citizens form at the bottom of the ladder work their way up through individual participation, deliberation, discussions, and electoral and legislative systems. To the extent that the policy that comes out the top of the ladder is related to the ideas and preferences at the bottom, we can say that the system seems to be working democratically. But there is no one-to-one correspondence between the levels of the ladder. Most citizens don't hold fixed and fast ideas or preferences, and if they do, those preferences may contradict one another or change when they are deliberated about. Deliberation serves both to clarify those views and to change them, and the electoral and legislative processes mold preferences into policies and convey those policies back to publics.

From these first three chapters, we can pull some important lessons about the nature of democratic representation:

1. **Representation is never transparent.** As political scientist Anne Norton declares, "representation alters the represented . . . representations (some more than others) alter the public world" (Norton 2004, 93–4). It is not just impractical – though it is – but also literally unthinkable for the ideas and preferences that citizens develop in their private lives to be transmitted unchanged through any democratic system. Some scholars say this is a reason to keep as many decisions as possible *outside* the

democratic process to avoid distortions (Pincione and Tesón 2006), but in fact that alteration is how publics are created and maintained. We should recognize the value of representation as a creative, not just transparent, process.

2. **Representation is never one-way.** Citizens do not just provide ideas to deliberative contexts; they also learn ideas from them. Deliberation does not just feed into elections, but elections bring fodder for citizens to deliberate about. Elections do not just instruct legislators in what to do, but legislation informs the progress of elections. And so on. For every step up the democratic ladder, there is a corresponding reach back down.

3. **The rules of participation are important** at every level, from individual opinion formation through deliberation, elections, and legislation.

4. However, **the ways these rules play out in practice are rarely straightforward.** Unintended consequences and attentive publics mean that changes in the rules of engagement often have effects that are unexpected and even paradoxical.

5. **All representation, and therefore all democracy, depends on practices and technologies** to represent and communicate ideas both up and down the ladder. Each of these practices and technologies, in turn, constrains and enables the democratic imaginations of its participants and the character of the publics they constitute.

In the next two chapters, we take a close look at two of the most important clusters of technologies and practices: public opinion (chapter 4) and the media (chapter 5). Both of these are in the middle of the democratic ladder, and both combine social practices and technological artifacts to synthesize ideas and preferences and constitute publics.

Public Opinion

Few techniques are more central to modern social science than the sample survey as a tool for measuring the opinion of a *public*. The technique has become so entrenched that the decisions, claims, and ideas that it represents are now hidden and forgotten. But developing these techniques required not just technical advances but also changes in how analysts and respondents imagined publics as they asked and answered questions on public opinion polls. As the new techniques became available, it made more sense to analysts just to adopt them than to consider carefully what assumptions they were making when they did so. And as the techniques took hold, they became progressively better representations of publics not only because the polls themselves became more technically proficient but also because people learned to imagine the public using polls and samples as indicators of publicness and therefore adapt their thought and behavior to the public opinion poll.

The idea that publics have stable preferences and that these can be revealed through adding up private, isolated opinions ought to make us very suspicious given what we have already learned about the cultures and practices of democratic citizenship. There are well-documented anomalies such as question wording, question order, non-response, and even fictional questions on surveys. These and other anomalies raise the possibility that responses are *produced*, not just represented, by the artificial interaction between interviewer and respondent. Public opinion, like the public that holds it, should be understood as collective, not just aggregated; dynamic, not static; and reactive, not unidirectional.

The Origins of Public Opinion Research

Chances are, when someone says "public opinion" you think of a poll: a person (or, more recently, a machine) calling you on the telephone (or, perhaps, knocking on your door or contacting you on the internet) to ask what you think of one or another matter, or for whom you plan to vote in the next election. And while you may be upset not to have been asked your opinion on a matter you particularly care about, or to have been bothered to ask what you think about something you don't find important, you probably understand the basics of the polling process. The person or machine who contacted you has a list of people to contact; that list of people has been selected at random from all the people whose opinions the poll is interested in gauging. Having gathered the answers from the prescribed list, the polling organization will calculate a set of percentages alongside a "margin of error," which explains to people reading the poll how many people believe each answer to the questions, and about how much confidence the polling company has in that number. Each of the people who actually provided answers to the poll effectively stands in for many others who weren't asked; the validity of the poll rests on the idea that all those others *could have* been asked, if only the selection had gone differently.

Modern public opinion polling didn't begin in earnest until the 1940s, as social science was becoming a more important area of academic study and social scientists were developing objective methods for assessing the growing populations of cities and regions. The growth of big cities, in particular, gave rise to a strain of sociological thinking about the role of the individual in society and the danger modern mass society posed to individual character. Sociology books of the time were obsessed with that dynamic: *Small Town in Mass Society* (Vidich and Bensman 2000 [1958]), *The Organization Man* (Whyte 1956), and studies of exemplary "normal" communities like Levittown (Gans 1982) and "Middletown" (Lynd and Lynd 1929) all expressed the promise and anxiety that came along with growing urbanization and the loss of the innocence of small-town life.

The most successful of the books in this vein was written by David Riesman with Nathan Glazer and Reuel Denney. That book, called *The Lonely Crowd: A Study of the Changing American Character*, identified higher education, higher urban life, and a decreasing birth rate as factors that changed American culture itself. Among many other elements of this change, Riesman noted that the political attitude people tended to adopt was what he called the "inside-dopester." No longer interested in deeply held beliefs, values about the national direction, or opinions about right and wrong, the newly ascendant urban sophisticate preferred to talk about what *others* would do. In other words, they wanted the inside dope: which party will win the next election? Whom will the governor pick for an important post? Will the president successfully negotiate a deal on a big piece of legislation? In a phrase, Riesman suggested that modern people were more interested in *knowing* than in *caring* about politics.

In this environment, the development of modern polling makes perfect sense. The public – which small-town citizens could conceptualize by walking outside and looking at their neighbors – was now enormous and anonymous. People wanted to know and understand what was likely to happen. And faith in science and technology was burgeoning as people looked to the marvels of modern technology to help them manage the newfound complexity.

The Gallup Organization, along with rival Elmo Roper and academic pioneers such as Paul Lazarsfeld of Columbia University (Fleck 2011), heavily promoted scientific polling, where results were based on relatively small, randomly selected samples who would be asked to report their views and thus stand in for the many similar others who were not questioned. Their practices were certainly controversial at the time, both among critics and among everyday people. Igo (2007) reports that citizens routinely wrote earnest letters to Gallup notifying the pollsters that they'd forgotten to poll their home; how else could they know with such accuracy how their block or town would vote? But over time the voices of most critics who concentrated on what the representation meant were drowned out by the sheer predictive power of the polls: who cared if the philosophy supporting the polls was sound when they were so good at predicting elections? And citizens learned to understand the random-sample scientific poll so thoroughly that, in the decades since its widespread introduction, most Americans think polling results *are* public opinion, and think reflexively of polls as the authoritative, indeed the only, way of evaluating what the public thinks. Defenders think of polls as synonymous with democracy itself, and as providing a key mechanism for governing leaders to be forced to pay attention to the desires of citizens (Newport 2004).

In 1949 a group of European social scientists who had been in exile in the United States returned to Germany hoping to rebuild the academic and political environment after World War II. These scholars – known as the "Frankfurt School" – were steeped both in European philosophy and in American social science, including the techniques of scientific polling championed by Gallup, Roper, Lazarsfeld, and others in the United States. The scene in Germany just after World War II was chaotic, and the American occupation authority was carrying out a series of public opinion polls to try to understand whether Nazi ideology was still prevalent in the West German population.

Meanwhile, the Frankfurt scholars, particularly Theodor W. Adorno, had spent their years in the United States writing deeply critical analyses of culture's effects on people's democratic independence (Horkheimer and Adorno 1969) as well as a pioneering survey analysis of authoritarianism in the United States (Adorno et al. 1950). For reasons that were both personal and theoretical, they were deeply skeptical of the conclusions the American pollsters were reaching: basically, that introducing an electoral democracy to West Germany had largely banished Nazi thinking from the population, and that the country was ready to rejoin world society as a full member (Olick 2005; Merritt 1995; Merritt and Merritt 1970, 1980). To determine whether they or the American pollsters were right, the Frankfurt scholars launched the Group Experiment (*Gruppenexperiment*): an ambitious project to discover any lingering or hidden influence of Nazi ideology in postwar Germany (Pollock et al. 2011).

The public opinion polls, wrote German lawyer Franz Böhm, encouraged people to answer as if they were in their "Sunday Best": putting forward the face they thought best. Under the surface of such survey-based public opinion research, he said, circulated another kind of "non-public opinion": the ideas, styles, skills, and habits that people might bring back up in order to handle new political and social issues that arise (Olick 2007). The important question, the Frankfurt scholars pointed out, was not what people said they believed when they were talking with a polling interviewer, but what they would say or do when confronted with a real-world situation. To evaluate this, the scholars gathered groups of Germans from various different walks of life, and they presented the groups with a made-up letter back to home from a made-up American or British soldier in Germany. The letter was designed to make the groups defensive about German guilt – and it did so. The groups demonstrated that Nazi-like attitudes and ideas lay just below the surface, and that groups of Germans were all too ready to bring them back out in conversations.

The Group Experiment is important today not just because of the striking differences between what it found and what the authorities were finding at the time, but also because of the ideas about publicness, authenticity, and public opinion that it pioneered. Although the study was largely unknown for 60 years after its publication, some of these ideas became important elements of our twenty-first-century criticisms and ideas about public opinion. I will outline the ideas here and then return to some of the ways public opinion research – and surveys in particular – have been used (and misused) since their introduction in the middle of the twentieth century.

Perhaps the most important theoretical discovery in the Group Experiment is the difference between public and non-public opinion – a distinction that maps closely onto the difference between collections of individuals and collectivities or publics, which we considered earlier in this book. Public opinion polling goes to great extremes to make sure the people being interviewed are isolated from one another: only the interviewer and the citizen are part of the interaction. While this mirrors the enforced isolation of modern voting (as discussed in chapter 2), it doesn't really represent the way people develop, hold, or express opinions. People may express one idea in one situation, then be convinced of another position or just feel another position is demanded by the situation in which they are discussing the same matter later on. The Group Experiment took seriously the idea that people's opinions come to matter in specific social situations. But the claim was not that Germans were still Nazis at their individual cores; it was that they had Nazi elements in their cultural repertoires, ready to deploy when they felt the situation called for it. So the first point about public opinion research to glean from the Group Experiment is that public opinion, shifting and changing, is best understood as being about groups of people (collectivities) expressing opinions, not about individuals stating them as fixed answers in a private discussion with an interviewer. In other words, public opinion is different from collected private opinions.

A related point is that opinions are not stable things sitting in individuals' heads, ready to be found by pollsters. (In a much later work, political scientist John Zaller [Zaller 1992] called this idea the "file drawer model," as if individuals' minds were file drawers full of opinions and pollsters just opened the drawers and pulled out the opinions.) People likely have relatively stable values and general ideas about the world, some of which may crystallize into specific opinions about political matters. In general, though, they have to do some work to translate these attitudes and general views into answers on specific questions: they need to be traced "to a deeper source of legitimacy" (Pollock et al. 2011, 22). Indeed, at times people can be tricked into providing answers to questions about fake issues, which implies that their minds are far from file drawers; instead, they are applying principles and approaches they hold to whatever questions are posed to them.

Finally, the Group Experiment raised the thorny issue of who has opinions to begin with. "The assumption of an opinion of every individual is questionable," the study pointed out. "Indeed, ... that everyone possesses his own opinion is a cliché of the Modern" (Pollock et al. 2011, 22), meaning that in previous historical periods we assumed that most people didn't actually know or care about many political matters. In a strange paradox, only after the innovation of widespread public opinion polling did it become obvious that everyone could have an opinion to be elicited in such polls. Most of the public opinion researchers of the time just assumed this change was legitimate. For example, an influential early practitioner of polling, Harwood Childs, wrote in 1939 as the practice was developing that "by public opinion we mean . . . simply any collection of individual opinions designated" (Childs 1939, 331). In other words: we don't really know what public opinion is, but we will just decide to name it whatever we measure using public opinion surveys.

By the late twentieth century, polling was an industry fully accepted by practitioners, politicians, and the public, and the criticisms that were prevalent were actually about doing too much of it. Politicians listen too much to the polls instead of their own principles and wisdom; polls can be manipulated to say anything you want them to say; and pollsters do as much to set the agenda as they do to listen to what citizens really care about (Moore 2008). Americans have a love–hate relationship with polling. On the one hand, people have learned to understand polling as a literal representation of what the people think (Igo 2007) – to "think with" polls. On the other hand, "pandering" to the polls is considered an indictment of a politician (Jacobs 2000), criticisms leveled at a wide range of people, famously including Bill Clinton and Mitt Romney.

Public opinion researchers are well aware of many of the technical shortcomings of polling. These shortcomings are challenges that prevent poll results from acting as transparent representations of citizens' opinions. Later in the chapter I will argue that transparency is the wrong thing to be looking for in polls, but for now it's important to grasp the threats to transparent representation in polls.

Non-Response

The first thing a pollster needs to do is get enough people to agree to answer. People who don't respond at all, or who refuse to answer particular questions, are often treated as "missing data" (Bogart 1967; Schuman and Presser 1980). But non-response may also be the result of nearly any underlying attitude, including mistrust of polls, being too busy to participate (which can be a marker for other things that do influence opinions), or lacking any attitude at all. It could also indicate that those who do respond are either more or less informed and engaged than those who do not.

Also, researchers have found many reasons for people answering "don't know" even if they do agree to participate in a poll. First, respondents may not know or care enough about an issue to offer an opinion. Giving a "don't know" response correlates with less knowledge, interest, and exposure to information (Atkeson and Rapoport 2003; Faulkenberry and Mason 1978; Rapoport 1982). When researchers first ask respondents if they know about an issue, roughly one-fifth admit to ignorance or disinterest (Bishop et al. 1983, 1986; Schuman and Presser 1996). Second, some may give a "don't know" response when they do not understand a question or their opinion is not represented in the answer choices (Converse 1976; Harmon 2001). Finally, Berinsky (1999, 2004) argues that some give a "don't know" response when their true opinions are socially undesirable. For example, people holding racist views may answer "don't know" instead of owning up to those views. In addition to underreporting undesirable opinions, Americans also overreport desirable ones. Americans overreport voting and attending religious services (Brenner 2011); in both cases the people who claim that they engaged in the behavior when they did not do so are similar to the people who did (Silver et al. 1986). People who report that they voted when they didn't are likely to be better educated, higher income, and more civically engaged than those who don't claim to have voted.

Respondents' willingness to answer "don't know" or "no opinion" on opinion polls also varies cross-nationally (Sicinski 1970). That suggests that citizens of different countries have different ideas about what it means to have an opinion and what areas people feel licensed to have opinions about (Jepperson 1992; see also Perrin and Olick's introduction to Pollock et al. 2011). Another possibility is that different people – whether from different countries, social classes, or races, or with different levels of education – are more and less likely to feel competent to have opinions (Bourdieu 1979, 1991, 2005). Daniel Laurison (2012) analyzed large amounts of public opinion data and concluded that, indeed, a person's feeling of competence to offer an opinion is one important element of the likelihood that she will answer as opposed to offering a "don't know" response. The fact that there are so many different reasons why people might not respond, or might answer "don't know," makes interpreting public opinion from them far from straightforward. If one person's "don't know" means "I don't feel I should have an opinion" while another's means "I never heard of that topic before," and a third's is "I know but I won't admit it to you," it is impossible to draw firm conclusions about what those answers mean for public opinion.

Fictional Questions and Proxy Responses

In related studies, researchers actually found that between 25 percent and 40 percent of respondents give opinions on issues that the researchers made up or that are so obscure that the respondents would have no knowledge of them (Bishop et al. 1980, 1983, 1986; Schuman and Presser 1980, 1996). People probably answer using these pseudo-opinions because the poll implies that respondents should have opinions; why else would the pollster be asking for them? Thus, while some respondents say "don't know," many other respondents are unwilling to admit that they either don't know or don't care about the matter (Bishop et al. 1986; see Althaus 2003 and Bishop 2005 for extended discussions of the implications of poorly informed respondents). Fictional responses may also reflect respondents' more general political opinions about things people assume are related. Bishop et al. (1980) argued that respondents likely inferred that the fictitious Public Affairs Act had something vaguely to do with government and thus based their responses on their feelings toward government. Thus answers to fictional questions don't necessarily mean that people are lying or ignorant; they are probably expressing their general attitudes toward issues they expect to be related.

There are several cases of patterned responses to fictional questions and other findings that make sense only by interpreting the responses in that way. For example, a 1991 experiment included "Wisian Americans" on a list of ethnic groups for respondents to rate favorably or unfavorably. It was included alongside, for example, African Americans, Italian Americans, and Hispanics. Fully 39 percent of respondents offered a rating (Lewin 1992). More recently, during the summer of 2010 between 18 percent and 24 percent of respondents said that they believed President Barack Obama is Muslim, a rate nearly double that of the previous two years. Thus, a substantial number of Americans apparently learned a "fact" that was untrue and that had been consistently reported to be false in the media. Further analysis of these polls strongly suggests that they reflect respondents' self-identification as members of a public that dislikes the president. Most of them probably do not actually believe him to be a Muslim. In both of these cases, the observed pattern of responses is either entirely implausible or very unlikely to reflect underlying public opinion.

Question Order

Numerous studies have uncovered significant differences in respondents' answer patterns based on the order in which questions are asked. One important example is in attitudes toward affirmative action. Whites asked about affirmative action for racial minorities *before* being asked about their opinions about those minorities express more racial hostility toward African Americans than those for whom the affirmative action question comes after the general questions about racial attitudes (Sniderman and Piazza 1993), and men even support affirmative action for women less strongly after being asked about affirmative action for racial minorities (Wilson et al. 2008). One explanation is that people feel compelled to be consistent. A person who is first asked about affirmative action may feel she should continue to answer in the same way later in the survey, even if she changes her mind or feels inconsistent later on. This is, in a sense, playing a role: responding to a series of questions from a pollster encourages people to stay in role, playing the kind of person they want to portray themselves as. Thus, much like voting and other forms of participation, answering a survey is at least as much about adopting a political identity as it is about answering a collection of separate questions.

However, in broader tests of question-order effects, Schuman and Presser (1996) found only mixed support for this "consistency hypothesis." Another explanation is that questions that appear earlier on a survey help set the criteria the respondent will use to evaluate later items. Experiments by Tourangeau and colleagues (Tourangeau and Rasinski 1988; Tourangeau et al. 1989) showed that respondents' attitudes toward abortion were influenced by whether the question followed items about religion or about women's rights. When questions about religion were asked first, respondents were more opposed to abortion, but when questions about women's rights were asked first they were more pro-choice. Similarly, analysis by Bartels (2002) showed that faith in elections appeared to drop after 1980, when a new question order put that item after questions about government waste and corrupt politicians. Question-order effects are evidence that it is very difficult, if not impossible, to achieve uniform meaning for any given public opinion item. That's not an error or a fault with surveys; it's evidence that questions have different true, authentic meanings depending on the context in which they're asked.

Question-Wording, Priming, and Framing

Important differences in results also come from sometimes very small differences in how questions are asked, how the survey and questions are explained, and what background respondents are provided before they answer. These are called question-wording, framing, and priming effects, respectively. For instance, asking about partisanship "today" encourages respondents to draw on current feelings about political parties and thus fluctuates over time, whereas asking "generally" solicits a longer-range view that is more stable (Abramson and Ostrom 1994; Borrelli et al. 1987). That's because the small change in the question, replacing "generally" with "today," clues respondents in to the idea that their answers might change from day to day. Respondents are encouraged to think about their answers in a much shorter-term way than if they are cued in to thinking about the same question "generally." Similarly, calling water-boarding "torture" vs. "enhanced interrogation," for example, may condition the responses. Different terms evoke very different responses, either because people may understand the question to be about something different, or just because different images are associated in their minds with the question. Water-boarding may be about national security, or it may be about unethical treatment of prisoners (Druckman 2001; Druckman and Holmes 2004).

In many cases, such different categorizations will lead to very different answers. A CBS News/*New York Times* (2010) poll showed a 17-point difference between strong support for "gay men and lesbians" serving in the military (51 percent) and for "homosexuals" serving (34 percent). Similarly, Conlon and McFarland (2010) found a significant difference between support for a law allowing "gays and lesbians to marry a partner of the same sex" (36.6 percent) and one allowing "two men to marry each other or two women to marry each other" (33.6 percent). Smith (1987) showed that across myriad surveys the term "welfare" invoked stronger negative opinions than the term "poor." In most cases, there is no neutral word for an issue, and thus getting accurate results from such polls representing the genuine opinions of the public is impossible. But like question-order effects, this should be understood as an authentic characteristic of polls: different wordings tap into different psychological states, and those are in turn the authentic ways respondents are thinking.

Media exposure (Althaus and Kim 2006; Scheufele 2000) and even late-night television (Moy et al. 2006) help respondents understand what questions might be about. For example, people who watched *The Late Show* with David Letterman were generally more negative toward President Bush – except in the week immediately following Bush's appearance on the show, when they became markedly more positive toward him (Moy et al. 2006). Because respondents "think with" these constructs (Perrin 2006, 64–5), their answers are really the result of an interaction between their prior views and experiences and the information environment from which the answers emerged. That information environment is the product of the various other influences

– frames, priming messages, different settings – that people have experienced that help them put questions into context.

Social Theoretical Criticisms

Sociologists Herbert Blumer and Pierre Bourdieu both argued that public opinion polling as it is usually practiced is insufficiently sociological. Polling ignores the social character and the power relationships of society, although it is possible to reduce that fact to some extent by asking people about their social environments: what their friends, neighbors, and colleagues believe. These power dynamics mean that some people's opinions matter more than others in having more ability to influence officials according to their opinion (Blumer 1948). Thus, polling obscures social inequality by assuming that everyone has an equally valued opinion about every subject (Bourdieu 1979). Polls, in Blumer's view, served mostly to legitimate public policy by creating the idea of a single public voice: the idea that there is, in fact, a public opinion, even if it is split. Bourdieu (1979) goes one step further, arguing that public opinion polls actually *create* public opinion more than discovering what is already out there.

Public opinion polling requires presuming that there are standardized political problems in order to standardize the questions. As the Frankfurt School sociologists argued:

> That everyone possesses his own opinion is a cliché of the Modern. In earlier social epochs, the spiritual cosmos was, on the one hand, much too strongly constructed and strictly controlled for everyone to be able to have or to have been able to develop a private opinion about everything . . . [O]n the other hand, the information and communications possibilities were too limited for the overwhelming majority of people to have been in the situation to have an opinion about everything imaginable. (Pollock et al. 2011, ch. 1; see also Adorno 2005; Alsina et al. 2001; Ginsberg 1986, 1989)

In a similar vein, critical political scientists have called public opinion a "fetish" (Bennett 1993, 109; Edelman 1993) and a "fiction" (Ginsberg 1986; Herbst 1998), albeit a "useful" one (Entman and Herbst 2001). First, what polls represent as public opinion is a construction, not an absolute reality (Duncan 1984; Cicourel 1964), and second, the way polls measure public opinion does not transparently represent the way people actually think.

Defenders of standardized public opinion research point to the fact that responding to a poll is very similar to voting: the choices are presented as fixed options, and you are asked simply to choose among them. They often suggest that this similarity makes polling fundamentally democratic in character (e.g., Newport 2004). Asher (2004, 189) sums up this democratic defense as follows: "Public opinion polling is a contemporary manifestation of classical democratic theory; it attests to the ability of the rational and wise citizen to make informed judgments on the major issues of the day." Lynn Sanders (1999), a political scientist and theorist, provides a thorough defense of this position. She claims that the democratic merits of public opinion polling outweigh the problems with representation that come about because of polling's fixed-choice approach. Sanders suggests that asking questions in different ways, different orders, and the like will provide us with better understandings of underlying public opinion. This position takes for granted the idea that the right way for public opinion research to represent is transparently – and that ever better technical practices can get us ever closer to that transparent ideal.

Some scholars have responded by arguing that polls are the true "voice of the people," the most democratic way for the public to speak to its leaders. Other forms of communication – directly writing or calling one's elected leaders, appearing in the mass media, or staging political demonstrations – suffer from selection bias. That means that only the most motivated citizens – and those generally with the most resources such as money, time, and education, along with those with the least to lose – are likely to have their voices heard through these mechanisms. This was the great promise of polling championed by Gallup (1940) and other early founders: polling so reduced the amount of energy, sophistication, and resources necessary to voice an opinion that it included far more of the population. Certainly in the news media public opinion polls are treated as the true, unadulterated voice of the people. They are routinely reported on as pure fact with minimal mention of problems resulting from question wording or other biases. This reporting, in turn, serves to "teach" citizens that polling is unquestionably the best way to represent the people.

In general, the scorched-earth critiques such as those of Blumer and Bourdieu miss the point of public opinion research, while the democratic defenses are overly rosy about its capacities (Schuman 2008, 21). The critics tend to indict public opinion research not for its internal practices, but for not being a different kind of research; they want to ask different kinds of questions, not to answer the same questions better! Because of this, these critiques rarely contain evidence or analysis of their own (although Herbst 1998 and Pollock et al. 2011 are two important exceptions). While Manza and Brooks (2012) offer an insightful review of public opinion research, they ignore the big-picture criticisms of polling by simply stating that public opinion is useful because it predicts how people will vote. The question remains: does polling predict how people will vote because it is a clear, transparent representation? Or, alternatively, does it predict how people will vote because those people have so learned to think with polling that that's how they imagine the relationship between their own views and the views of the public? I believe that at least some of polls' accurate predictions are due to that latter effect: what researchers call *performativity*. Public opinion polling does not just represent how people think; it also *causes* people to think in particular ways by teaching them what kinds of questions and answers are most appropriate (MacKenzie 2006).

Polling and the Choice-Making Citizen

Recall Horkheimer and Adorno's distinction between the telephone and the radio, discussed in chapter 3. The introduction of the telephone into social life, they argued, encouraged people to interact with one another; each person on a telephone call[1] is able to speak as well as to listen (see Fischer 1992). This, in turn, means that people using telephones can be subjects, not just objects. In contrast, the main way people interact with radio shows is by listening to them. Listeners cannot really participate, so they are primarily objects or consumers: they consume the radio show but cannot actively engage with it.

The idea that particular communications technologies affect what they communicate is well supported in many areas. Consider, for example, an area that is seemingly very far from public opinion: music. Before the widespread introduction of long-playing records, those who listened to music had to do so live, whether in the context of a formal concert or informal folk or street music. The story of technologies for music listening since then has been a steady progression of devices for recording music and transporting it to other places: first through expensive record players that allowed the wealthy to share music with smaller groups of people in their homes (Barnett 2006), then through stereo systems, "boom boxes," Walkman-style portable music players, and finally the iPod and similar digital players. Each of these innovations allowed listeners to choose ever more closely what they heard and with whom they heard it. They are basically *privatizing* technologies, and by the 1980s if not earlier, musicians were creating music with these technologies in mind.

Current popular music is, in many ways, designed to be played on portable players: it uses electronic instruments and mixing devices, and the tracks created are about the right length to be easily compiled into personal playlists. Privatized music listening encourages a kind of multitasking like that many people practice at work: much of the music people listen to is consumed as background for other activities. Technologies for recording music, then, served also to change that music; by enabling "low-attention" listening, they encouraged people to change their relationships with music and, eventually, artists to change their music to match (Katz 2010). Without these technologies, music listening would be limited to far fewer people, and those people would be active, careful, and committed listeners; this would be "high-attention" listening. By contrast, low-attention listening is enjoyed by nearly everyone, and it is mostly passive, careless, and uncommitted.

In important ways, the technologies of public opinion polling follow a similar logic. In a world in which public opinion polling didn't exist, having an opinion would be difficult, committed, and restricted to relatively few people: high-attention citizenship. People would have to decide what to develop an opinion about, learn enough to develop that opinion, and find a way to express it. By contrast, in the real world, since polling does exist, polling firms provide all the infrastructure: what to have an opinion about, what the possible answers are, and how to make that opinion known to others. This is low-attention citizenship, and like listeners and artists in a low-attention listening environment, citizens and political actors in a low-attention citizenship environment learn their approaches to political activity, in part, from those technologies.

Benjamin Ginsberg (1986, 1989) compared the work involved in having an opinion (opining) in an environment of public opinion polling with that of doing so in an environment without such polling. In order to opine – to have a real opinion – in a world without the apparatus of routine public opinion polling, a citizen must decide that an issue is worth developing an opinion about, use one or more decision processes to develop that opinion, and choose to articulate it in some way, whether that be in person or in writing. Opining in that vast landscape would be active and difficult. By contrast, opining in the context of a polling-savvy public is passive and easy. The poll-taker decides what is important to have an opinion about and offers the opportunity to articulate that opinion. This transformation in the practice of opining, Ginsberg argues, leads to a significant shift in what it means to be a citizen. Citizens learn to be *choice-making citizens* (Paley 2001): their primary job is to select the option from a multiple-choice list that best represents their views and preferences.

Thinking With Polls: The Contemporary Public

One of the most important observations made by critics of public opinion polling is that public opinion research is *reactive*. Citizens and publics express their ideas, preferences, and views through polls and other public opinion research, but they also consume that same research: they read about it in newspapers, watch it on television, share it via social media like Facebook and Twitter. In part, that's because polling research is what's available to the public. News media are some of the biggest institutions producing polling, and they report poll results routinely, both during election seasons and in non-election periods. Carrying out polls and reporting poll results is very attractive to the modern news media for various reasons, covered more thoroughly in the next chapter. Perhaps the most important reason is that it allows the media and the public to fulfill the "inside-dopester" role David Riesman and colleagues identified over a half-century ago. Normal polling allows commentators and consumers alike to think about politics without thinking about differences in values and moral concerns that underlie such political struggles. Polling, in other words, makes *values* into *facts*, thereby refocusing attention away from big differences in philosophy.

In consuming polls, people also learn what expectations fall to citizens of a modern public. This effect is called *reactivity*: the thing being measured – in this case, public opinion – changes due to the very fact of its being measured. This principle exists in many areas of science; in social science particularly, the feedback between measurement and the people being measured means that people form their ideas and opinions partly in response to how they are measured and publicized (see Sauder and Espeland 2009 for a related version of this finding).

Because of the ways polling is experienced, reported, and consumed, though, its influence goes far beyond simple reactivity. Reactivity just means that people who are measured or affected by research respond in some way to being measured by it. Public opinion polling goes a step further in being *performative*: to some extent, public opinion polling actually *creates* the type of reality it is trying to measure. "In short, across a range of different measures of opinion quality, the empirical record consistently supported the view that, in surveying public opinion, we do not simply reveal a pre-existing public mood but, to some extent, we serve to create it as well" (Sturgis and Smith 2010, p. 67).

Many critics (e.g., Ginsberg 1986, 1989) assume the active, expressive citizen who might predominate if there were no polling to be preferable to the choice-making citizen (Paley 2001, 135) that emerges from the environment of public opinion polling. Similarly, Peer's (1992) deep critique of public opinion polling charges the technique with "manipulating" and even "manufacturing" public opinion (see also Beniger 1992). These critiques probably go too far because they fail to recognize the benefits of polling to democratic practice and the extent to which polling creates a genuine, authentic democratic public even as it also prevents the development of other, potentially better, publics. The concepts of "manufactured" and "manipulated" public opinion imply that there is something foundational that is being manipulated. Instead, polling methods, like other technologies, have constituted publics *de novo* in particular ways, evoking some modes of citizenship behavior (such as answering a survey) while discouraging others (such as mass demonstrations; see Tilly 1983; Osborne and Rose 1999).

Understanding the extent to which polling helps create its reality – the extent to which polling is performative – explains how both the enormous advances in, and predictive validity of, polling techniques and the equally trenchant and convincing critiques of those techniques can be correct. The idea is that technical practices have social outcomes (Latour 2005; Law 2009) and that, in particular, theoretical and measurement apparatuses designed to represent a social phenomenon transparently often also encourage people to act in accordance with the theory (Callon 2007; Callon et al. 2009). Theories and measurement devices such as polling, that is, are "an engine, not a camera" (MacKenzie 2006): they don't just record human behavior, they drive it.[2]

Publics are born, shaped, and changed, and individuals made part of them, through practices that represent and address those publics (Warner 1992, 2002; Anderson 2006; Saward 2006). Public opinion polling is certainly one of those practices, and likely one of the best understood and most widely accepted. These practices represent the public and thereby make the otherwise abstract notion of the public concrete. Just as the ritual practice of voting helps citizens imagine themselves as part of a polity they cannot visualize, the representational practice of public opinion polling helps with that same important imagination.

Because of this, we should understand the empirically demonstrated problems with conventional survey research not as technical problems to be fixed, but as substantive observations about public opinion itself. The fact that people answer the same questions differently based on things like question wording, question order, and other context is evidence that responding to a given question reflects a respondent's position in a complicated, multidimensional web of symbolism and group identification (e.g., Conlon and McFarland 2010). When contacted by a pollster, respondents choose identities to represent themselves; most people have lots of such identities they can choose among, representing their membership in many different publics. Generally, we don't know where people are or what they're doing when they answer a poll: at home, alone, with their families, in groups, churches, hospitals, etc., each of which might well affect how they reason and therefore answer the poll. One among the list of identities respondents draw upon is the abstract identity of poll-respondent: an identity that did not exist, and therefore a mode of behavior that was unavailable, before the widespread adoption of polling techniques for representing public opinion.

Because people often confuse public opinion itself with the measurements of public opinion surveys, the illusion is easily conveyed of a public that is collectively "opinionated" – committed to strongly held views. The publication of opinion poll results undoubtedly acts as a reinforcing agent in support of the public's consciousness of its own collective opinions as a definable, describable force. These published poll data may then become reference points by which the individual formulates and expresses his opinions (Bogart 1967, 335).

As an example of interpreting polling performatively, consider public opinion about same-sex marriage. The standard approach would interpret the results of 33 years of polling as a gradual shift of Americans' true opinions on same-sex marriage, brought to light through the standardized techniques (Andersen and

Fetner 2008; Sherkat et al. 2011). Instead, we can interpret them as a shift in where respondents tend to place themselves on a predefined spectrum of opinion. We cannot know whether those who "strongly oppose" laws allowing same-sex marriage do so because they have carefully considered these laws, because they do not like gays and lesbians, or because they identify as social conservatives. Rather than trying to guess which of these identities is operating, it makes most sense to interpret their responses as authentic but, at the same time, completely dependent on the context in which the respondents were answering. They are indications of the respondents' identification with one or another social group they recognize. Because their responses are dynamic, reactive, and collective, it is less useful to seek to isolate their individually authentic opinions than it is to understand the social cues they are giving off. Understanding these cues requires other kinds of research such as interviews, media analysis, political discussion networks (Huckfeldt et al. 2004), and group discussions (Lezaun 2007) that offer insight into how opinions fit in social contexts.

People focused narrowly on forecasting election outcomes (such as referenda on same-sex marriage) may well choose to stick with traditional polling strategies. But if we want to understand how public opinion actually works, what its genuine contours are, we should strongly consider adopting a performative viewpoint. This approach has several important advantages as well. It takes seriously the fundamentally collective character of publics as more than the aggregation of their constituent individuals, as previous chapters of the book have established. It recognizes the information gathered through polling as real information, relevant to the social and political life of the public, without making the untenable assumption that this information is transparent or authoritative or that its representation goes only one way. We turn next to the question of how representation runs in both directions on the democratic ladder.

Policy Responsiveness and Feedback: Back to the Democratic Ladder

If we take seriously the idea that public opinion research is performative – that is, that it helps to *create* the kind of public we experience – we can place public opinion on the democratic ladder as an institution that bridges gaps between individuals' experiences and ideas and the policies enacted in the name of the public. But we can do so under two important conditions. First, we need to understand its role on the ladder as *creative*, not just straightforward. Public opinion as expressed through polling ought to be understood as genuine and real, but as created through a technological process that changes opinions as it makes them public. Therefore, public policy is *responsive* to public opinion, but it is responsive to public opinion in specific, technologically mediated ways, not in absolute or unfiltered ways. Second, we need to recognize that public opinion, like other elements of the democratic ladder, is a two-way system. Polling provides crucial information to policy makers for them to make decisions, but it also provides key information to citizens about who they and their publics are. It therefore facilitates policy *feedback* as well.

Policy responsiveness refers to the extent to which policies adopted by the government are the policies the public wants. In general, most studies of policy responsiveness find fairly high levels, meaning that public policies often reflect public opinion as represented by polls (Brooks and Manza 2006; Burstein 2003; Erikson et al. 2002). In general, when polling results are compared to public policy outcomes, public policy looks quite responsive (Manza and Cook 2002). This raises a new puzzle: why do so few Americans trust government when government, in turn, generally produces policies that most Americans favor (see Hetherington 2005)? Indeed, in many cases people don't know that they agree with laws that are enacted, even when they agree with the policies the laws actually put in place (Coggins and Stimson 2012)! The answer to that question is two-fold. To some extent, it lies in the structure of the media, which we take up in the next chapter.

Another important point, though, is that overall responsiveness masks an important reality: affluent and wealthy Americans have their views represented far more thoroughly and regularly than do middle-, working-, and lower-class Americans. This is true across many policy domains and probably goes a long way toward explaining disaffection with government (Gilens 2012).

The main message is that public policy is responsive to public opinion *as represented through conventional polls*. And we have seen that these polls represent the public's opinions creatively, not transparently. So some portion of the public's mistrust in government is probably the result of the fact that people's opinions are distorted and changed as they become public, and thus the feedback they get from watching policies being implemented focuses more on the changes needed than on the ways government has responded.

A contemporary example of this process took place at the end of 2012, when the Democrats and the Republicans entered tense negotiations to try to avoid the so-called "fiscal cliff," a package of federal spending cuts and tax increases that many expected to send the economy into a recession. Many Americans answer public opinion polls with consistent preferences for cutting spending, but they are rarely able to name *any* public programs they would like to cut that would even make a dent in the federal budget. This disconnect – supporting budget cuts in general but having no particular programs to cut – is often interpreted as evidence for the public's fickle nature, or Americans' inability to make tough choices about public policy. And, in fact, it is one source of the breakdown in governance in Washington, as politicians seek to balance the competing, even contradictory, demands of public opinion and opposing policies. It would be reasonable to say that public policy was responsive to public opinion regardless of the outcome, since the public seems both to support and to oppose budget cuts.

That dysfunction brings up the other important element of public opinion on the democratic ladder: *policy feedback*. Policy feedback is the learning process that allows citizens who pay attention to government policy to adjust their ideas and preferences based on the policies that are adopted. Some forms of policy feedback – particularly surrounding tax incentives – are assumed as part of policy making. For example, tax deductions for home mortgage interest or for charitable donations are in the law precisely to *encourage* people to own homes and make charitable donations. Thus the policy feeds back: citizens learn about the laws they prompted in the first place, and then change their behaviors to match.

Policy feedback extends well beyond tax policy, though. Andrea Louise Campbell (2011) highlights three health policies that created new constituencies because groups of people were coalesced into publics by virtue of being treated similarly by health policies. Their status as publics was created because they were addressed in common. So just as publics make policy through policy responsiveness, policy can create publics through policy feedback. People develop preferences not just from the bottom up, from private life into public opinion and policy, but also from the top down, from policy through observation and public opinion to reconfigure their existing opinions (Valelly 1993).

To sum up: public opinion polling has in many ways structured the culture and practice of democracy since World War II. As I have argued, most Americans now "think with" polls as the very definition of public opinion, and with public opinion as the obvious connection between individual preferences and public policies. Appreciating these roles, it's important to recognize two things about public opinion: first, that public opinion polling really is a democratic practice. It helps create and constitute publics, and these publics are real, genuine, and democratically interactive. In other words: societies do become more democratic because of the presence of public opinion polling. But second: just as other technologies – from scientific to cultural, musical, and communications – create new possibilities while also closing off others, public opinion polling severely limits the democratic imaginations of citizens while creating others. It needs to be carried out and interpreted carefully and thoughtfully to understand the complicated and nuanced ways respondents' social and cultural patterns affect the answers they give. The next chapter takes up the other crucial institution along the democratic ladder, the way most citizens learn about and express issues: the mass media.

5

Media, Communications, and Political Knowledge

In any modern polity, the communication of political ideas, beliefs, and facts is of paramount importance. The connection between print media and democracy has long been recognized, and important updates have followed for radio, television, film, e-mail, and social networking. This chapter considers the impact of these methods: how do citizens learn what they know (even the knowledge that, as Ronald Reagan famously quipped, "isn't so" [Reagan 1964])? Since I have conceptualized democracy as essentially a communicative system, transmitting citizen preferences to governmental and other actors and vice versa, it makes sense to conclude our study with a focus on old and new media.

Beyond their immediate communicative function, media also help create publics in large societies where people cannot meet and deliberate in person. The proliferation of new forms of media, and with them new audiences and new opportunities for the public to splinter, means the contours and boundaries of publics are constantly changing. While there are important promises in the new media environment that has emerged since about 1990, the media environment is the weakest link in my otherwise optimistic view of the social and cultural bases of democracy and their future outlook. Practices and publics that have formed around new media technologies and new patterns of ownership of the media do not provide sufficient cross-cutting public discourse to support democratic practices, although there are promising signs that new practices could form to play this role.

As we have seen above, one important effect of media changes since 1990 is epistemic closure: the tendency for citizens and leaders alike to be insulated from opposing opinions and even inconvenient facts (Sanchez 2010). The trend in communications technologies is to offer greater access but also greater choice in what media individuals consume. The natural outcome of this has been a reduction in individuals' access to disagreement. This chapter considers the bridging and bonding functions of media and the ways different communications forms affect these distinct roles. Changing technologies and the social and political opportunities they afford, the increasing ownership of media by a few very large companies, and practices of isolation and audience fragmentation on the part of both media producers and the public make the current media landscape an area of concern for democracy.

In the context of small-town communities like the one Rockwell's *Town Meeting* imagines, the function of the local newspaper was relatively simple: to make sure the routine goings-on of the town were recorded and distributed to the population. Secondarily, community newspaper editors were the sometimes-controversial opinion leaders. They knew what was going on and thought about it, ideally in a more dispassionate way than others who were more intimately involved.

Although this small-town ideal persists in the thousands of local newspapers that continue to exist and even thrive (Lauterer 2006), it is a far cry from the structure, role, and experience of the contemporary mass media. Many of the national and international media are now owned by large corporations that often own many other news and entertainment outlets. The audiences for mass media are widely dispersed, whether over large metropolitan areas or across whole countries or beyond. And audiences are often very distrustful of these media, even as they pay close attention to them.

In addition to these processes, huge changes in media technologies and the practices that have grown up around them mean that the publics constituted by media are dramatically different than they were a generation ago. The mass public created by the twentieth-century mass media has been replaced by multiple, fragmented publics created by multiple, fragmented media sources.

Several characteristics of media in general combine to allow each form of media to afford different opportunities and threats to democratic practices. I propose considering several dimensions of media outlets to evaluate these democratic risks and potentials:

- **Bandwidth:** how much information is available? Print media are in the middle here, as a newspaper can carry long stories and photographs but not video or audio. Video (internet and broadcast) is high bandwidth, as it carries a lot of information at once, whereas the Twitter social media engine is extremely low bandwidth, allowing only 140 characters in a given message.
- **Interactivity:** to what extent is the public involved in creating and disseminating the message? Traditional mass media cast the audience – the public – as only listening or reading, although that relationship has changed over time. Various technologies of *mediated public spheres* like letters to the editor and online commenting engage the audience in a conversation still driven by professionals, and social media like Twitter and Facebook offer the opportunity to interact among friends and networks without professional involvement.
- **Synchronicity:** how much time is there between the creation and the reception of a message? Live broadcasts are synchronous, meaning that audiences hear them at the time they are produced. Social media are generally nearly synchronous, as messages are available as soon as they are produced. Print media and websites are asynchronous: recipients of media must wait a period of time after a message is created in order to receive it, although that time is shorter than in previous eras and is growing ever shorter.
- **Partisanship:** to what extent are messages committed to a political position? Traditional mass media make a claim to objectivity – avoiding partisanship – while nearly every other

form of media is driven by partisanship, by competition between rival ideologies.

* **Access to disagreement:** to what extent do audiences receive ideas they expect to disagree with? Again, traditional media such as mass-market, broadcast news and newspapers tend to provide more opportunities for people to run across information they disagree with than newer media forms.

Using these characteristics, we can evaluate different media sources. None is necessarily better or worse; successful fostering of democratic publics should make use of all the different characteristics. Partisan cable channels like Fox News and MSNBC, for example, are high in bandwidth, low in interactivity, high in synchronicity, high in partisanship, and low in access to disagreement. Mainstream print sources such as the *New York Times* or the *Wall Street Journal* are moderate in bandwidth, low in interactivity, low in synchronicity, low in partisanship (in their news sections, not their editorial pages), and high in access to disagreement. And social networking tools like Twitter are low in bandwidth, high in interactivity, high in synchronicity, high in partisanship, and low in access to disagreement.

Why do Media Matter?

The media play two separate roles on the democratic ladder (see figure 6). The first is mostly a vertical role: media carry information and ideas from government, business, and elites to everyday citizens, providing the basic news of the moment, information about the agendas being considered in government, and the performance of officials, government, and other institutions. In their vertical role, media are similar to the newspaper's character; as Benedict Anderson (2006) pointed out, newspapers tie together imagined publics for specific points in time:

> The date at the top of the newspaper, the single most important emblem on it, provides the essential connection – the steady onward

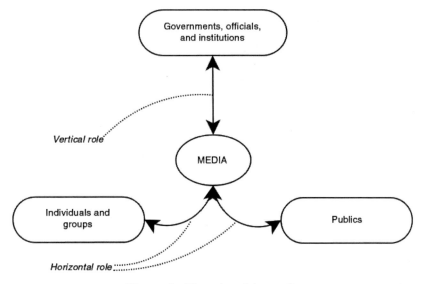

Figure 6 The roles of the media

clocking of homogeneous, empty time ... The second source of imagined linkage lies in the relationship between the newspaper, as an odd form of book, and the market ... The newspaper is merely an "extreme form" of the book, a book sold on a colossal scale, but of ephemeral popularity. Might we say: one-day best-sellers? (Anderson 1992, 33–5)

Media in their vertical role may also carry messages and ideas from people back "up" to governmental officials and elites. Particularly since the advent of "public journalism" (Haas 2007; Rosenberry 2010), in which newspapers endeavored to bring community voices into the elite conversation, the media have sought to represent the needs and desires of the public instead of only bringing information down to the public.

The media play an entirely different role too: a horizontal role. Beginning with letters to the editor and continuing through a wide variety of mediated public spheres, media have provided the space for citizens to interact, deliberate, and argue with one another. Here the communication is among citizens and groups of citizens, not between citizens and governments and institutions. Mediated public spheres offer the opportunity for citizens to act as if they were in a physical public sphere, something like the one discussed in chapter 2. They can express their views, listen to the ideas of others, and potentially change their own opinions to respond to what others say.

Different kinds of horizontal media work differently. Letters to the editor, for example, have a set of characteristics that influence the kinds of ideas and arguments that are put forward there. Letters are *asynchronous*, which means that people read them at a later time than when they are written. They are also subject to *gatekeeping*, meaning that letter writers have to write a letter that will first convince the newspaper's editor to print it, then go on to convince readers of its point. Finally, like most mediated public spheres, letters to the editor address an *anonymous* public: writers could not possibly meet, see, or even really imagine the entire audience for their letters.

Other mediated public spheres work differently; call-in talk radio, for example, sometimes features gatekeepers analogous to letters editors, who decide which calls make it to the air. But the communications themselves are synchronous, meaning that listeners hear the comments at the same time they are spoken (though, of course, *reactions* to the comments take a bit longer as other listeners call in to respond). And online comments on news stories – a very popular mediated public sphere – are asynchronous but feature no gatekeeping, a combination that can lead to heated arguments and incivility. Other forms of mediated public spheres are much more constrained. CNN, for example, used a device called the Perception Analyzer[1] during the 2012 presidential debates. The device continuously monitored the reactions of a group of voters during the debate, providing an external "read" on how a specific, if small, public felt about each moment (Boyd 2008). This form of feedback provides precious little opportunity for real deliberation, but allows viewers to see how an apparently ordinary group of voters responds in real time. That, in turn, may affect how viewers feel as well.

Returning to the image of deliberation from chapter 2, one

feature of the town meeting is that it took place within a town, and in general a small one. So participants in this scene likely knew one another, probably interacted before the town meeting, and likely expected to interact again afterward. The social network of the public was, therefore, dense; there were consequences for taking extreme positions, public insults, and uncivil behavior. That society is mostly gone; in its place are neighborhoods that are parts of much larger metropolitan areas, full of people who move often (Oishi 2010) and who, increasingly, choose neighborhoods and communities where others are like them both demographically and politically (Bishop 2008). The most important thing about the horizontal function of media is that it brings media technologies to bear on the crucial task of forming publics in an increasingly anonymous society.

The media have had a key role in forming "communities of discourse" (Nord 2001) for a long time. In postcolonial societies in Asia and Africa, a key tool allowing people to imagine themselves as parts of a single nation was the advent of "print culture" (Anderson 2006).

Already by the eighteenth century, American newspapers were places for debate about public matters, first in general and in the later eighteenth century as active partisan promoters (Starr 2004, 57). By the early twentieth century, overtly partisan newspapers had declined and the principles of objectivity and professionalism had become the standard for media behavior – part of the more general faith in objectivity, science, and detachment that the Progressive era brought in the rest of the political realm as well. The main exception to this was the Muckraking movement, in which many reporters saw themselves as the bulwark against corruption in politics. In that sense, they campaigned for that very Progressive point: promoting authentic, individualist democracy against its perversion by corrupt, private interests:

> The muckrakers asserted that democracy was a moral good and that any perversion of what they called democracy was evil . . . When the muckrakers turned their attention to American life and politics, they discerned moral flaws . . . they argued that political parties were often

the tools of special interests rather than the means of majority rule. They decried the reign of urban bosses whom they claimed controlled the public at will. (Schultz 1965, 529)

Throughout the twentieth century, the American newspaper looked relatively uniform: a front page and front section containing articles and information about current events, reported in a way that at least claimed objectivity; an opinion/editorial page at the end of that section, containing editorials from the newspaper's leadership, columns from other experts, letters from readers, and often a political cartoon; and other sections focusing on business, sports, the arts, and so on.

In the post-World War II era, several changes occurred. One was the emergence of competition among elite, nationally oriented newspapers such as the *New York Times*, the *Washington Post*, and the *Wall Street Journal*. These papers competed for readers in various ways, including by seeking "scoops": new stories the others didn't yet have. This focus, in turn, helped produce a generation of journalists who saw their job as providing professional scrutiny and oversight for public figures – a practice that earned the press the memorable term "nattering nabobs of negativism" from Vice-President Spiro Agnew. During the Watergate scandal that eventually brought down President Nixon and after which public trust in government dropped dramatically (Hetherington 2005), among the most memorable heroes were *Washington Post* reporters Bob Woodward and Carl Bernstein. Their quest to uncover the scandal, memorialized in the 1975 movie *All the President's Men*, ushered in an era of greater distrust between government and the mass media (Schudson 1992b).

Under this "traditional" version of the news media, newspapers, editors, and reporters used their networks of contacts, access, and expertise to uncover, report, and explain the news; audiences received and read the news in a relatively homogeneous way. This institutional organization of the news media established a professional cadre of journalists. The other thing it did was to produce a particular kind of audience – as we have discussed earlier in the book, a particular kind of public. In the era of the mass media (relatively similar news messages broadcast through print or electronic means), one of the products was the mass itself: the kind of audience and the bonds among members of that audience. Although often referred to as "traditional" media, the primacy of the objectivity-driven, professionalized mass media really lasted only about half a century, perhaps less. In fact, perhaps the main constant in the history of the media is that everything changes: technologies, practices, ownership patterns, and public attitudes (Schudson 2013). The "traditional" relationship began to crumble with the engagement of the electronic media in the protests of 1968 (Gitlin 1980), and new communications and media technologies since then have dramatically transformed the kinds of publics evoked by the media.

What gets called the "traditional" mass media, then, is a relatively short-term phenomenon in historical perspective. Indeed, the term "media," whose root implies that the job is to be in the middle of other things (generally, the government and the public), became the predominant name for newspapers, television, and radio only in the 1970s in reaction to the Watergate scandal. Before that, they were generally referred to as "the press," implying a role as disseminators of information, not go-betweens. The salient characteristics of the so-called traditional media environment were:

1. **for-profit ownership** of media outlets, so that viewers and advertisers had to be attracted in order to pay for news coverage and sufficient profits to maintain the parent businesses;[2]
2. a commitment to **objectivity as the standard**, which required that editorial commentary be accorded its own page and that advertisers' demands be carefully insulated from journalistic practices; and
3. mostly **one-way communication**, wherein journalists and editors with expertise explained matters to the listening public without much in the way of responses back. (The main exception to this is the letters-to-the-editor column, a venerated element of the opinion page [Perrin 2012; Perrin and Vaisey 2008]).

These characteristics combined to produce an attention-paying public that was subject, overall, to similar messages regardless of which broadcast or print news source they paid attention to. The kind of public this media arrangement evoked was a *mass public*: as consumers of media, the public was relatively similar in the information and viewpoints they had access to, and to a significant extent their main relationship with news and information was with expert producers of information with whom they had no back-and-forth interaction. The first element – for-profit ownership – has stayed the same since the golden era of the mass media. In fact, media conglomeration has meant more media outlets and sources owned by fewer, larger corporations (Bagdikian 2004; McChesney and Pickard 2011; Press and Williams 2010). The other two elements – the professional commitment to objectivity and the one-way character of media communication – have changed in various ways, and several times, in the past few decades.

Of course, this image of the mass created by the mass media was never literally true. In a famous argument against the "mass" model, Katz and Lazarsfeld (1955) showed that the influence of mass media messages was often carried through "opinion leaders": people within communities to whom others looked to help interpret and understand the news coming from the mass media. These writers criticized what they called the "hypodermic needle" view in which the media injected ideas into the public, which passively took them in. In a novel experiment, political scientist Katherine Cramer Walsh showed that the way a group of "old timers" talked about current issues went well beyond the facts and ideas they encountered in all the media they consumed (Walsh 2004). So even in the context of a truly mass media, interpersonal contacts and communications between people come between the media and people's beliefs and ideas. But these observations are about the particular ways messages were heard and communicated; they do not address the more general point that the mass media's structure gave it:

> the power . . . to define normal and abnormal social and political activity, to say what is politically real and legitimate and what is not;

to justify the two-party political structure; to establish certain political agendas for social attention and to contain, channel, and exclude others; and to shape the images of opposition movements. (Gitlin 1978, 205)

In other words: the golden-era mass public was *collective*, since it was addressed in a fairly uniform way (Warner 2002). In terms of media, it was not very deliberative, since strongly oppositional voices were rare (Page 1996), and audiences had little opportunity to "talk back" to the media. The flow of information was therefore mostly in one direction, and it was mostly "vertical": communicated from media to audiences, not among members of audiences.

Recall Horkheimer and Adorno's distinction between two then-prominent communications technologies: the telephone and the radio (Horkheimer and Adorno 2002 [1946], 95–6). In calling radio democratic, they emphasized its creation of a collective public: addressing the mass as a single whole, a *demos* of the kind discussed in chapter 1. That collectivity, though, was vulnerable to manipulation because of the trust the audience placed in the personality. For example, Adorno (2000) provides a thorough critique of a very successful radio personality, Rev. Martin Luther Thomas, who used his radio program to incite his audience to authoritarian and intolerant views, a pattern that has continued through twentieth-century talk radio (Apostilidis 2000; Herbst 1995). With few exceptions, political talk radio is extremely partisan, seeking to agitate and motivate its audience through name-calling, divisive language, and mobilization talk, and shares more with talk radio about sports than it does with deliberative talk about civic matters (Dempsey 2006; Bobbitt 2010). This is not to say that this kind of talk is inherently bad – such partisan talk may well inspire listeners to get involved in politics even as it discourages their being respectful of citizens who disagree (Mutz 2006). But talk radio succeeds mostly in playing to divided, niche audiences, and far more conservative audiences than liberal for reasons of corporate ownership (Halpin et al. 2007).

Since the 1970s, a series of social and technological changes have wreaked havoc with the golden-era, mass-media model. Overwhelmingly, the technologies that have emerged have been liberal in character more than democratic; they have tended toward privatizing and individualizing communication, entertainment, and information. The trend began in earnest with the introduction of cable television, which meant that viewers suddenly had the ability to select their particular news source, which in turn encouraged television producers to create "niche news" tailored to specific sub-groups of viewers (Stroud 2011). This change, in turn, led fairly quickly to declining political knowledge, as evening television audiences were no longer forced by technological necessity to pay attention to a nationally oriented news broadcast if they were to pay attention to anything at all (Prior 2007). Fox News Channel was founded in 1996 on the heels of the strong success of CNN's cable-only 24-hour news model. From the beginning FNC was to offer a conservative alternative to mainstream news, and by 2002 its ratings surpassed CNN's. In 2002, then-struggling cable channel MSNBC sought to revitalize ratings, first by mimicking Fox's conservative brand before settling on its current trademark as the liberal alternative to Fox (Richey 2012). Formally, the difference is in the way the technological change to cable television combined with people's tendency to prefer material they find comfortable, such as that they already agree with. The technological opportunity, the business decisions, and the cultural practice – each a positive development on its own – combined to produce an outcome that was clearly bad for democratic life (Sunstein 2007, 2009).

Cable television was only the beginning. In fact, the relationship between broadcaster and audience is formally similar for cable and over-the-air broadcasters. It remains essentially vertical, in that on-air personalities make statements that are carried to the entire audience without audience involvement or conversation. The social and technological changes that came later have been overwhelmingly individualizing: the affordances they provide allow for dramatically more individual expression on the part of citizens but dramatically less collective; more horizontal, less cross-cutting. In addition, the distinction between entertainment and information became increasingly blurred, as both were combined into what industry insiders call "content."

Entertainment technologies following this model began with the introduction of the long-playing record in 1948, which Adorno predicted would ultimately change the content of music itself by changing what it meant to listen to music (Adorno 1990a [1928], 1990b [1934]; Levin 1990). Traditional music listening, he reasoned, required a certain degree of work; audiences at live performances of classical music were focused on the performance and their attention was engaged in the task of listening and interpreting it. By moving the task of listening out of the concert hall and into private spaces (Barnett 2006), and by affording the possibility of listening to music while engaged in other activities, the long-playing record and similar recording devices changed what it meant to listen to music and, eventually, the content of music itself. As we saw in chapter 4, the history of devices to afford increasingly private, easy, and low-cost music listening since then is well known, extending from the car radio through the cassette, compact disc, Walkman, MP3 player, and electronic music distribution systems like iTunes, Pandora, and Spotify. Each of these has had effects on the music itself, as artists adapt musical styles to the constraining and enabling affordances of the technologies (Katz 2010).

Like entertainment devices, devices for reading, learning about, and reacting to public events have become increasingly private, easy, and low-cost. Cable television gave way to proliferating all-news channels and later to channels identified with specific political ideologies. The introduction of the web allowed readers to pick and choose their news and information without regard to geography, isolating individual news stories and columns from the newspapers, magazines, and broadcasts they would previously have been published in. Websites and blogs allow virtually anyone not only to read the news and opinion of her choice but to publish her own news and opinions. The tradeoff? Nobody needs to listen, so the price of individual expression might be utter obscurity or total inanity. The advent of "social media" (principally microblogs like Facebook and Twitter) added to these tendencies by affording networks of friends and followers – essentially, people who often read one another's writings and comment on them, or simply ignore them and move on. A 2009 study found that the majority of Twitter traffic was devoted to self-promotion, unwanted commercial messages, and the overall winner, "pointless babble" (Pear Analytics 2009, 5). Each of these technologies, to use Horkheimer and Adorno's language, has been increasingly "liberal": they encourage individual self-expression to the detriment of broader, collective publics.

Adorno worried about recorded music requiring too little work to consume, thus lowering the quality of listening. Similarly, news, information, and ideas have become so individualized through contemporary technologies that they may be too easy to read, requiring relatively little attention or intellectual commitment by citizens. Psychological research demonstrates that people generally prefer, and are better at, understanding information that accords with their existing schemas: the system of ideas that they already believe (Fiske and Linville 1980). It is easier to consume information and ideas that you are likely to agree with. In turn, reading material that one is predisposed to agree with – whether because it is distributed by friends on social media or because it is broadcast over niche media outlets tailored to the audience's existing political preferences – reduces the likelihood of encountering new or dramatically different ideas. Technologies that change music shape only the direction of musical change (Lena 2012); technologies that facilitate this "epistemic closure" in news, information, and ideas threaten democratic citizenship by dividing publics into "echo chambers" (Jamieson and Cappella 2008). In particular, mediated public spheres like talk radio, internet chat, and social media, as well as targeted television stations, have produced a new mode of media audiences, saturated with competing opinions that form the primary sources for many citizens' thinking about politics (Jacobs and Townsley 2011).

At the same time as these practices and technologies close off the development of some of the kinds of publics essential to democracy, they also open new frontiers for the development of new kinds of publics. Those citizens who are particularly interested in politics – attentive publics – have more access now to information, ideas, and diverse interpretations than did similar citizens at any prior point in history. Increasing sources of news and information may encourage citizens to narrow their outlook, but they also provide the opportunity for citizens to resist that trend and broaden their outlook instead. And beyond the distribution of news and information, social media afford new ways of mobilizing citizens and potential publics that have not yet been fully understood (Halpern and Gibbs 2012). Activist citizens in the Tea Party movement, Occupy Wall Street, and, internationally, in the Arab Spring all used new social media technologies to help organize protests (Tufekci and Wilson 2012), and electoral campaigns have mobilized the web and social media as new ways to inform and engage citizens (Klinenberg and Perrin 2000; Kreiss 2012; Nielsen 2012). So these technological advances afford new possibilities for democratic publics while foreclosing old ones. The challenge – which is covered in more detail in the final chapter of the book – is to match practices, institutions, and rules with the kinds of publics afforded by our current technical and practical environment. Mismatches between current technological styles and public practices can lead to mistakes in citizenship practices. As one example, Sobieraj (2011) found activists so focused on trying to get coverage in traditional mass media that they ignored opportunities for face-to-face interaction with interested members of the public who approached the protests. Meanwhile, it is the most extreme movement actors that tend to get noticed by mainstream media outlets (Bail 2012), so the attention to media as the site of political activism may push activists to extreme messages or tactics in order to be noticed.

Privatizing technologies have important effects on horizontal media functions as well as vertical ones. Many online commenting engines are tied to media with ideological commitments. Conservatives can feel comfortable posting their opinions about stories on the Fox News website, while the *Huffington Post* caters to a more liberal demographic and its comments follow along. There is no requirement that commenters stick with sites full of those they agree with; indeed, one of the relatively few sources of access to disagreement is that some people cross over, preferring to post comments on sites they expect to disagree with. Many sites have frequent commenters who oppose the site's main theme, and these commenters become "regulars" in the conversations, pigeon-holed but vocal in their contributions.

Technology is only half the story, though. As media scholars Andrea Press and Bruce Williams write: "even though new technologies may have built-in potentials for affecting social relations in one way or another, which potentials are actually realized is a function of the specific political and economic systems in which they are actually deployed" (Press and Williams 2010, 34). The other half of the story is about the first element in the list of characteristics of the traditional media: the fact that virtually all news media outlets in the United States are owned by for-profit companies for which the provision of news, information, and ideas is often no different from the provision of any other product. Large media conglomerates control an enormous proportion of the country's broadcast and print media. Unlike other large-corporation industries, though, "media products are unique in one vital respect. They do not manufacture nuts and bolts: they manufacture a social and political world" (Bagdikian 2004, 9). But large corporations control virtually all radio broadcasting in the United States (Klinenberg 2007), along with cable television, newspaper (Meyer 2009), and television news. Technological change, corporate profit-seeking, and cultural and psychological tendencies to prefer easy information to complicated ideas combined to produce major changes in the media landscape. These corporate drivers have shaped internet news and information too, making the internet and social media corporate-friendly as well (McChesney 2013).

Earlier in the book, I detailed why an agonistic approach to democracy – embracing true conflict and differences of position and opinion – is the best way to represent the reality of current society in democratic publics. The question now is: how can we reconcile that vision with my contention here that a fractured, polarized media environment damages democratic practice? The answer lies in the question of public attention. An agonistic public sphere allows – in fact, may even *require* – citizens to hear one another out, to pay attention to the fact of their disagreement even if they would rather not. An agonistic public is, then, still a collective public, albeit one in which civility may be swamped by frank conflict.

Sociologists Ron Jacobs and Eleanor Townsley, following Mutz (2006), suggest that these emotional appeals to fragmented publics actually spur viewers into political activity:

> More playful forms of argument, such as the clever use of dramatic techniques to place moral conflict into bold (and usually overstated) relief, the careful cuing of recognizable genres, and the elaborate identification of contemporary public figures with mythic archetypes – all [. . .] increase the level of civic involvement, in official as informal publics . . . if an individual "hates" George Will or Paul Krugman or Bill O'Reilly, it is more likely that that person will participate in the public sphere. (Jacobs and Townsley 2011, 69)

To be sure, many media intellectuals such as O'Reilly, or former MSNBC host Keith Olbermann, set themselves up to be the objects of such hatred. But in some cases, this hatred gets in the way of considering the actual claims made by the personalities. To the extent that this media environment spurs political engagement, that engagement is in a public that is itself fragmented. Participants are hard-pressed to find enough common ground even to have a productive argument with those they disagree with.

The Fragmented Public

Technological development favoring privatization and niche news over public, collective, and cross-cutting news is one of the processes driving the contemporary media public. Audience expectations of easy-to-consume ideas and opinions mesh with these technological changes to produce unprecedented fragmentation of audiences and therefore publics. And corporations whose bottom lines are driven by how many viewers or readers they can attract help drive these tendencies and take advantage of their outcomes.

This is an example of the paradox of choice (Schwartz 2004): too many options for consumers means many such consumers make choices that are ultimately bad for the public. Most people do not want to experience disagreement with others; they prefer, quite reasonably, to have their views validated and expressed. But their ability to put that preference into action results in precious little access to disagreement. As discussed in chapter 4, while most Americans do know someone they disagree with (Huckfeldt 2007; Huckfeldt et al. 2004), they often do not actually talk about politics with those people (Klofstad et al. 2013; Wojcieszak and Mutz 2009). Corporate decisions to drive and use technologies to encourage niche news have served to impoverish the ability of citizens to consider and express opinions across social, cultural, and ideological divides (McChesney 1999).

The media's ability to form publics – even niche publics – can be a useful, even foundational, element of democratic practice. That's because publics exist at many levels, and it's important to have publics that are attentive and paying attention to specific issues ("issue publics"), which are sometimes deeply partisan and divisive, *alongside* publics that are broad-based, deliberative, and open to consideration of alternative points of view. To borrow terms from the study of social capital, the first of these is a *bonding* public, in which people who are similar to one another and share similar principles bond with one another. The second is a *bridging* public, in which people who share commitments to a broad public like a state, region, or country consider one another's views, ideas, and concerns even if they do so with emotional and partisan commitments (Putnam 2000). Democratic practice requires *both* bridging and bonding publics. The problem I've identified in this chapter is that the current technological and corporate media environment strongly encourages bonding publics but provides little opportunity for bridging publics. Bridging publics are often built out of "weak culture" (Schultz and Breiger 2010): connections between people because of not-very-important interests they have in common, such as preferences for particular music or hobbies rather than politics.

A particularly strong example of this was in the final days of the 2012 presidential election campaign, in which numerous Republican commentators made strong and unequivocal claims that Romney was sure to win, the polling results notwithstanding. Pundits asserted that "independent" voters were breaking for Romney, and that for various other reasons biased media meant that Obama's support was being overstated (see, for example, Franc 2012). Indeed, reports indicated that Romney himself and top advisers believed this story, in large part because it was broadcast by Fox News, the network of choice for the Republican campaign and voters, and circulated around conservative blogs and websites (Peters and Stelter 2012). In fact, conservative commentator and strategist Karl Rove – famous for having engineered George W. Bush's electoral success – refused to believe the results as they came in on national television on the Fox News set, he himself apparently the victim of this niche-news error.

This example of niche-news publics did not just lend itself to embarrassing errors. It also provided fodder for partisan readers and commenters to foster greater social and political divisions in the future. Consider, for example, this comment posted on the *Cleveland Plain Dealer's* website by a reader:

> I get the impression that justification for street violence is being established in the event of a loss. When people scream suppression and vote rigging all the time, you have to wonder where their heart is? Adding fuel to that fire are pollsters who have polled the President ahead consistently, because they totally miss the intensity of the Republican vote. This will result in the Obama base feeling like the election was stolen. Street violence is bad for everyone and will even further reduce our standing in the world.[3]

The commenter was, of course, wrong about the outcome of the election. But his or her concern highlights the problem of such strong divisions among publics in the current media environment: partisan news and opinion can drive factual mistakes, which in turn are interpreted not as mistakes but as undeserved victories for the opposing side.

The emergence of the new media environment since about 1990 is the story of fragmented audiences for broadcast media and separate networks participating in conversations on blogs and social media. There is a lot positive about these developments: citizens have better access to the arguments they can use to understand and explain their views and preferences, and they can use these networks to build their confidence in their efficacy as citizens. Indeed, since in many cases social and broadcast media provide outlets for participation in government through contacting representatives, signing petitions, and similar actions, these networks provide the direct means for citizens to participate in this public sphere.

An important case in point is the Tea Party movement that emerged in 2009 following the election of Barack Obama as president. The movement's origin is usually located in the "Santelli rant," an emotional protest by CNBC business commentator Rick Santelli. On February 19, 2009, Santelli complained from the floor of the Chicago Mercantile Exchange about the proposed mortgage relief program: "How many people want to pay for your neighbor's mortgages that has [sic] an extra bathroom and can't pay their bills? Raise their hand!" He called for "another Tea Party" to protest the policies. The Tea Party movement grew quickly, encompassing economic populism alongside other conservative hot button issues (Perrin et al. 2011, forthcoming; Zernike 2010). Tea Party activists were strongly encouraged by Fox News reporters and commentators, who played overtly supportive roles in publicizing and covering the movement. Fox (and, to a lesser extent, CNBC) played the role, then, of horizontal more than vertical media. Its main role was to support the movement and mobilize the movement's supporters, and all indications are that it did this job with great success. Since citizen participation is a positive feature of democracy, that role was valuable – it just isn't the role we tend to expect from traditional media.

What's missing in this new media environment is the cross-cutting opportunities for communication: the publicness constituted by common address. We expect two different, sometimes contradictory, things from the media: a mobilizing, empowering function, largely a function of the horizontal feature of the media, and an informing, public-creating function, largely the role of the vertical feature. Ladd (2012, 194–220) outlines these two functions as coalition-building and citizen-informing functions. The media of the mid-twentieth century did an admirable job of the vertical function, offering little in the way of the horizontal function. The new, fractured media presents virtually the opposite strengths: ample opportunity to mobilize already-convinced citizens, but little commitment to informing the public.

This effect is not uniform, though. Some media outlets do a better job of informing their audiences than do others. It is difficult to tease apart what is cause and effect, since people who are more inclined to want objective information may be more likely to select certain media sources to begin with, and they may have better information as well. However, several important studies have demonstrated that media attention and political knowledge go hand in hand. For example, an important study showed that viewers of Fox News had significantly worse political knowledge about the then-current Iraq War than did viewers of virtually every other media source, including CNN, National Public Radio, and the *New York Times* (Kull et al. 2004). There is some dispute as to whether this political knowledge outcome is unique to Fox – which is also the most blatantly partisan of the news networks – or if it attaches to other politically biased outlets as well. A 2012 Farleigh Dickinson University study (Cassino et al. 2012) found that people who watched only Fox News or MSNBC had similar, low levels of political knowledge. The most knowledgeable were listeners to National Public Radio (a notoriously high-education, high-status audience), as well as those watching Comedy Central's *The Daily Show with Jon Stewart* and the Sunday morning talk shows, which feature competing opinions, not traditional news (Jacobs and Townsley 2011).

The polarized media environment has brought with it an ever-declining trust in the media as reported in public opinion polls. Trust in the news media, which was high for a brief period during the golden era of the mid-twentieth century, declined sharply between 1970 and 2000, to the point that only 9 percent of Americans said they had "a great deal" of trust in the media, and trust in the media has declined much more quickly than has trust in other major social institutions (Ladd 2012, 88–9).

These findings suggest that:

- the new media environment provides ample opportunities for citizens to gain political knowledge and information if they seek it; however,
- it also provides ample opportunities for citizens to reinforce their existing views and avoid challenges to these if that is what they seek; and, finally,
- it affords new opportunities for citizens to be mobilized and build efficacy, as audiences for partisan broadcasts but particularly as members of social media networks.

This fragmentation is closely associated with the much-discussed decline of civil discourse in the United States. Nearly every political commentator bemoans the incivility of political discussions, but incivility continues and grows. To some extent that is because of media fragmentation: when people do have an opportunity to engage with people they disagree with, they are disposed to consider those people enemies and to react to them with anger instead of consideration. A reasonable reaction is to point out that civility is not necessarily the right goal, as it's more important to be *frank*: to get your point across, even if that means not being polite (Herbst 2010; Schudson 1997). Indeed, recent research shows that most citizens don't want their representatives to compromise, even as they blame opponents' representatives for failing to do so (Wolf, Strachan, and Shea 2012).

The Internet and Media Publics

The advent of the internet – and, in particular, the web in 1994 – ushered in huge changes to the ways information was provided, both by campaigns and through the media. Indeed, internet provision of news and news aggregation is one of the major forces driving the fast decline of newspaper readership in the United States (Meyer 2009).

The first presidential campaigns to have websites were those in 1996, when several Republican candidates sought the nomination to run against Bill Clinton's re-election bid. Bob Dole eventually won the nomination and went on to lose to Clinton in the general election. As we saw in chapter 1, by our current measure, those campaigns' web presence was primitive. Each campaign essentially used its website to distribute materials they would otherwise have sent out in the mail – an efficiency, but hardly the game-changing move that the internet has brought since (Klinenberg and Perrin 2000). By the 2004 election, Howard Dean's campaign had brought enormous innovations in the use of internet media, including the web as well as nascent social media such as Facebook and Twitter (Nielsen 2012; Kreiss 2012).

Social media built upon the blogs that preceded them by allowing anyone with adequate technology – which has become very widespread in the United States – to offer ideas and opinions. Campaigns, activist groups, media, businesses, and friends can send messages quickly about events, demonstrations, articles, and new ideas. Facebook and Twitter provide new opportunities for people to experience political voice: to express their ideas, potentially to an audience that is far-flung geographically. In short, as a tool for political mobilization and the horizontal function of media, social media represent a tremendous leap, and their effectiveness has been demonstrated in several important campaigns already.

The promise of the internet as a new public sphere, though, has not been realized. Instead, the capacity of the internet to let each citizen consume a "daily me" – a specific selection of information, news, and ideas tailored to her pre-existing preferences – is part of the more general tendency of audiences, technologies, and corporations to evacuate the common public. In a country as big as the United States – or, truly, any modern democracy – the ability to exchange ideas, opinions, and emotions among the population is absolutely essential. It remains to be seen whether media and communications technologies can be devised that will be able to support such a common public.

6

Democratic Culture and Practice in Postmodern America

The preceding five chapters establish a platform from which to consider the democratic ladder in its entirety. At the bottom of the ladder remains the public: individuals in their private lives, combined through common concerns as neighbors, audiences, or people with related interests or ideas. Moving up the ladder, these individuals and publics encounter a series of mediators: institutions, practices, and technologies that refine, constitute, enable, and constrain the kinds of publics they can form and the ideas that can be transmitted.

These mediators (e.g., communications technologies and practices, electoral and legislative systems, public opinion representation, deliberation) all have both vertical and horizontal aspects. In their vertical aspects, these mediators carry ideas and preferences up *and down* the ladder. They help transmit people's preferences up to the governmental agencies that make and implement policy, and they help transmit the policy decisions and effects back down the ladder so publics and people develop and refine their ideas, opinions, and preferences in light of policy decisions. In their horizontal aspects, they provide the core around which publics are formed. These institutions, technologies, and practices are the means of communication among members of publics that form the publics' character, boundaries, and capacities. Figure 7 shows the completed democratic ladder, including both its horizontal and vertical aspects.

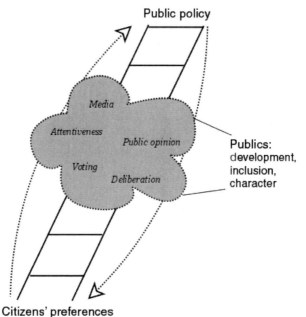

Public policy

Media

Attentiveness

Public opinion

Voting

Deliberation

Publics:
development,
inclusion,
character

Citizens' preferences

Figure 7 The complete democratic ladder

The Postmodern Moment Complicates Publics and Representation

Democracy as we know it is a modern practice. It emerged out of the culture and ideas of modernity, and the systems, assumptions, approaches, and values it contains are modern values. Writing about the worldwide experience of modernity, Marshall Berman (1982) begins with a famous statement about the dynamic character of modern culture from Karl Marx and Friedrich Engels:

> uninterrupted disturbance of all social conditions, everlasting uncertainty and agitation distinguish the bourgeois epoch from all earlier ones. All fixed, fast-frozen relations, with their train of ancient and venerable prejudices and opinions, are swept away, all new-formed ones become antiquated before they can ossify. All that is solid melts into air, all that is holy is profaned. (Marx and Engels 1848)

While Marx and Engels may have thought they were describing capitalism in particular, Berman shows that the experience of the modern world as a whole was summed up in that passage: the experience of big systems, bureaucratic efficiency, and constant change.

The modern world brought with it the fundamental ideas of fairness and procedural efficiency that we associate with democracy. Modernist social thought, especially in capitalist democracies like ours, holds that the people *should* govern themselves because imposing systems of hierarchy and royalty is wrong. And it holds that the people *can* govern themselves because in the modern world people believed they could develop systems and practices to implement their values. The development of bureaucracy – complicated, fair, dispassionate offices that implement the policies the people expect without fear or favor – is a perfect example of this modern faith in fairness and efficiency (Weber 1978, vol. 2, 956–9).

Anthony Giddens identifies trust in abstract institutions as a key element of modernity: "the nature of modern institutions is deeply bound up with the mechanisms of trust in abstract systems, especially trust in expert systems" (Giddens 1990, 83). These provide for "large areas of secure, coordinated actions and events that make modern social life possible" (113). These coordinated actions and events are social institutions that let people live complex lives without needing complicated expertise in many areas.

Under the general cultural style of modernity, Americans developed an amazing democratic structure of elections, legislative processes, media institutions, and more. Some of these were designed by the Founders, others by other leaders and groups, particularly the Progressives who championed cultural and electoral reforms that further rationalized and bureaucratized the process of democratic representation. These Progressive reforms expressed the height of modernism, at once "the assertion of increasing independence from the authority of traditional figures like parents and priests ... [and] belief in the efficacy of science" (Inkeles 1969, 210). Together, they formed one of Giddens' "expert systems": a collection of powerful tools for democratic participation and representation, checks and balances that were generally assumed, on the whole, to make political representation work.

Under modernity, people see such institutions as relatively unproblematic, designed to enhance the faithful representation of the public. But as the modernist trust in institutions has dissipated since about the 1970s, and modernity has begun to give way to "postmodernity," the tools of representation become available not just to represent but actually to change and form the public. Since we've already used technology and music as examples in the book, we'll return to music as an analogy here.

Writing about a "DJ battle" in which rival DJs "attempt to vanquish . . . [each other] with superior skill and showmanship," musicologist Mark Katz observes that this new musical form, which emerged in the late 1990s, depended upon technology originally developed simply to record and play back music made on traditional instruments:

> The machinery on stage was never intended to produce music, but to *reproduce* it: the performers use turntables, records, and a mixer. But instead of merely letting the machines play, these Djs – also known as turntablists – bend the equipment to their will, altering existing sounds and producing a wide range of new ones. (Katz 2010, 124–5)

The ability to record music – and other art – and re-present it at different times and different places was a modern innovation, as discussed earlier in the book (Adorno 1990a [1928], 1990b [1934]; Benjamin 2008). And as I argued before, that ability on its own changed what it meant to listen to music, and therefore changed the music itself, because how people listen to music changes what kind of audience they form. But something was new with turntablism. Now devices that were designed to represent music were turned on their head, used to *create* music. That change indicated a shift into *postmodernity*, in which the rules, practices, and techniques developed under modernity become active tools that can help create what they once represented.

A similar dynamic emerged around the same time, with several tools of political representation. For example, as discussed above, the 1998 impeachment of President Clinton in the wake of a sex scandal was only the second presidential impeachment in American history. Most observers agreed that, however seamy, the scandal did not rise to the level of "high crimes and misde-meanors" contemplated in the Constitution, and public opinion opposed the impeachment (Moore 1998). The votes were split nearly completely along party lines, indicating that the impeach-ment was a political strategy; the Republicans had repurposed impeachment – a tool designed for protecting representation from presidential misconduct – and used it to change the political scene (Sarfatti-Larson and Wagner-Pacifici 2001), not to represent the public. To recap: similar cases of postmodern political crises included the 2000 Florida election; the recall of California gov-ernor Gray Davis; several state legislators' decisions to flee their states instead of casting votes they expected to lose; the increas-ingly strategic use of congressional district boundary drawing for political purposes; and the dramatic increase in the use of the filibuster and other legislative techniques for partisan gain (Perrin et al. 2006; Forest 2004).

These postmodern political crises arise from the fact that, in postmodern times, no element of society is truly stable; every-thing is subject to change. Ideas and practices that were once kept separate, reserved for extraordinary moments, are considered not particularly different from any other political tool. Social theorist Zygmunt Bauman has called this "liquid modernity" (Bauman 2000), in which "social forms [. . .] can no longer (and are not expected) to [sic] keep their shape for long, because they decompose and melt faster than the time it takes to cast them" (Bauman 2007, 1). Political opportunities are re-used and re-interpreted willy-nilly without respect to their original purposes or the potential social, cultural, and representative effects of these uses.

The very mention of postmodernity, or postmodernism, can scare readers away from the argument. The theory of the origins and characteristics of postmodernity is much broader than just this point, and well beyond the scope of this book, so there's no need to consider the much bigger question of whether postmodernity is a distinct period or what constitutes it.[1] For now, what's important is to recognize that democracy and its practices and rules emerged during modern times, and that democracy itself is very much a modern project. The technologies developed during modernity helped bring in the postmodern era, which presents a new set of challenges and opportunities for democracy. The challenges and opportunities faced by contemporary democracy emerge out of the degree of fragmentation and uncertainty that accompanies this postmodern environment. In the remainder of this final chapter, I outline some of the lessons of the book with special attention to the cultural dimensions of publics in these conditions.

Democracy Always Concerns Representation

In order for ideas and preferences to move up the democratic ladder and be put into practice as policy, they have to be represented. No citizen – and certainly no public – has ideas or preferences that are so thoroughly considered, so minutely worked out, that they could go literally and seamlessly from preference to policy, even if there were no disagreement from other citizens and publics. No matter the specific rules and approaches, democracy is at its core a process of representation: a way of communicating material back and forth among citizens, publics, and leaders.

Because of this fact, it's wrong to consider representative democracy, such as the systems in place in virtually every democratic society, as somehow second-best. Often, people imagine that representative democracy is necessary because it would be impossible to implement direct democracy in a society the size of any modern country. But the practices that get called "direct democracy," such as referenda, "electronic town halls," and town meetings, are representative too. First, not everyone participates in these, so the people who actually do participate become, by default, representatives for the broader public. Second, people who participate in them hope that their views and ideas will be represented in the decision-making process and, ultimately, in the decisions themselves.

Representation is Active and Bi-Directional

Because democracy is always representative, the question to ask is: what do the technologies, practices, and rules of a given democracy do to distill, change, and communicate what they represent? As Anne Norton notes, "representation alters the represented" (Norton 2004, 93) – representation is *never* a transparent process. In every kind of representation – political, artistic, even scientific – the process of representation is active and adds something to the represented. Embracing that reality means finding a better way of evaluating democratic practices and structures than determining how transparent they are. This task is particularly urgent in the contemporary world, in which we confront what the French scholar Pierre Rosanvallon calls an "enormous deficit of representation." Because our societies are profoundly individualistic, representation has to be all the more deliberate and active: "In modern societies ... positive steps have to be taken in order for the representation of society to be instituted. Visible and tangible appearance has to be given to the society of individuals, and the people must be given a face" (Rosanvallon 2006, 61–2).

Instead of searching for transparency, I suggest that effective democratic representation represents and fosters the growth of broad publics. Representation that takes into account the publics that have formed in society is more faithful to social conflicts and concerns than representation that seeks the unattainable ideal of transparency (see Saward 2006, 2008). Indeed, Saward (2006) shows that the acts of seeking and accomplishing representation can themselves lead to publics forming or strengthening.

Building on that idea, representation goes in both directions as well. Preferences and ideas are carried up the ladder, but ideas, experiences, and information are carried down it too. Over time, we should understand representation as repeated communication and interaction between publics and governments that simultaneously constrains and enables action by each.

Another way of saying this is that representation is *creative*. That makes sense if we think back to other kinds of representation discussed in chapter 1. Imagine, for example, homeowners in a coastal community potentially affected by climate change impacting their homes and livelihoods. At the bottom of the democratic ladder, their concerns are private: each homeowner, separately, has interests, some in common, others different. Those who live in the homes may worry more about the homes themselves, while those who rent their homes out to vacationers may be more concerned about entertainment, boardwalks, and other amenities that make the community attractive to visitors. But as the group forms a public through a meeting, communications, or conversations, these diverse interests can morph into common concerns over climate change and coastal management. A complicated, multifaceted issue – the kind Walter Lippmann reserves for the public: "Where the facts are most obscure, where precedents are lacking, where novelty and confusion pervade everything, the public in all its unfitness is compelled to make its most important decisions" (Lippmann 2002 [1927], 121). This issue has "spark[ed] a public into being" (Marres 2005, 208), and in so doing it has *created* political interests in that collective. These interests will shift as they make their way up the ladder, as each moment of representation creates new elements and does away with others. The fact that representation is creative does not make it less representative – it means representation in politics, like that in art, literature, even science, takes the thing being represented and draws out some important themes, de-emphasizing others.

Different Publics Form and Act Differently

Publics are fundamentally collectives, not just collections, to revisit the distinction from chapter 1. That fact is a direct result of what we learned about representation: because there is no way for individuals' private desires to be represented transparently, the publics that get represented must be able to act, even speak, as collectivities, at least sometimes.

Publics do not just appear out of nowhere. Rather, publics form as people understand themselves to be connected in some way. Publics are "communicative sites that emerge at the points of connection among social and/or cognitive networks" (Ikegami 2000, 997). Such connections are formed around the intersections of practices, technologies, and structures. Practices such as reading, viewing, listening, talking, discussing, voting, and demonstrating are oriented toward, and constrained and enabled by, the affordances of technologies ranging from public opinion polling to the telephone and the internet. And structures that set the rules of elections and legislative processes orient publics toward goals they may set and self-images as publics. The existence of the electoral college, for example, encourages people to think their votes don't directly "count" – even in races where the electoral college isn't relevant, such as for Senate seats (Perrin 2006, 80–2). So electoral and legislative structures affect publics by teaching them how to think about publicness, not only by channeling their views into particular political activities but by offering the cultural tools to imagine the public.

Practices, rules, and technologies work together to form publics out of the shifting social structure of modern society. Daniel Dayan (2005, 12) distinguishes among three different kinds of publics, each of which forms in different conditions and around different ideas:

- taste publics, formed around people's shared preferences for particular "works, texts, or programmes";
- issue publics, formed around particular concerns (like the public imagined above among seashore homeowners), "aimed at determining certain courses of action"; and
- identity publics, formed around common characteristics "in order to endow themselves with a visible identity."

Each of these kinds of publics forms through shared attention to something, whether that is a media source, a political concern, a sense of self-identity, or common interests in a given technological or entertainment practice.

Some practices – such as voting and public opinion research – are very widespread and help constitute publics on a national scale that would otherwise be nearly impossible to imagine, all the more so to form. Other practices, such as the extent and boundaries of informal political conversation, or arguing about politics, may be much more specific to geographic areas, cultural tendencies, or historical periods.

Technologies, too, may be widespread or specific. In particular, technologies are often very time-dependent, as new technologies rest on the combination of social preferences and previous technologies. Technologies do not, in themselves, determine how people will use them or what their effects will be. But new technologies do facilitate some social practices and hamper others. The tendency of most twentieth-century communication technologies was toward privatization: allowing individuals to choose their own environments in increasing isolation. Social media invented in the early years of the twenty-first century are not privatizing, in that they encourage connections among people. However, by allowing people to choose exactly their own networks, social media afford more bonding than bridging connections: more opportunities to build publics based on shared beliefs and agreement than those that connect opposing viewpoints.

Democratic Culture Can Transcend Antidemocratic Systems

In the Florida presidential election of 2000, an extraordinarily small difference between the vote counts for candidates Al Gore and George W. Bush, combined with the very close election nationwide, focused the nation on the arcane questions of voting methods and laws. It seemed that the future of the country hung on these obscure questions: butterfly ballots, hanging chads, and provisional ballots. In one sense it really was the specific voting systems used across Florida's 67 counties that threw the state's electors, and therefore the presidential election, to Bush (Wand et al. 2001; Mebane 2004). Had each Florida county used the "best" voting method available, argues Mebane (2004), Gore would have won the state, and therefore the presidency, handily. Democrats also debated whether the third-party candidacy of Ralph Nader "spoiled" the election for Gore by siphoning off votes that would otherwise have gone to Gore. The likelihood is that Nader did not tip the election (Herron and Lewis 2007), but the influence of his voters is another technical consideration of the election.

Americans went to sleep the night of November 7, 2000, recognizing that the election was unusually close (as many observers had predicted [e.g., Milligan 2000]), but fully assuming it would be resolved by morning. They woke the next morning to CNN anchor Bernie Shaw declaring: "We are in a state of political suspended animation . . . It's not over. It is simply not over!" The month that followed was filled with legal motions and counter-motions, discussions of how voting machines worked, and claims about the right legal standards to use in evaluating the validity of votes (Brinkley 2001). Ultimately, the US Supreme Court decided the election (*Bush v. Gore*, 531 U.S. 98 (2000)), emphasizing that the Court was concerned only with this election and not with setting a precedent (Posner 2004; Scheppele 2001), though the principle the court used showed up soon thereafter in cases involving the California gubernatorial recall (Perrin et al. 2006; Brady 2004; Alvarez et al. 2004). Soon thereafter, Supreme Court Chief Justice William Rehnquist published a book about the contested election of 1876, which many saw as a defense of his court's controversial decision in *Bush v. Gore* (Rehnquist 2004).

Since that election, political activists and media have focused considerable attention on voting methods. Many states have implemented systems allowing more citizens to vote early and reducing the difficulty of registration. Democratic activists cried foul when Diebold, the largest manufacturer of electronic voting machines, was also a contributor to Republican campaigns (Fitrakis and Wasserman 2004). In 2010 and 2012, Republicans began concerted efforts to tighten requirements for voting, including laws requiring photographic identification ("Voter ID") to vote and even policies reducing the number of voting districts in certain areas in swing states such as Ohio and Florida (Overton 2007).

This concentration on the technical mechanisms of voting is misplaced, important as it can be in very tight elections. The main reality that needed to be represented in the Florida case was that the population (of the state and of the country) was very evenly divided, with a tiny fraction of the population making the difference between those preferring the Democratic and the Republican candidates. The complication that resulted in the 2000 Florida debacle was not primarily a technical one: it was the fact that the public being represented held conflicting preferences. Focusing on democratic culture – on developing publics with a stronger collective understanding and preferences – might well have allowed a more decisive victory in the election and avoided the technical breakdowns.

In 2012, some of the biggest debates surrounded Florida's reductions in voting opportunities, particularly in poor and minority communities. Some journalists (e.g., Wang 2012) argued that the changes could mean the difference between Florida's result being for Obama or for Romney, and in turn could mean the national election. As it turned out, voters in the affected areas made extra efforts to vote, in some cases standing hours in line to do so. In his 2013 State of the Union Speech, Obama highlighted one such voter, Desiline Victor, a 102-year-old Florida voter who waited for hours to vote. He held her up as a symbol of the need to make voting easier (Southall 2013). But again, the focus on the systems and mechanics of voting masked an important, deeper reality: Ohio, Florida, and Pennsylvania alike, all states that had been criticized for enacting voter suppression measures, eventually voted for Obama, with turnout figures in line with the rest of the country. This was a triumph of democratic culture over structure: voters determined to vote overcame many structural impediments to do so. Indeed, they may well have been encouraged to do so because the publicity around voter suppression measures convinced them their vote was important.

This is not to suggest that electoral systems and legislative processes don't matter. Certainly they do. An important example is the process of drawing the boundaries of congressional districts, which is carried out by state legislatures following each US Census. Because legislatures are made up of elected politicians who, themselves, have interests in specific political outcomes, the party that controls a state's legislature during the redistricting process has a big advantage in affecting the outcome of future elections. In the 2012 congressional elections, these district lines made a huge difference in the outcome of House races, potentially determining the majority in the House. This process leads to unfair distributions of votes, and is clearly antidemocratic. My argument, though, is that technologies, practices, and rules that encourage the formation of true, active publics are more important than rules and systems that alter the representation of those publics. Creative, motivated publics can often transcend suppression rules and technicalities.

Structural Reforms Invite Unanticipated Consequences

Of course, ideally we would have *both* active, creative publics *and* electoral and legislative systems that represent those publics fairly. It's reasonable to advocate reforms like uniform and inclusive voting rules, unbiased boundaries on political districts, and other technical changes that would make for fairer elections and legislation. But if we take seriously the idea that representation always alters the represented, few if any such reforms will be straightforward. Rather, nearly any decision about rules of legislation and representation is likely to have complicated effects and unanticipated consequences: results that are not what proponents intended or even imagined when they pushed for the reforms.

We saw in chapter 2 that efforts to make voter registration easier through the Motor-Voter law (Piven and Cloward 1988) and early-voting initiatives have had minimal impact on voter turnout, probably because most non-voters don't vote because they aren't motivated to do so, not because they are frustrated in their attempts. Taken as cultural and symbolic policies, these reforms may have unintended consequences. For example, by expanding the "electoral moment" (Geddis 2003), the reforms may change the meaning of an election, since people voting at the beginning of an early-voting period cannot possibly take into account events or information that emerge after their vote but before election day itself. More subtly, they may convey to potential voters that the value of voting is low, since it must be made convenient in order to be worth doing. Making voting seem like a trivial errand to be done when convenient might interfere with voters' experiencing voting as the important ritual connecting them to the public they are participating in. Making voting seem important may have the opposite effect. Again, I am not suggesting that these reforms are necessarily bad ideas, but rather that they could have unintended negative cultural and technical effects. Although it is too early to determine, the Supreme Court's evisceration of the Voting Rights Act (*Shelby County v. Holder*, 2013) could well teach potential voters that their representation is unimportant, reducing voter participation.

During the Progressive era, reformers sought to change systems they saw as corrupt and unfair, substituting apparently objective, populist measures like recall elections, referenda and ballot questions, and even the secret ballot (Goebel 1997). At first glance, it would appear that allowing voters to recall governors and legislators by popular vote would afford greater representation, and that government policies would therefore be more responsive to public concerns. And, in fact, it appears that ballot initiatives do "have positive effects on citizens . . . Citizens living in states with frequent ballot initiatives are more motivated to vote, are more interested and better informed about politics, and express more confidence in government responsiveness than do citizens living in noninitiative states" (Smith and Tolbert 2004, 137–8). But as it turns out, actual policies adopted in these states are no more responsive to public opinion than those adopted in states without initiative processes (Lascher et al. 1996), and the sheer amount of money required to mount a successful initiative or recall campaign often increases inequality in access to the public sphere (Goebel

2002; Gerber 1999) – certainly not the ideas the reformers had in mind. In California in particular – a state in which these populist measures are very common – the result has been the greater influence of wealthy actors and an often bewildering ballot presented to voters (DeBow and Syer 1997).

Americans have long been excited by the ideal of direct democracy, whether by town meeting, electronic plebiscite, or ballot initiative. What could be more democratic than bringing an issue directly to the people to decide for themselves instead of relying on a clumsy, hierarchical system of representation? Similarly, the idea of some sort of national conversation – whether by town meetings, public forums, or electronic debates – sparks Americans' ambitions to improve democratic practice. But if direct democracy allows citizens to answer questions more directly, who gets to ask the questions? How do citizens sort themselves into groups when deliberating? How do these groups help determine the outcome of deliberation?

None of this means voting reforms – whether institutional, "direct," or deliberative – should be off the table. But none will be successful unless they take into account both faces of the curious practice of voting in America. The ritual face of American democracy is every bit as important as its procedural face.

Popular reforms and unintended consequences

There are many proposals for reforming democracy. Some of these are technical, such as changes to election laws. Others emphasize grassroots deliberation on specific policy matters: what Fung and Wright call "empowered participatory governance" (Fung and Wright 2003, 5). Still others call for paying more attention to social movements and protest as the real sources of democratic engagement (Blee 2012). Graham Smith (2009) recommends a set of goals democratic innovations should strive for: inclusiveness, popular control, considered judgment, transparency, efficiency, and transferability (Smith 2009, 162).

It would be impossible even to list, let alone evaluate, all the proposals for democratic reform that have been circulated. Instead,

I examine a few particularly popular ones and one unusual idea. Among the most popular reforms proposed are imposing rules on campaign financing; providing fact checks on candidates' and politicians' claims; imposing term limits on elected officials; and abolishing the electoral college method of electing the president and vice-president. Each of these possibilities contains not only real promise in terms of Smith's goals, but also dangers that threaten to turn into unintended consequences.

When the Constitution was written, the Founders designed the electoral college as a buffer between the popular vote and the enormous decision of who would lead the country. Writing in the *Federalist* 68, Alexander Hamilton explained the idea:

> It was ... desirable, that the immediate election should be made by men most capable of analyzing the qualities adapted to the station, and acting under circumstances favorable to deliberation, and to a judicious combination of all the reasons and inducements which were proper to govern their choice. A small number of persons, selected by their fellow-citizens from the general mass, will be most likely to possess the information and discernment requisite to such complicated investigations.

The electoral college was designed specifically to insure that impartial electors, "most capable of analyzing the qualities adapted to the station" of president, would mediate between the people and the choice of president:

> The process of election affords a moral certainty, that the office of President will never fall to the lot of any man who is not in an eminent degree endowed with the requisite qualifications. Talents for low intrigue, and the little arts of popularity, may alone suffice to elevate a man to the first honors in a single State; but it will require other talents, and a different kind of merit, to establish him in the esteem and confidence of the whole Union, or of so considerable a portion of it as would be necessary to make him a successful candidate for the distinguished office of President of the United States. It will not be too strong to say, that there will be a constant probability of seeing the station filled by characters pre-eminent for ability and virtue. (Hamilton 1788)

In American history, there have been only two elections in which the final decision from the electoral college was different from the national popular vote. These were the elections of 1876 (Rehnquist 2004) and 2000 (Toobin 2001). So in the vast majority of presidential elections, the presence of the electoral college does not directly influence the outcome of the election.

Nevertheless, large majorities of Americans support abolishing the electoral college: approximately 62 percent, a proportion that has remained quite stable for more than a decade following the 2000 election (Saad 2011; Carlson 2004). "In Gallup polls that stretch back over 50 years, a majority of Americans have continually expressed support for the notion of an official amendment of the U.S. Constitution that would allow for direct election of the president" (Newport 2001). The objections are two-fold. First is the fact that voters are not voting for the president directly, but for a substitute; many voters see this as one way their votes don't count, even though there has never been an election outcome that changed due to electors changing their votes. This objection is symbolic: voting for electors "teaches" some voters that their votes are less important.

The more substantial issue comes about because nearly every state awards all its electoral votes to the candidate who won that state. As of this writing, the only exceptions are Maine and Nebraska, which split theirs based on the candidates' proportions of votes in the state. That means that candidates have little incentive to campaign in, or address issues that matter to, states that are likely to vote heavily for either party. Instead, they concentrate on "swing states": those in which the election is expected to be close enough that one's vote matters. Indeed, voter turnout in swing states is substantially higher than in other states (McDonald 2008, 2). Certain states get disproportionate attention, both from candidates and from the media – and voters in those states get a disproportionate voice.

Abolishing the electoral college in favor of a direct vote for president would certainly make voters believe their votes mattered more, and in most states they would be right. Actually abolishing the college would require a constitutional amendment, but the National Popular Vote movement (http://www.nationalpopularvote.com) offers a mechanism for bringing about a popular vote without recourse to an amendment.[2] But abolishing the electoral college would likely also have unintended consequences, and these should be considered carefully. First, the state-by-state process helps contain voting problems; if the 2000 election had been nationalized, we might have had to recount every vote in every state, not just Florida! Second, and more important, making every part of every state count in the election would mean that candidates would need to visit or communicate with all those places. That would likely make campaigns far more expensive, further increasing the role of money in politics. And it would probably mean more campaigning would be done via television and other media instead of in person. Since both of these consequences would have the effect of *reducing* popular influence on the election, it's important to consider them and other possible "paradoxical effects": ways in which reforms might end up resulting in exactly the opposite of their intentions (Beahrs 1992).

A similar analysis makes sense for the popular idea of term limits for politicians. As many Americans believe part of the problem is professional politicians who are out of touch with the people they represent, the idea of limiting representatives to a few terms in office is popular (Karp 1995; Saad 2013). Like abolishing the electoral college, limiting terms seems pro-democratic. Rotating people in and out of Congress might provide for more communication between people and their representatives and prevent the kind of "inside-Washington" attitude that angers many Americans. And since incumbent representatives enjoy a substantial advantage in elections against challengers (Ansolabehere and Snyder 2002), reducing the number of incumbents would open up more competitive races each time.

Like abolishing the electoral college, though, term limits could backfire too. One reason is that in a system as complicated as the US federal government, there will always be a need for people with experience and deep knowledge. If the politicians don't have that experience, it could well be provided by unelected staff members and aides who have spent their whole careers in Washington. We would be exchanging elected career politicians for *unelected* career staffers: another paradoxical effect that might diminish popular influence in Washington.

These are just a couple of the reforms that have been suggested. Fact-checking during campaigns helps make sure the truth is communicated – but also teaches voters that there is a "right answer" and trains them to listen for true vs. false instead of right vs. wrong. Campaign spending limits would increase popular involvement, but they, too, would likely have unintended consequences, including cumbersome reporting regulations and candidates spending more time raising funds from smaller donors. Abolishing the filibuster rule in the Senate would grant less influence to minority parties while increasing the efficiency and transparency of the legislative process. Many observers, though, credit the Senate with offering voice to minority parties, so such a decision would reduce one of the main features of the Senate.

Many of these popular reforms may still be the right thing to do to preserve and reinvigorate the culture of democracy. But my point is that, in general, reforms, rules, and technologies that encourage voters to form into vibrant, democratic publics are more important than technical reforms that try to make representation more transparent without considering possible unintended consequences. As in the previous section, culture trumps structure; voters learn from these systems how to think and act about politics. Encouraging a democratically vibrant culture, in which vigorous, spirited, and committed debate comes to the fore, is far more important than reforming the electoral or legislative systems that represent the outcomes of that debate.

One potential reform that has received virtually no attention (one exception is Issenberg 2012b) is abandoning the secret ballot in favor of a system that encourages or even requires voters to state publicly their positions. The introduction of the so-called Australian Ballot (the secret ballot) was a Progressive reform that served at once to rationalize voting and to make it much less exciting than it had been during the turbulent, corrupt nineteenth century (Issenberg 2012a; Green and Gerber 2008). In fact, many Americans don't know, or believe, that their vote choices are actually kept secret, and most discuss their choices with others anyway (Gerber et al. 2009). Moving voting back into the open could have significant cultural benefits: it would teach voters that their votes were to be taken seriously as public matters, not solely private; and it would help shame non-voters, which could increase overall participation (Gerber et al. 2008).

Of course, abolishing the secret ballot would certainly have unintended consequences. The most obvious of these would be the possibility of intimidation ahead of time or retaliation afterward by political opponents and other powerful actors. The secret ballot was introduced when voting was opened up to more vulnerable populations like immigrants and the poor, and later women and African Americans. The secret ballot may be particularly necessary to protect these voters from intimidation. In the 2012 presidential election, some employers warned their employees of bad consequences if Obama were re-elected; one responded: "There's no way I can pressure anybody. I'm not in the voting booth with them" (Greenhouse 2012). As with the other reforms, the point is not to claim that abolishing the secret ballot is definitely a good idea, but rather to push for considering its cultural effects, not just its technical ones.

Modern, Individualist Societies Demand Agonistic Publics

In his nineteenth-century observations of American democratic culture (Tocqueville 1969), Alexis de Tocqueville observed the individualist culture combined with the tendency to join together to form associations: the individualist and the collective. In *The Democratic Wish*, James A. Morone argues that American democratic life bridges two incompatible cultural desires: the desire for less government and the desire for communal problem solving (Morone 1998). While much has changed since Tocqueville's writing (and even since Morone's), the same basic tension exists now. The cultural shift from the eighteenth century to now has been almost entirely a shift toward individualism and privatization through law, beliefs, expectations, and technology. Expectations and demands for privacy have developed alongside technologies both allowing and threatening that privacy (Gumpert and Drucker 1998).

Where a nineteenth-century public might have been relatively easy to represent because the ideal of community was still strong, the twenty-first-century ideal of individualism requires extra work in order to assemble a public to represent. "How to give form – one open to description and recognition – to an agglomeration of individuals? . . . it is at the very moment [in history] that the principle of popular sovereignty triumphs that its face, in a sense, becomes problematic" (Rosanvallon 2006, 85). In addition to becoming more individualistic since the nineteenth century, the American public has also become enormously more diverse, incorporating people from race, religious, gender, class, and nationality groups the Founders would never have imagined. Along with this diversification of the public comes the reality of frank, deep disagreements among parts of the public. These disagreements may be based on material interests or on fundamental values, but either way they are realities of social life.

The best way to represent such a conflict-ridden, multifaceted society is by embracing that conflict and all its facets. That means reflecting the underlying social conflicts in public discourse and deliberation: the *agonistic* approach discussed in chapter 3, with everyone invited and encouraged to speak the ideas they choose in the form and style that best fits them. An agonistic public sphere is noisy, uncomfortable, inefficient, and sometimes even scary. As Barack Obama put it, "democracy . . . can be noisy and messy and complicated" (Obama 2012b). But it is forthright and honest, and it encourages people to pay attention to and consider the points of view of other groups. In a deeply divided, wonderfully diverse society, that is the best way to represent that diversity.

Democratic discourse: frank, civil, thorough, accurate, and substantive

It is popular to bemoan the fact that politics has lost its civility and to call for politicians and all Americans to become more civil. As Susan Herbst notes, concerns over incivility in politics are nearly as old as the country, and these concerns may serve as much to scold people seen as "uncivil" as to promote actual dialogue (Herbst 2010). But the agonistic style I endorse suggests that the most important element of democratic speech is actually its *frankness*: above all else, citizens should seek to be genuine and honest in the things they say, even if that means abandoning the desire for civility. Tolerance and understanding are to be valued only when the tolerance is warranted and when they don't get in the way of making one's own point (Marcuse 1965).

Civility is, of course, valuable too. The biggest problem with incivility is the possibility that an angry or overbearing speaker might intimidate or scare another into remaining silent. Ideally, people should be able to be frank *and* civil. Setting ground rules for how to have "difficult dialogues," a first-year seminar class I taught came up with five standards for political speech: it should be frank, civil, thorough, accurate, and substantive.

The final three standards (thorough, accurate, and substantive) deal with the factual content of public speech. To be responsible, it's important not to leave out thoughts, ideas, or facts one knows, and it's important to speak these thoughts, ideas, and facts faithfully. Those are the *thorough* and *accurate* standards, respectively. The *substantive* standard emphasizes that whatever is said be about the substance of the matter being discussed, not about other issues including the personality, character, or background of others participating in the discussion. These standards do *not* include some others: that speech should be *calm*, *rational*, or *fact-based*, for example. All of these have been proposed as elements of good deliberation, but all of them put undue burdens on citizens and thereby keep them from speaking their minds. Collective, creative, and expressive speech is, in general, good for democratic publics; individual, repetitive, and instrumental speech tends to shut down debate and undermine the formation of publics.

Audience Fragmentation Encourages Undemocratic Qualities

One of the principal ambitions of American democracy, going back to the earliest days, is summed up by John Adams in a letter he wrote home to his wife:

> I *must study politics and war, that our sons may have liberty to study mathematics and philosophy.* Our sons ought to study mathematics and philosophy, geography, natural history and naval architecture, navigation, commerce and agriculture in order to give their children a right to study painting, poetry, music, architecture, statuary, tapestry and porcelain. (Adams 1780)

Politics and war, Adams seems to suggest, ought to recede over time, making way for intellectual and creative pursuits that are less urgent, but (Adams suggests in his hopes for his grandchildren) more valuable than the necessities of politics and war. This desire to leave behind the needs of politics and pay attention to the other parts of life continues. Berger (2011) suggests that widespread engagement is the wrong goal to pursue: "liberal democracies' top priority should be preventing radical *disengagement* . . . and also to promote political attention and activity among those segments of the population most likely to suffer when disengaged" (Berger 2011, 20). In other words, demanding focused attention to democracy may be too much to ask of today's multitasking, overburdened citizens.

The problem with this tendency – as genuine as it is – is that it suggests that publics can be represented without their active participation. But as I have demonstrated in the previous chapters, publics come into existence as publics only through their active engagement with rules, practices, and technologies. And the tendency of those technologies has been to enable more and more selectivity in whom one encounters, what messages one sees, and to whom one speaks. Berger proposes a remedy focusing on "accomplishing more with our limited resources of energy, attention, and tastes than we have done in recent years, while trying to avoid paternalism and coercion" (Berger 2011, 147). His proposal is to use current cultural tendencies (which he calls "tastes") as political elements, forging new publics around new ways of being political.

The problem we face is that paying attention to political matters is difficult. It's difficult to understand, and it's difficult to sort through the volumes of information and opinion that are increasingly available. The desire to make politics easy, to make governance efficient, or to ignore politics altogether, undermines democratic citizenship by teaching citizens that their participation in publics ought to be simple, straightforward, seamless. Just as Adorno and colleagues worried that making art and music easy to consume would ruin the aesthetic experience of art, making democracy easy to participate in can threaten the thick democratic imaginations that form the basis of strong publics (Perrin 2006, 5). These dangers are magnified in the context of a media environment that encourages people to pick news, information, and opinions they expect to agree with, since engaging with ideas one agrees with is cognitively simple – far from the difficulty of paying full attention to public matters.

In 2012, musician Kid Rock, a Republican activist and Mitt Romney supporter, teamed up with liberal movie star Sean Penn on a widely viewed video called *Americans* (Rock and Penn 2012). In the video, Penn is at a bar watching a concert video of Rock and grows visibly disgusted with the patriotic imagery in the concert. He succeeds in getting the bartender to change the channel to an episode of *Ellen*. Rock himself shows up at the bar and confronts Penn, calling him a "commie."

Penn: Commie? At least I'm not a seal-clubbing, confederate flag-waving, oil whoring, Chick-fil-A-eating, water-boarding, NASCAR-loving, Cayman Island bank account-having, endangered species-hunting, war mongering, redneck, toothless, Wall Street troglodyte.
Rock: Yeah, I guess not, that's because you are basically a tofu-munching, welfare-loving, Prius-driving, Obama-sucking, tree-hugging, whale-saving, gay marriage-fantasizing, big government-voting, PETA-chasing, Oprah Winfrey masturbating, flag-burning, socialist, ACLU, whiney-ass granola-crat.

The insults continue until both men see a news report on the bar television announcing the 2,000th American soldier killed in the Afghanistan war. The two join in a toast to freedom and embark on a tour together in which each encounters the other's cultural style. Rock buys a Toyota Prius (quickly hanging a gun rack on the back) and cries at a same-sex wedding, and Penn gives up his high-class cocktail for a beer bottle and proudly dons a NASCAR tee-shirt. Patriotism brings them together to gloss over their very real differences in favor of "what really matters," as the film's website says: "that we're all Americans, with diverse thoughts, opinions and stances on issues." At the end of the video comes a message: "Don't let our differences divide us. Thinking differently is what made America great." The combination of the two men's cultural symbols is presented as a powerful message about the importance of a bridging, common public, embracing genuine, frank disagreement within the context of common cultural connections.

As we've seen throughout this book, nearly two centuries after Tocqueville showed the tight relationship between Americans' democratic culture and the growth of our democratic system of government, many of the insights he set down remain fundamental elements of American culture and politics. From the micro-level practices of voting and deliberation; to the public-forming activities of Twitter, Sean Penn and Kid Rock, and mediated public spheres; to the macro-level processes of representation and legislation; cultural patterns and shared practices truly drive democratic life. Technologies like public opinion polling, the mass media, and social media organize not just formal representation but the shared understandings that help Americans imagine the publics we comprise. In the final analysis, the question of democracy is a question of culture and society. I believe our practices, technologies, and institutions have the potential to build and maintain vibrant publics and lend those publics voice. Democracy is alive in American culture and society, but efforts to remain an engaged and thoughtful public need to continue in order to insure that practices, institutions, and technologies can serve that public faithfully.

Notes

Chapter 1 History and Theory of Democracy

1 People who design and support democracy are "democrats" with a lower-case *d*. By contrast, members of the Democratic Party in the United States are "Democrats" with an upper-case *D*.

Chapter 2 Voting, Civil Society, and Citizenship

1 Hegel's definition of civil society, based on the modern development of capitalism, includes participation in economic markets (Hegel 1991), but later thinkers have tended to separate civil society from the market to recognize civil society as an area in which people's interactions are free of their specific interests and needs.

2 We will return to the idea of agonism in greater depth in the next chapter. Essentially, agonism is the principle of allowing real and deep disagreement and even conflict to animate democratic deliberations.

3 It's important to recognize that the twenty-first-century vision is different from the eighteenth-century version contemplated by the Founders. Partially because of the limited scope of "the people" (as discussed in chapter 1) and partially because the matters they expected government to consider were not nearly as complex as those of the current day, the problem of becoming an "informed citizen" – a very high value espoused by twenty-first-century students and thinkers – was not part of the world the Founders imagined (Schudson 1998).

4 One way, of course, is that many of the candidates' sites are happy to provide information as to what's wrong with the other candidate – a form of negative advertising that can be very instructive, since this kind of competition provides incentives for the candidates to make the strongest, most convincing arguments (Jacobs 2000; Geer 2006). In the 2012 presidential election, Mitt

Romney's website contained sections called "Obama's Failure" and "Mitt's Plan" for each policy area.

5 We will consider the ways in which electoral regimes create incentives for different kinds and numbers of candidates (which explains the fact that most American elections have only two serious candidates) in chapter 3.

6 Some people claim that the Republican Party tricks people into voting for Republicans by adopting these values-voter positions. The argument, essentially, is that Republican economic policies are bad news for middle- and lower-class voters, so in order to win the Republican Party has to convince some of these voters that their values are best served by paying attention to something other than economic policies (Frank 2004). But the success these platforms have in mobilizing voters through numerous election cycles suggests that the beliefs are genuine and may even be the result of particular styles of thought (Hetherington and Weiler 2009). Republican efforts to mobilize them are strategic behavior to be sure, but not trickery.

Chapter 3 Deliberation, Representation, and Legislation

1 Kloppenberg (2011) shows that this tendency to compromise, and to value diverse voices and conciliation, is a long-running trait of Obama's character at least since his days as a student at Harvard Law School.

2 The question of whether mass media *actually* contain liberal bias is hotly contested (Herman and Chomsky 1988; Groseclose 2011).

3 I will refer to people entering mediated public spheres as "speakers" even though in many cases they are actually writing or typing, not literally speaking.

4 Geddis (2003) defines the electoral moment slightly differently: "the entire *electoral moment* leading up to and including the actual casting of ballots . . . is claimed to legitimate the majority's final choice" (61). That conception is similar to Tocqueville's discussion of election season, an extended ritual that leads up to the specific moment I refer to as the electoral moment.

Chapter 4 Public Opinion, Policy Responsiveness, and Feedback

1 Of course, Horkheimer and Adorno did not anticipate ways these two media eventually merged: the modern conference call, for example, in which one speaker may broadcast to many listeners over a telephone, or the modern call-in radio show, in which listeners may use the telephone to contribute to a radio program in real time.

2 It is reasonable to argue, as art historians have (e.g., Bolt 2004, 2006) that cameras, too, change the world they try to record, but that question is well beyond the scope of our consideration here.

Chapter 5 Media, Communications, and Political Knowledge

1 The Perception Analyzer is a product of the Dialsmith company.
2 The only significant exception to this rule – National Public Radio – emerged in the 1970s in the aftermath of Watergate. This pattern is very different from many other advanced democracies, which have nationally subsidized broadcast media such as the BBC in Britain.
3 http: //www.cleveland.com/metro/index.ssf/2012/11/ohio_secretary_of_state _jon_hu_1.html.

Chapter 6 Democratic Culture and Practice in Postmodern America

1 Interested readers should read Jameson (1990) or Baudrillard (1994) as introductions to the broader theory.
2 In 2013 some Republican state legislators in "blue" states proposed apportioning electors based on vote totals in each congressional district – a move that would give Republicans a vast advantage in those states because of the strategic ways those district boundaries are drawn. However, the idea is unlikely to succeed, if only because even the Republican beneficiaries recognize it as antidemocratic (Hasen 2013).

References

Abramson, Paul R., and Charles W. Ostrom. 1994. "Question Wording and Partisanship: Change and Continuity in Party Loyalties During the 1992 Election Campaign." *Public Opinion Quarterly* 58: 21–48.

Achen, Christopher H., and Larry M. Bartels. 2006. "It Feels Like We're Thinking: The Rationalizing Voter and Electoral Democracy." Presented at the Annual Meeting of the American Political Science Association, Philadelphia. Retrieved August 21, 2013, from http://www.princeton.edu/csdp/events/AchenBartels011107/AchenBartels011107.pdf.

Ackerman, Bruce. 1991. *We, the People*. 2 vols. Cambridge, MA: Harvard University Press.

Ackerman, Bruce, and James S. Fishkin. 2004. *Deliberation Day*. New Haven, CT: Yale University Press.

Adams, John. 1776. "Thoughts on Government." Retrieved August 21, 2013, from http://www.heritage.org/initiatives/first-principles/primary-sources/john-adams-thoughts-on-government.

Adams, John. 1780. "Letter to Abigail Adams." May 12. Retrieved February 24, 2013, from http://www.thefederalistpapers.org/founders/adams/john-adams-letter-to-abigail-adams-12-may-1780.

Adorno, Theodor W. 1990a [1928]. "The Curves of the Needle." Trans. Thomas Y. Levin. *October* 55: 48–55.

Adorno, Theodor W. 1990b [1934]. "The Form of the Phonograph Record." Trans. Thomas Y. Levin. *October* 55: 56–61.

Adorno, Theodor W. 2000. *The Psychological Technique of Martin Luther Thomas' Radio Addresses*. Stanford, CA: Stanford University Press.

Adorno, Theodor W. 2005. "Opinion Research and Publicness." Trans. and intro. A.J. Perrin and L. Jarkko. *Sociological Theory* 23: (1): 116–23.

Adorno, Theodor W., Else Frenkel-Brunswik, Daniel J. Levinson, and R. Nevitt Sanford. 1950. *The Authoritarian Personality*. New York, NY: W.W. Norton.

References

Aldrich, Howard. 1999. *Organizations Evolving*. 2nd edn. Thousand Oaks, CA: Sage.

Alexander, Jeffrey C. 2006. *The Civil Sphere*. New York, NY: Oxford University Press.

Allen, Austin. 2007. "Coalitions Without Compromise: Reconsidering the Political Abolitionists." *Reviews in American History* 35: (1): 57–64.

Allen, Danielle S. 2004. *Talking to Strangers: Anxieties of Citizenship Since Brown v. Board of Education*. Chicago, IL: University of Chicago Press.

Alsina, Cristina, Philip John Davies, and Bruce E. Gronbeck. 2001. "Preference Poll Stories in the Last 2 Weeks of Campaign 2000: Uses of the Massed Opinions of Numbered Citizens." *American Behavioral Scientist* 44: 2288–305.

Althaus, Scott L. 2003. *Collective Preferences in Democratic Politics: Opinion Surveys and the Will of the People*. New York, NY: Cambridge University Press.

Althaus, Scott L., and Young Mie Kim. 2006. "Priming Effects in Complex Information Environments: Reassessing the Impact of News Discourse on Presidential Approval." *Journal of Politics* 68: 960–76.

Alvarez, R. Michael, Melanie Goodrich, Thad E. Hall, D. Roderick Kieweiet, and Sarah M. Sled. 2004. "The Complexity of the California Recall Election." *PS: Political Science and Politics* XXXVIII: 23–6.

Andersen, Robert. 2012. "Support for Democracy in Cross-national Perspective: The Detrimental Effect of Economic Inequality." *Research in Social Stratification and Mobility* 30: (4): 389–402.

Andersen, Robert, and Tina Fetner. 2008. "Cohort Differences in Tolerance of Homosexuality: Attitudinal Change in Canada and the United States, 1981–2000." *Public Opinion Quarterly* 72(2): 311–30.

Anderson, Benedict R. 2006. *Imagined Communities: Reflections on the Origin and Spread of Nationalism*. London, UK: Verso.

Ansolabehere, Stephen, and James M. Snyder, Jr. 2002. "The Incumbency Advantage in US Elections: An Analysis of State and Federal Offices, 1942–2000." *Election Law Journal* 193: 315–38.

Apostolidis, Paul. 2000. *Stations of the Cross: Adorno and Christian Right Radio*. Durham, NC: Duke University Press.

Archibugi, Daniele. 2008. *The Global Commonwealth of Citizens: Toward Cosmopolitan Democracy*. Princeton, NJ: Princeton University Press.

Arnold, R. Douglas. 1990. *The Logic of Congressional Action*. New Haven, CT: Yale University Press.

Asher, Herbert B. 2004. *Polling and the Public: What Every Citizen Should Know*. Washington, DC: CQ Press.

Atkeson, Lonna Rae, and Ronald B. Rapoport. 2003. "The More Things Change the More They Stay the Same: Examining Gender Differences in Political Attitude Expression, 1952–2000." *Public Opinion Quarterly* 67: 495–521.

References

Bagdikian, Ben H. 2004. *The New Media Monopoly*. Boston, MA: Beacon Press.

Bageant, Joe. 2007. *Deer Hunting With Jesus: Dispatches from America's Class War*. New York, NY: Crown Books.

Bail, Christopher A. 2012. "The Fringe Effect: Civil Society Organizations and the Evolution of Media Discourse about Islam." *American Sociological Review*, 77(7): 855–79.

Barnett, Kyle S. 2006. "Furniture Music: The Phonograph as Furniture, 1900–1930." *Journal of Popular Music Studies* 18(3): 301–24.

Bartels, Larry M. 2002. "Question Order and Declining Faith in Elections." *Public Opinion Quarterly* 66: 67–79.

Baudrillard, Jean. 1994. *Simulacra and Simulation*. Trans. Sheila Faria Glaser. Ann Arbor, MI: University of Michigan Press.

Bauman, Zygmunt. 2000. *Liquid Modernity*. Cambridge, UK: Polity.

Bauman, Zygmunt. 2001. *Modernity and the Holocaust*. Cambridge, UK: Polity.

Bauman, Zygmunt. 2007. *Liquid Times: Living in an Age of Uncertainty*. Cambridge, UK: Polity.

Beahrs, John O. 1992. "Paradoxical Effects in Political Systems." *Political Psychology* 13(4): 755–69.

Bellah, Robert N., Richard Madsen, William M. Sullivan, Ann Swidler, and Steven M. Tipton. 1985. *Habits of the Heart: Individualism and Commitment in American Life*. Berkeley, CA: University of California Press.

Beniger, James R. 1992. "The Impact of Polling on Public Opinion: Reconciling Foucault, Habermas, and Bourdieu." *International Journal of Public Opinion Research* 4(3): 204–19.

Benjamin, Walter. 2008. "The Work of Art in the Age of its Technological Reproducibility." Pp. 19–55 in *The Work of Art in the Age of its Technological Reproducibility and Other Writings On Media*, eds. Michael W. Jennings, Brigid Doherty, and Thomas Y. Levin; trans. Edmund Jephcott, Rodney Livingstone, Howard Eiland, and Others. Cambridge, MA: Belknap/Harvard University Press.

Bennett, Michael. 2005. *Democratic Discourses: The Radical Abolition Movement and Antebellum American Literature*. New Brunswick, NJ: Rutgers University Press.

Bennett, W. Lance. 1993. "Constructing Publics and Their Opinions." *Political Communication* 10: 101–20.

Bensel, Richard Franklin. 2004. *The American Ballot Box in the Mid-Nineteenth Century*. Cambridge, UK: Cambridge University Press.

Berger, Benjamin. 2011. *Attention-Deficit Democracy: The Paradox of Civic Engagement*. Princeton, NJ: Princeton University Press.

Berinsky, Adam J. 1999. "The Two Faces of Public Opinion." *American Journal of Political Science* 43: 1209–30.

Berinsky, Adam J. 2004. *Silent Voices: Public Opinion and Political Participation in America*. Princeton, NJ: Princeton University Press.

References

Berman, Marshall. 1982. *All that is Solid Melts into Air: The Experience of Modernity*. New York, NY: Penguin.

Bickford, Susan. 2001. "Anti-Anti-Identity Politics: Feminism, Democracy, and the Complexities of Citizenship." Pp. 56–77 in *Theorizing Feminism: Parallel Trends in the Humanities and Social Sciences*, eds. Anne C. Hermann and Abigail J. Stewart. Boulder, CO: Westview Press.

Bing Team, The. 2012. "Introducing Bing Elections: News, Results, Conversation, Nonstop." October 26. Retrieved August 21, 2013, from http://www.bing.com/community/site_blogs/b/search/archive/2012/10/26/elections.aspx.

Bishop, Bill. 2008. *The Big Sort: Why the Clustering of Like-Minded America is Tearing Us Apart*. Boston, MA: Houghton Mifflin Harcourt.

Bishop, George F. 2005. *The Illusion of Public Opinion: Fact and Artifact in American Public Opinion Polls*. Lanham, MD: Rowman & Littlefield.

Bishop, George F., Robert W. Oldendick, Alfred J. Tuchfarber, and Stephen E. Bennett. 1980. "Pseudo-Opinions on Public Affairs." *Public Opinion Quarterly* 44(2): 198–209.

Bishop, George F., Robert W. Oldendick, and Alfred J. Tuchfarber. 1983. "Effects of Filter Questions in Public Opinion Surveys." *Public Opinion Quarterly* 47(4): 528–46.

Bishop, George F., Alfred J. Tuchfarber, and Robert W. Oldendick. 1986. "Opinions on Fictitious Issues: The Pressure to Answer Survey Questions." *Public Opinion Quarterly* 50(2): 240–50.

Blee, Kathleen M. 2012. *Democracy in the Making: How Activist Groups Form*. New York, NY: Oxford University Press.

Blokker, Paul. 2009. "Democracy Through the Lens of 1989: Liberal Triumph or Radical Turn?" *International Journal of Politics, Culture, and Society* 22(3): 273–90.

Blumer, Herbert. 1948. "Public Opinion and Public Opinion Polling." *American Sociological Review* 13(5): 542–9.

Bobbitt, Randy. 2010. *Us Against Them: The Political Culture of Talk Radio*. Lanham, MD: Lexington Books.

Bogart, Leo. 1967. "No Opinion, Don't Know, and Maybe No Answer." *Public Opinion Quarterly* 31(3): 331–45.

Bolt, Barbara. 2004. *Art Beyond Representation: The Performative Power of the Image*. London, UK: I.B.Tauris.

Bolt, Barbara. 2006. "Materializing Pedagogies." *Working Papers in Art and Design* 4.

Bonilla-Silva, Eduardo. 2010. *Racism Without Racists: Color-Blind Racism and the Persistence of Racial Inequality in the United States*. 3rd edn. Lanham, MD: Rowman & Littlefield.

Borrelli, Stephen A., Brad Lockerbie, and Richard G. Niemi. 1987. "Why the Democrat–Republican Partisanship Gap Varies from Poll to Poll." *Public Opinion Quarterly* 51: 115–19.

References

Bourdieu, Pierre. 1979. "Public Opinion Does Not Exist." In *Communication and Class Struggle. Vol. 1: Capitalism and Imperialism*, eds. A. Mattelart and S. Siegelaub. New York, NY: International Mass Media Research Center.

Bourdieu, Pierre. 1991. *Language and Symbolic Power*. Cambridge, MA: Harvard University Press.

Bourdieu, Pierre. 1999. *On Television*. Trans. Priscilla Parkhurst Ferguson. Cambridge, UK: Polity.

Bourdieu, Pierre. 2005. "The Mystery of Ministry: From Particular Wills to the General Will." Pp. 55–63 in *Pierre Bourdieu and Democratic Politics*, ed. L. Wacquant. Cambridge, UK: Polity.

Boyd, Sam. 2008. "What Are Those Squiggly Lines on CNN Telling You?" *American Prospect*, October 15. Retrieved February 1, 2013, from http://prospect.org/article/what-are-those-squiggly-lines-cnn-telling-you.

Brady, Henry E. 2004. "Postponing the California Recall to Protect Voting Rights." *PS: Political Science and Politics* XXXVII: 27–32.

Breed, Warren, and Thomas Ktsanes. 1961. "Pluralistic Ignorance in the Process of Opinion Formation." *Public Opinion Quarterly* 25(3): 382–92.

Brenner, Philip S. 2011. "Identity Importance and the Overreporting of Religious Service Attendance: Multiple Imputation of Religious Attendance Using the American Time Use Study and the General Social Survey." *Journal for the Scientific Study of Religion* 50(1): 103–15.

Brinkley, Douglas. 2001. *36 Days: The Complete Chronicle of the 2000 Presidential Election Crisis*. New York, NY: Times Books.

Brooks, Clem, and Jeff Manza. 2006. "Social Policy Responsiveness in Developed Democracies." *American Sociological Review* 71: 474–94.

Brooks, Clem, and Jeff Manza. 2013. *Whose Rights? Counterterrorism and the Dark Side of American Public Opinion*. New York, NY: Russell Sage Foundation.

Brown, Robert D., and Justin Wedeking. 2006. "People Who Have Their Tickets But Do Not Use Them: 'Motor Voter,' Registration, and Turnout Revisited." *American Politics Research* 34(4): 479–504.

Bryan, Frank M. 2004. *Real Democracy: The New England Town Meeting and How It Works*. Chicago, IL: University of Chicago Press.

Burden, Barry C., David T. Canon, Kenneth R. Mayer, and Donald P. Moynihan. 2012. "Election Laws, Mobilization, and Turnout: The Unanticipated Consequences of Election Reform." Unpublished manuscript, University of Wisconsin. Retrieved March 21, 2013, from http://papers.ssrn.com/sol3/papers.cfm?abstract_id=1690723.

Burke, Edmund. 1790 [1993]. *Reflections on the Revolution in France*. Oxford, UK: Oxford University Press.

Burstein, Paul. 2003. "The Impact of Public Opinion on Public Policy: A Review and an Agenda." *Political Research Quarterly* 56: 29–40.

Burstein, Paul. 2006. "Why Estimates of the Impact of Public Opinion on Public

References

Policy are Too High: Empirical and Theoretical Considerations." *Social Forces* 84: 2273–89.

Bush v. Gore. 531 U.S. 98 (2000).

Callon, Michel. 2007. "What Does It Mean to Say that Economics Is Performative?" Pp. 311–57 in *Do Economists Make Markets? On the Performativity of Economics*, eds. D. MacKenzie, F. Muniesa, and L. Siu. Princeton, NJ: Princeton University Press.

Callon, Michel, Pierre Lascoumes, and Yannick Barthe. 2009. *Acting in an Uncertain World: An Essay on Technical Democracy.* Trans. G. Burchell. Cambridge, MA: MIT Press.

Campbell, Andrea Louise. 2011. "Policy Feedbacks and the Impact of Policy Designs on Public Opinion." *Journal of Health Politics, Policy, and Law* 36(6): 961–73.

Campbell, Angus, Philip E. Converse, Warren E. Miller, and Donald E. Stokes. 1960. *The American Voter.* Ann Arbor, MI: University of Michigan Survey Research Center.

Carlson, Darren K. 2004. "Public Flunks Electoral College System." *Gallup*, November 2. Retrieved February 22, 2013, from http://www.gallup.com/poll/13918/public-flunks-electoral-college-system.aspx.

Cassino, Dan, Peter Woolley, and Krista Jenkins. 2012. "What You Know Depends On What You Watch: Current Events Knowledge Across Popular News Sources." Farleigh Dickinson University, May 3. Retrieved February 4, 2013, from http://publicmind.fdu.edu/2012/confirmed.

CBS/*New York Times* Poll. 2010. "Gays in the Military." Retrieved September 13, 2013, from http://www.cbsnews.com/htdocs/pdf/poll_021110_2pm.pdf.

Childs, Harwood L. 1939. "'By Public Opinion I Mean': Professional Services." *Public Opinion Quarterly*, April: 327–36.

Cicourel, Aaron. 1964. *Method and Measurement in Sociology.* Glencoe, IL: Free Press.

Citizens United v. Federal Election Commission. 558 US 310. 2010. Retrieved August 21, 2013, from http://www.supremecourt.gov/opinions/09pdf/08-205.pdf.

Coggins, K. Elizabeth, and James A. Stimson. 2012. "Understanding the Decline of Liberal Self-Identification in America." Unpublished manuscript. Retrieved December 21, 2012, http://www.unc.edu/~cogginse/Curriculum_Vitae.html.

Cohen, Joshua. 1986. "An Epistemic Conception of Democracy." *Ethics* 97(1): 26–38.

Cohen, Patricia. 2010. "'Epistemic Closure'? Those are Fighting Words." *New York Times*, April 27. Retrieved August 21, 2013, from http://www.nytimes.com/2010/04/28/books/28conserv.html.

Cohn, Alicia M. 2012. "Romney Surrogate Rebukes Crowley for 'Fact-Check' on Libya During Debate." *The Hill.* Retrieved August 21, 2013, from http://

References

thehill.com/blogs/blog-briefing-room/news/262489-rep-chaffetz-confronts-can
dy-crowley-on-libya-fact-check-.

Conley, Dalton. 2010. *Being Black, Living in the Red: Race, Wealth, and Social Policy in America*. 10th anniversary edn. Berkeley, CA; London, UK: University of California Press.

Conlon, Ian, and Katherine McFarland. 2010. "Concrete Language and Sexual Prejudice: The Effect of Question Wording on Opinion of Same-Sex Marriage." Presented at the Annual Meeting of the American Sociological Association Atlanta, August 13.

Converse, Jean M. 1976. "Predicting No Opinion in the Polls." *Public Opinion Quarterly* 40(4): 515–30.

Coontz, Stephanie. 1992. *The Way We Never Were: American Families and the Nostalgia Trap*. New York, NY: Basic Books.

Coser, Lewis A. 1954. *The Functions of Social Conflict*. Glencoe, IL: Free Press.

Coser, Rose Laub. 1994. *In Defense of Modernity*. Stanford, CA: Stanford University Press.

Cottrol, Robert J. 1991. "Reconstruction Amendment Historiography: The Quest for Racial and Intellectual Maturity." *Rutgers Law Journal* 23: 249–52.

Daniels, Roger. 2002. *Coming to America: A History of Immigration and Ethnicity in American Life*. 2nd edn. New York, NY: Perennial.

Dayan, Daniel. 2005. "Paying Attention to Attention: Audiences, Publics, Thresholds and Genealogies." *Journal of Media Practice* 6(1): 9–18.

DeBow, Ken, and John C. Syer. 1997. *Power and Politics in California*. 5th edn. Boston, MA: Allyn and Bacon.

DellaVigna, Stefano, and Ethan Kaplan. 2007. "The Fox News Effect: Media Bias and Voting." *Quarterly Journal of Economics* 122: 1187–234.

Delli Carpini, Michael X., and Scott Keeter. 1997. *What Americans Know about Politics and Why It Matters*. New Haven, CT: Yale University Press.

Dempsey, J.M. (ed.). 2006. *Sports-Talk Radio in America: Its Context and Culture*. New York, NY: Haworth.

DiMaggio, Paul. 1982. "Cultural Entrepreneurship in Nineteenth-Century Boston: The Creation of an Organizational Base for High Culture in America." *Media, Culture & Society* 4(1): 33–50.

Dobson, Andrew. 2012. "Listening: The New Democratic Deficit." *Political Studies* 60(4): 843–59.

Downs, Anthony. 1957. *An Economic Theory of Democracy*. New York, NY: Harper and Row.

Druckman, James N. 2001. "The Implications of Framing Effects for Citizen Competence." *Political Behavior* 23: 225–56.

Druckman, James N., and Justin W. Holmes. 2004. "Does Presidential Rhetoric Matter? Priming and Presidential Approval." *Presidential Studies Quarterly* 34: 755–78.

References

Dryzek, John S. 2005. "Handle With Care: The Deadly Hermeneutics of Deliberative Instrumentation." *Acta Politica* 40: 197–211.

Duncan, Otis D. 1984. *Notes on Social Measurement.* New York, NY: Russell Sage Foundation.

Durkheim, Emile. 1984. *The Division of Labor in Society.* Trans. W. D. Halls; intro. Lewis A. Coser. New York, NY: Free Press.

Durkheim, Emile. 1995. *The Elementary Forms of Religious Life.* Trans. and intro. Karen E. Fields. New York, NY: Free Press.

Economist Intelligence Unit. 2011. "Democracy Index 2011: Democracy Under Stress." London, UK: Economist Intelligence Unit. Retrieved March 3, 2013, from https://www.eiu.com/public/topical_report.aspx?campaignid=Democracy Index2011.

Edelman, Murray. 1993. "Contestable Categories and Public Opinion." *Political Communication* 10(3): 231–42.

Edlin, Aaron, Andrew Gelman, and Noah Kaplan. 2007. "Voting as a Rational Choice: Why and How People Vote to Improve the Well-Being of Others." *Rationality and Society* 19: 293–314.

Eliasoph, Nina. 1996. "Making a Fragile Public: A Talk-Centered Study of Citizenship and Power." *Sociological Theory* 14(3): 262–89.

Eliasoph, Nina. 1998. *Avoiding Politics: How Americans Create Apathy in Everyday Life.* New York, NY: Cambridge University Press.

Eliasoph, Nina, and Paul Lichterman. 2002. "Culture in Interaction." *American Journal of Sociology* 108(4): 735–94.

Entman, Robert M., and Susan Herbst. 2001. "Reframing Public Opinion As We Have Known It." Pp. 203–25 in *Mediated Politics: Communication in the Future of Democracy*, eds. W.L. Bennett and R. Entman. Cambridge, UK: Cambridge University Press.

Erikson, Robert S., Michael B. MacKuen, and James A. Stimson. 2002. *The Macro Polity.* New York, NY: Cambridge University Press.

Erisen, Elif, and Cengiz Erisen. 2012. "The Effect of Social Networks on the Quality of Political Thinking." *Political Psychology* 33(6): 839–65.

Faulkenberry, G. David, and Robert Mason. 1978. "Characteristics of Nonopinion and No Opinion Response Groups." *Public Opinion Quarterly* 42: 533–43.

Ferree, Myra Marx, William A. Gamson, Jürgen Gerhards, and Dieter Rucht. 2002. "Four Models of the Public Sphere in Modern Democracies." *Theory and Society* 31: 289–324.

Fields, Karen E. 1995. "Translator's Introduction: Religion as an Eminently Social Thing." Pp. xvii–lxxiii in Emile Durkheim, *The Elementary Forms of Religious Life*, trans. and intro. Karen E. Fields. New York, NY: Free Press.

Fischer, Claude S. 1992. *America Calling: A Social History of the Telephone to 1940.* Berkeley, CA: University of California Press.

References

Fishkin, James S. 2009. *When the People Speak: Deliberative Democracy and Public Consultation*. New York, NY: Oxford University Press.

Fishkin, James, and Robert Luskin. 2005. "Experimenting with a Democratic Ideal: Deliberative Polling and Public Opinion." *Acta Politica* 40(3): 284–98.

Fiske, Susan T., and Patricia W. Linville. 1980. "What Does the Schema Concept Buy us?" *Personality and Social Psychology Bulletin* 6: 543–57.

Fitrakis, Bob, and Harvey Wasserman. 2004. "Diebold's Political Machine." *Mother Jones*, March 5. Retrieved February 17, 2013, from http://www.motherjones.com/politics/2004/03/diebolds-political-machine.

Fleck, Christian. 2011. *A Transatlantic History of the Social Sciences: Robber Barons, the Third Reich and the Invention of Empirical Social Research*. London; New York, NY: Bloomsbury Academic.

Foner, Eric. 1989. *Reconstruction: America's Unfinished Revolution, 1863–1877*. New York, NY: Harper and Row.

Foner, Eric. 1999. "The Strange Career of the Reconstruction Amendments." *Yale Law Journal* 108(8): 2003–9.

Forest, Benjamin. 2004. "Information Sovereignty and GIS: The Evolution of 'Communities of Interest' in Political Redistricting." *Political Geography* 23: 425–51.

Fowler, James H., and Christopher T. Dawes. 2008. "Two Genes Predict Voter Turnout." *Journal of Politics* 70(3): 579–94.

Franc, Michael G. 2012. "Parsing the Polls: If Gallup is Right, Tuesday Will Be a Long Night for the Democratic Party." *National Review Online*, November 3. Retrieved February 4, 2013, from http://www.nationalreview.com/articles/332386/parsing-polls-michael-g-franc.

Frank, Thomas. 2004. *What's the Matter with Kansas? How Conservatives Won the Heart of America*. New York, NY: Metropolitan Books.

Friedan, Betty. 1963. *The Feminine Mystique*. New York, NY: W.W. Norton.

Friedman, Lionel E. 1968. *The Australian Ballot: The Story of an American Reform*. Lansing, MI: Michigan State University Press.

Fukuyama, Francis. 1991. *The End of History and the Last Man*. New York, NY: Free Press.

Fung, Archon, and Erik Olin Wright. 2003. "Thinking About Empowered Participatory Governance." Pp. 3–43 in *Deepening Democracy: Institutional Innovations in Empowered Participatory Governance*, eds. A. Fung and E.O. Wright. London, UK: Verso.

Gallup, George H. 1940. *The Pulse of Democracy: The Public Opinion Poll and How It Works*. New York, NY: Simon & Schuster.

Gans, Herbert. 1982. *The Levittowners: Ways of Life and Politics in a New Suburban Community*. New York, NY: Columbia University Press.

Gastil, John. 2000. *By Popular Demand: Revitalizing Representative Democracy Through Deliberative Elections*. Berkeley, CA: University of California Press.

References

Geddis, Andrew. 2003. "Three Conceptions of the Electoral Moment." *Australian Journal of Legal Philosophy* 28(53).

Geer, John G. 2006. *In Defense of Negativity: Attack Ads in Presidential Campaigns.* Chicago, IL: University of Chicago Press.

Geertz, Clifford. 1984. "Distinguished Lecture: Anti Anti-Relativism." *American Anthropologist* 86(2): 263–78.

Gelman, Andrew. 2010. *Red State, Blue State, Rich State, Poor State: Why Americans Vote the Way They Do.* Expanded edn. Princeton, NJ: Princeton University Press.

Gerber, Alan S., Donald P. Green, and Christopher W. Larimer. 2008. "Social Pressure and Voter Turnout: Evidence from a Large-Scale Field Experiment." *American Political Science Review* 102(1): 33–48.

Gerber, Alan, Gregory Huber, David Doherty, and Conor Dowling. 2009. "Is There a Secret Ballot? Ballot Secrecy Perceptions and Their Implications for Voting Behavior." American Political Science Association Annual Meeting Paper. Retrieved February 24, 2013, from http://ssrn.com/abstract=1451254.

Gerber, Elisabeth R. 1999. *The Populist Paradox: Interest Group Influence and the Promise of Direct Legislation.* Princeton, NJ: Princeton University Press.

Gerhardt, Michael J. 2001. "Impeachment Defanged and Other Institutional Ramifications of the Clinton Scandals." *Maryland Law Review* 60: 59–96.

Giddens, Anthony. 1990. *The Consequences of Modernity.* Stanford, CA: Stanford University Press.

Gilens, Martin. 2012. *Affluence and Influence: Economic Inequality and Political Power in America.* Princeton, NJ: Princeton University Press.

Ginsberg, Benjamin. 1986. *The Captive Public: How Mass Opinion Promotes State Power.* New York, NY: Basic Books.

Ginsberg, Benjamin. 1989. "How Polling Transforms Public Opinion." Pp. 271–93 in *Manipulating Public Opinion: Essays on Public Opinion as a Dependent Variable,* eds. M. Margolis and G.A. Mauser. Pacific Grove, CA: Brooks-Cole.

Girard, Monique, and David Stark. 2007. "Socio-Technologies of Assembly: Sense Making and Demonstration in Rebuilding Lower Manhattan." Pp. 145–76 in *Governance and Information: The Rewiring of Governing and Deliberation in the 21st Century,* eds. Viktor Mayer-Schönberg and David Lazer. Oxford, UK; New York, NY: Oxford University Press.

Gitlin, Todd. 1978. "Media Sociology: The Dominant Paradigm." *Theory and Society* 6(2): 205–53.

Gitlin, Todd. 1980. *The Whole World Is Watching: Mass Media in the Making and Unmaking of the New Left.* Berkeley, CA: University of California Press.

Goebel, Thomas. 1997. "'A Case of Democratic Contagion': Direct Democracy in the American West, 1890–1920." *Pacific Historical Review* 66: 213–30.

Goebel, Thomas. 2002. *A Government By the People: Direct Democracy in America, 1890–1940.* Chapel Hill, NC: University of North Carolina Press.

References

Green, Donald P., and Alan S. Gerber. 2008. *Get Out the Vote: How to Increase Voter Turnout*. 2nd edn. Washington, DC: Brookings Institution Press.

Greenhouse, Steven. 2012. "Here's a Memo from the Boss: Vote This Way." *New York Times*, October 26. Retrieved February 24, 2013, from http://www.nytimes.com/2012/10/27/us/politics/bosses-offering-timely-advice-how-to-vote.html.

Grennes, Thomas. 2001. "Free Trade's Benefits." (Letter to the Editor). *News & Observer* (Raleigh, NC), October 23.

Gronke, Paul, Eva Galanes-Rosenbaum, and Peter A. Miller. 2007. "Early Voting and Turnout." *PS: Political Science and Politics* 40(4): 639–45.

Groseclose, Timothy. 2011. *Left Turn: How Liberal Media Bias Distorts the American Mind*. New York, NY: St. Martin's Press.

Guinier, Lani. 1994. *The Tyranny of the Majority: Fundamental Fairness in Representative Democracy*. New York, NY: Free Press.

Gumpert, Gary, and Susan J. Drucker. 1998. "The Demise of Privacy in a Private World: From Front Porches to Chat Rooms." *Communication Theory* 8(4): 408–25.

Haas, Tanni. 2007. *The Pursuit of Public Journalism: Theory, Practice, and Criticism*. New York, NY: Routledge.

Habermas, Jürgen. 1962. *The Structural Transformation of the Public Sphere: An Inquiry into a Category of Bourgeois Society*. Trans. Thomas Burger. Cambridge, MA: MIT Press.

Haidt, Jonathan. 2007. "The New Synthesis in Moral Psychology." *Science* 316: 998–1002.

Halpern, Daniel, and Jennifer Gibbs. 2012. "Social Media as a Catalyst for Online Deliberation? Exploring the Affordances of Facebook and YouTube for Political Expression." *Computers in Human Behavior* 29(3): 1159–68.

Halpin, John, James Heidbreder, Mark Lloyd, Paul Woodhull, Ben Scott, Josh Silver, and S. Derek Turner. 2007. "The Structural Imbalance of Political Talk Radio." Center for American Progress and Free Press, June 22. Retrieved February 4, 2013, from http://www.americanprogress.org/issues/media/report/2007/06/20/3087/the-structural-imbalance-of-political-talk-radio.

Hamilton, Alexander. 1788. "The Mode of Electing the President." *Federalist* 68. Retrieved February 22, 2013, from http://www.constitution.org/fed/federa68.htm.

Harmon, Mark D. 2001. "Poll Question Readability and 'Don't Know' Reply." *International Journal of Public Opinion Research* 13: 72–9.

Hasen, Richard L. 2013. "Democrats, Don't Freak Out!" *Slate*, January 25. Retrieved February 22, 2013, from http://www.slate.com/articles/news_and_politics/politics/2013/01/republican_plans_for_electoral_college_reform_democrats_shouldn_t_worry.html.

Hatemi, Peter K., and Rose McDermott. 2012. "Broadening Political Psychology." *Political Psychology* 33(1): 11–25.

References

Havel, Václav. 1985. "The Power of the Powerless." Pp. 23–96 in Václav Havel et al., *The Power of the Powerless: Citizens Against the State in Central-Eastern Europe*. Ed. John Keane; intro. Steven Lukes. Armonk, NY: M.E. Sharpe.

Hayden, Tom. 1962. "Port Huron Statement." Retrieved August 21, 2013, from http://www2.iath.virginia.edu/sixties/HTML_docs/Resources/Primary/Manifestos/SDS_Port_Huron.html.

Hayes, Chris. 2012. *Twilight of the Elites: America After Meritocracy*. New York, NY: Crown.

Heater, Derek. 2004. *A Brief History of Citizenship*. New York, NY: New York University Press.

Hegel, Georg F.W. 1991. *Philosophy of Right*. Ed. Allen W. Wood. Cambridge, UK: Cambridge University Press.

Herbst, Susan. 1995. "On Electronic Public Space: Talk Shows in Theoretical Perspective." *Political Communication* 12: 263–74.

Herbst, Susan. 1998. *Reading Public Opinion: How Political Actors View the Democratic Process*. Chicago, IL: University of Chicago Press.

Herbst, Susan. 2004. "Illustrator, American Icon, and Public Opinion Theorist: Norman Rockwell in Democracy." *Political Communication* 21: 1–25.

Herbst, Susan. 2010. *Rude Democracy: Civility and Incivility in American Politics*. Philadelphia, PA: Temple University Press.

Herman, Edward S., and Noam Chomsky. 1988. *Manufacturing Consent: The Political Economy of the Mass Media*. New York, NY: Pantheon.

Herron, Michael, and Jeffrey Lewis. 2007. "Did Ralph Nader Spoil a Gore Presidency? A Ballot-Level Study of Green and Reform Party Voters in the 2000 Presidential Election." *Quarterly Journal of Political Science* 2(3): 205–26.

Hetherington, Marc J. 2005. *Why Trust Matters: Declining Political Trust and the Demise of American Liberalism*. Princeton, NJ: Princeton University Press.

Hetherington, Marc J., and Jonathan Weiler. 2009. *Authoritarianism and Polarization in American Politics*. New York, NY: Cambridge University Press.

Hirschmann, Albert O. 1970. *Exit, Voice, and Loyalty: Responses to Decline in Firms, Organizations, and States*. Cambridge, MA: Harvard University Press.

Horkheimer, Max, and Theodor W. Adorno. 2002 [1946]. *Dialectic of Enlightenment: Philosophical Fragments*. Ed. Gunzelin Schmid Noerr; trans. Edmund Jephcott. Stanford, CA: Stanford University Press.

Huckfeldt, Robert. 2007. "Unanimity, Discord, and the Communication of Public Opinion." *American Journal of Political Science* 51(4): 978–95.

Huckfeldt, Robert, Paul E. Johnson, and John Sprague. 2004. *Political Disagreement: The Survival of Diverse Opinions Within Communication Networks*. Cambridge, UK: Cambridge University Press.

References

Igo, Sarah E. 2007. *The Averaged American: Surveys, Citizens, and the Making of a Mass Public*. Cambridge, MA: Harvard University Press.

Ikegami, Eiko. 2000. "A Sociological Theory of Publics: Identity and Culture as Emergent Properties in Networks." *Social Research* 67(4): 989–1029.

Inkeles, Alex. 1969. "Making Men Modern: On the Causes and Consequences of Individual Change in Six Developing Countries." *American Journal of Sociology* 75(2): 208–25.

Issenberg, Sasha. 2012a. *The Victory Lab: The Secret Science of Winning Campaigns*. New York, NY: Crown.

Issenberg, Sasha. 2012b. "Abolish the Secret Ballot." *Atlantic Monthly*, July/August. Retrieved February 24, 2013, from http://www.theatlantic.com/magazine/archive/2012/07/abolish-the-secret-ballot/309038.

Jacobs, Lawrence R. 2000. *Politicians Don't Pander: Political Manipulation and the Loss of Democratic Responsiveness*. Chicago, IL: University of Chicago Press.

Jacobs, Ronald N., and Eleanor Townsley. 2011. *The Space of Opinion: Media Intellectuals and the Public Sphere*. New York, NY: Oxford University Press.

Jameson, Fredric. 1990. *Postmodernism, or the Cultural Logic of Late Capitalism*. Durham, NC: Duke University Press.

Jamieson, Kathleen Hall, and Joseph N. Cappella. 2008. *Echo Chamber: Rush Limbaugh and the Conservative Media Establishment*. Oxford, UK; New York, NY: Oxford University Press.

Jasanoff, Sheila. 2005. *Designs on Nature: Science and Democracy in Europe and the United States*. Princeton, NJ: Princeton University Press.

Jenemann, David. 2007. *Adorno in America*. Minneapolis, MN: University of Minnesota Press.

Jensen, Tom. 2013. "Congress Somewhere Below Cockroaches, Traffic Jams, and Nickelback in Americans' Esteem." *Public Policy Polling*, January 8. Retrieved March 3, 2013, from http://www.publicpolicypolling.com/main/2013/01/congress-somewhere-below-cockroaches-traffic-jams-and-nickleback-in-americans-esteem.html.

Jepperson, Ronald L. 1992. "National Scripts: The Varying Construction of Individualism and Opinion Across the Modern Nation-States." PhD dissertation, Department of Sociology, Yale University.

Jepperson, Ronald L., and Ann Swidler. 1994. "What Properties of Culture Should We Measure?" *Poetics* 22: 359–71.

Johnson-Hanks, Jennifer A., Christine A. Bachrach, S. Philip Morgan, and Hans-Peter Kohler, with contributions by Lynette Hoelter, Rosalind King, and Pamela Smock. 2011. *Understanding Family Change and Variation: Toward a Theory of Conjunctural Action*. New York, NY: Springer.

Kaledin, Arthur. 2011. *Tocqueville and His America: A Darker Horizon*. New Haven, CT: Yale University Press.

References

Karp, Jeffrey A. 1995. "Explaining Public Support for Legislative Term Limits." *Public Opinion Quarterly* 59(3): 373–91.

Katz, Elihu, and Paul Lazarsfeld. 1955. *Personal Influence: The Part Played by People in the Flow of Mass Communications.* New York, NY: Free Press.

Katz, Mark. 2010. *Capturing Sound: How Technology Has Changed Music.* Berkeley, CA: University of California Press.

Katznelson, Ira. 2013. *Fear Itself: The New Deal and the Origins of Our Time.* New York, NY: Liveright.

Kaufman, Jason. 1999. "Three Views of Associationalism in 19th-Century America: An Empirical Examination." *American Journal of Sociology* 104(5): 1296–345.

Keith, Bruce E. 1992. *The Myth of the Independent Voter.* Berkeley, CA: University of California Press.

Kelly, Michael. 1992. "The 1992 Campaign: Third-Party Candidate; Perot's Vision: Consensus by Computer." *New York Times*, June 6.

King, Martin Luther, Jr. 1963. "Letter from a Birmingham Jail." April 16. Retrieved July 24, 2013, from http://mlk-kpp01.stanford.edu/kingweb/popular_requests/frequentdocs/birmingham.pdf.

Klatch, Rebecca E. 1999. *A Generation Divided: The New Left, the New Right, and the 1960s.* Berkeley, CA: University of California Press.

Klinenberg, Eric. 2007. *Fighting for Air: The Battle to Control America's Media.* New York, NY: Metropolitan Books.

Klinenberg, Eric, and Andrew J. Perrin. 2000. "Symbolic Politics in the Information Age: The 1996 Presidential Campaign in Cyberspace." *Information, Communication, and Society* 1(3): 17–38.

Klofstad, Casey A., Anand Edward Sokhey, and Scott D. Mcclurg. 2013. "Disagreeing about Disagreement: How Conflict in Social Networks Affects Political Behavior." *American Journal of Political Science* 57(1): 120–34.

Kloppenberg, James T. 2011. *Reading Obama: Dreams, Hope, and the American Political Tradition.* Princeton, NJ: Princeton University Press.

Kreiss, Daniel. 2012. *Taking Our Country Back: The Crafting of Networked Politics from Howard Dean to Barack Obama.* New York, NY: Oxford University Press.

Kull, Steven, Clay Ramsay, and Evan Lewis. 2004. "Misperceptions, the Media, and the Iraq War." *Political Science Quarterly* 118(4): 569–98.

Kunda, Ziva. 1990. "The Case for Motivated Reasoning." *Psychological Bulletin* 108(3): 480–98.

Ladd, Jonathan M. 2012. *Why Americans Hate the Media and How it Matters.* Princeton, NJ: Princeton University Press.

Lascher, Edward L., Jr., Michael G. Hagen, and Steven A. Rochlin. 1996. "Gun Behind the Door? Ballot Initiatives, State Policies and Public Opinion." *Journal of Politics* 58(3): 760–75.

References

Lasswell, Harold. 1936. *Politics: Who Gets What, When, How.* New York, NY: McGraw-Hill.

Latour, Bruno. 2005. *Reassembling the Social.* New York, NY: Oxford University Press.

Laurison, Daniel. 2012. "The Willingness to State an Opinion: Don't Know Responses and Political Participation." Unpublished manuscript.

Lauterer, Jock. 2006. *Community Journalism: Relentlessly Local.* 3rd edn. Chapel Hill, NC: University of North Carolina Press.

Law, John. 2009. "Seeing Like a Survey." *Cultural Sociology* 3(2): 239–56.

Lawrence, Eric, John Sides, and Henry Farrell. 2010. "Self-Segregation or Deliberation? Blog Readership, Participation, and Polarization in American Politics." *PS: Political Science and Politics* 8(1): 141–57.

Lee, Caroline W. 2012. "From Political to Institutional Change: A New Agenda for Research on Deliberative Democracy." Political Sociology Session on Civil Society and Political Culture, American Sociological Association Annual Meeting, Denver.

Lena, Jennifer C. 2012. *Banding Together: How Communities Create Genres in Popular Music.* Princeton, NJ: Princeton University Press.

Lepore, Jill. 2010. *The Whites of Their Eyes: The Tea Party's Revolution and the Battle over American History.* Princeton, NJ: Princeton University Press.

Levin, Thomas Y. 1990. "For the Record: Adorno on Music in the Age of Its Technological Reproducibility." *October* 55: 23–47.

Lewin, Tamar. 1992. "Study Points to Increase in Tolerance of Ethnicity." *New York Times*, January 8. Retrieved March 22, 2013, from http://www.nytimes.com/1992/01/08/us/study-points-to-increase-in-tolerance-of-ethnicity.html.

Lewis-Beck, Michael S., William G. Jacoby, Helmut Norpoth, and Herbert F. Weisberg. 2008. *The American Voter Revisited.* Ann Arbor, MI: University of Michigan Press.

Lezaun, Javier. 2007. "A Market of Opinions: The Political Epistemology of Focus Groups." *Sociological Review* 55(s2): 130–51.

Liberal Outposts. 2011. "How Can We Trust Republicans, Who Presided Over 74% of Our National Debt?" *Daily Kos*, August 11. Retrieved March 15, 2013, from http://www.dailykos.com/story/2012/08/11/1119099/-How-Can-We-Trust-Republicans-Who-Presided-Over-74-of-Our-National-Debt.

Lienesch, Michael. 2007. *In the Beginning: Fundamentalism, the Scopes Trial, and the Making of the Antievolution Movement.* Chapel Hill, NC: University of North Carolina Press.

Lincoln, Abraham. 1865. "Gettysburg Address." Retrieved August 21, 2013, from http://avalon.law.yale.edu/19th_century/gettyb.asp.

Lippmann, Walter. 2002 [1927]. *The Phantom Public.* New Brunswick, NJ: Transaction.

Lynd, Robert Staughton, and Helen Merrell Lynd. 1929. *Middletown: A Study in Contemporary American Culture.* New York, NY: Harcourt, Brace.

References

MacKenzie, Donald A. 2006. *An Engine, Not a Camera: How Financial Models Shape Markets*. Cambridge, MA: MIT Press.

MacKenzie, Jean. 2012. "International Election Observers Rile Americans." Retrieved August 21, 2013, from http://www.globalpost.com/dispatches/globalpost-blogs/highway-2012/international-election-observers-rile-texas-iowa.

Mann, Thomas E., and Norman J. Orenstein 2012. *It's Even Worse Than It Looks: How the American Constitutional System Collided with the New Politics of Extremism*. New York, NY: Basic Books.

Mansbridge, Jane J. 1980. *Beyond Adversary Democracy*. New York, NY: Basic Books.

Mansbridge, Jane J. 1986. *Why We Lost the ERA*. Chicago, IL: University of Chicago Press.

Manza, Jeff, and Clem Brooks. 2012. "How Sociology Lost Public Opinion: A Genealogy of a Missing Concept in the Study of the Political." *Sociological Theory* 30(2): 89–113.

Manza, Jeff, and Fay Lomax Cook. 2002. "The Impact of Public Opinion on Public Policy." Pp. 17–32 in *Navigating Public Opinion*, eds. Jeff Manza, Fay Lomax Cook, and Benjamin I. Page. New York, NY: Oxford University Press.

Marcuse, Herbert. 1965. "Repressive Tolerance." Pp. 81–118 in *A Critique of Pure Tolerance*, by Robert Paul Wolff, Barrington Moore, Jr., and Herbert Marcuse. Boston, MA: Beacon Press.

Marres, Noortje. 2005. "Issues Spark a Public into Being: A Key but Often Forgotten Point of the Lippmann–Dewey Debate." Pp. 208–17 in *Making Things Public: Atmospheres of Democracy*, eds. Bruno Latour and Peter Weibel. Cambridge, MA: MIT Press.

Marx, Karl, and Friedrich Engels. 1848. *Manifesto of the Communist Party*. Retrieved February 25, 2013, from http://www.marxists.org/archive/marx/works/1848/communist-manifesto.

Maxwell, Angie, and T. Wayne Parent. 2012. "The Obama Trigger: Presidential Approval and Tea Party Membership." *Social Science Quarterly* 93(5): 1384–401.

Mayeri, Serena, Ryan Brown, Nathaniel Persily, and Son-Ho Kim. 2008. "Gender Equality." Pp. 139–61 in *Public Opinion and Constitutional Controversy*, eds. Nathaniel Persily, Jack Citrin, and Patrick J. Egan. New York, NY: Oxford University Press.

McChesney, Robert 1999. *Rich Media, Poor Democracy: Communication Politics in Dubious Times*. Urbana, IL: University of Illinois Press.

McChesney, Robert. 2013. *Digital Disconnect: How Capitalism is Turning the Internet Against Democracy*. New York, NY: New Press.

McChesney, Robert, and Victor Pickard (eds.). 2011. *Will the Last Reporter Please Turn Out the Lights: The Collapse of Journalism and What Can Be Done to Fix It*. New York, NY: New Press.

References

McConnell, Michael W. 1994. "The Forgotten Constitutional Moment." *Constitutional Commentary* 11(1): 115–44.

McDonald, Michael P. 2008. "The Return of the Voter: Voter Turnout in the 2008 Presidential Election." *Forum* 6(4): article 4.

McGowan, John. 2012. *Pragmatist Politics: Making the Case for Liberal Democracy.* Minneapolis, MN: University of Minnesota Press.

McPherson, Miller, Lynn Smith-Lovin, and James M. Cook. 2001. "Birds of a Feather: Homophily in Social Networks." *Annual Review of Sociology* 27: 415–44.

Mebane, Walter R., Jr. 2004. "The Wrong Man is President! Overvotes in the 2000 Presidential Election in Florida." *Perspectives on Politics* 2(3): 525–35.

Merritt, Anna J., and Richard L. Merritt (eds.). 1970. *Public Opinion in Occupied Germany: The OMGUS Surveys, 1945–1949.* Urbana, IL: University of Illinois Press.

Merritt, Anna J., and Richard L. Merritt (eds.). 1980. *Public Opinion in Semisovereign Germany: The HICOG Surveys, 1949–1955.* Urbana IL: University of Illinois Press.

Merritt, Richard L. 1995. *Democracy Imposed: US Occupation Policy and the German Public, 1945–1949.* New Haven, CT: Yale University Press.

Merton, Robert K. 1936. "The Unanticipated Consequences of Purposive Social Action." *American Sociological Review* 1(6): 894–904.

Meyer, David S., and Nancy Whittier. 1994. "Social Movement Spillover." *Social Problems* 41(2): 277–98.

Meyer, Philip. 2009. *The Vanishing Newspaper: Saving Journalism in the Information Age.* 2nd edn. Columbia, MO: University of Missouri Press.

Miller, Norman. 2009. *Environmental Politics: Stakeholders, Interests, and Policymaking.* 2nd edn. New York, NY: Routledge.

Milligan, Susan. 2000. "Campaign 2000/Electoral College; Several Tight Races May Make for Strange Election Day Fallout." *Boston Globe.*

Mills, Charles W. 1997. *The Racial Contract.* Ithaca, NY: Cornell University Press.

Mische, Ann. 2009. "Projects and Possibilities: Researching Futures in Action." *Sociological Forum* 24(3): 694–704.

Moore, David W. 1998. "Public Leans Against Impeachment Hearings; Holds Fast Against Removal From Office." *Gallup*, October 10. Retrieved February 28, 2013, from http://www.gallup.com/poll/4156/Public-Leans-Against-Impeachment-Hearings-Holds-Fast-Against-Removal.aspx.

Moore, David W. 2008. *The Opinion Makers: An Insider Exposes the Truth Behind the Polls.* Boston, MA: Beacon Press.

Morone, James A. 1998. *The Democratic Wish: Popular Participation and the Limits of American Government.* Rev. edn. New Haven, CT: Yale University Press.

References

Morris, Aldon D. 1986. *Origins of the Civil Rights Movement*. New York, NY: Simon & Schuster.

Mott, Frank Luther. 1941. *American Journalism: A History of Newspapers in the United States Through 250 Years: 1690 to 1940*. New York, NY: Macmillan.

Mouffe, Chantal. 2005. *On the Political*. London: Routledge.

Moy, Patricia, Michael Z. Xenos, and Verena K. Hess. 2006. "Priming Effects of Late-Night Comedy." *International Journal of Public Opinion Research* 18: 198–210.

Moyers, Bill. 2004. *Moyers on America: A Journalist and His Times*. New York, NY: New Press.

Munro, Neil. 2011. "Veep Pitches Plan to Hill Dems." *Daily Caller*, August 1. Retrieved March 15, 2013, from http://dailycaller.com/2011/08/01/veep-pitches-plan-to-hill-dems.

Mutz, Diana C. 2006. *Hearing the Other Side: Deliberative vs. Participatory Democracy*. New York, NY: Cambridge University Press.

Negroponte, Nicholas. 1995. *Being Digital*. 1st edn. New York, NY: Knopf.

Newman, Nathan, and J.J. Gass. 2004. *A New Birth of Freedom: The Forgotten History of the 13th, 14th, and 15th Amendments*. New York, NY: Brennan Center for Justice.

Newport, Frank. 2001. "Americans Support Proposal to Eliminate Electoral College System." *Gallup*, January 5. Retrieved February 22, 2013, from http://www.gallup.com/poll/2140/Americans-Support-Proposal-Eliminate-Electoral-College-System.aspx.

Newport, Frank. 2004. *Polling Matters: Why Leaders Must Listen to the Wisdom of the People*. New York, NY: Warner.

Nie, Norman H., Jane Junn, and Kenneth Stehlik-Barry. 1996. *Education and Democratic Citizenship in America*. Chicago, IL: University of Chicago Press.

Nielsen, Rasmus Kleis. 2012. *Ground Wars: Personalized Communication in Political Campaigns*. Princeton, NJ: Princeton University Press.

Nord, David Paul. 2001. *Communities of Journalism: A History of American Newspapers and Their Readers*. Urbana, IL: University of Illinois Press.

Norton, Anne. 2004. *95 Theses on Politics, Culture, and Method*. New Haven, CT: Yale University Press.

Nowotny, Stefan. 2003. "The Condition of Becoming Public." Trans. Aileen Derieg. *Transversal*, September. Retrieved March 6, 2013, from http://eipcp.net/transversal/1203/nowotny/en.

Obama, Barack H. 2004. Speech at the Democratic National Convention, Boston, Massachusetts. Retrieved March 5, 2013, from http://www.washingtonpost.com/wp-dyn/articles/A19751-2004Jul27.html.

Obama, Barack H. 2012a. "Remarks Accepting the Presidential Nomination at the Democratic National Convention in Charlotte, North Carolina." September 6. Retrieved September 10, 2013, from http://www.presidency.ucsb.edu/ws/index.php?pid=101968.

References

Obama, Barack H. 2012b. "Remarks by the President on Election Night." November 6. Retrieved August 21, 2013, from http://www.whitehouse.gov/the-press-office/2012/11/07/remarks-president-election-night.

Obama, Barack H. 2013. "State of the Union." Speech, February 12. Retrieved March 5, 2013, from http://www.nytimes.com/2013/02/13/us/politics/obamas-2013-state-of-the-union-address.html.

Oishi, Shigehiro. 2010. "The Psychology of Residential Mobility Implications for the Self, Social Relationships, and Well-Being." *Perspectives on Psychological Science*, 5(1): 5–21.

Olick, Jeffrey K. 1999. "Collective Memory: The Two Cultures." *Sociological Theory* 17(3): 333–48.

Olick, Jeffrey K. 2005. *In the House of the Hangman: The Agonies of German Defeat, 1943–1949*. Chicago, IL: University of Chicago Press.

Olick, Jeffrey K. 2007. "Collective Memory and Nonpublic Opinion: An Historical Note on a Methodological Controversy about a Political Problem." *Symbolic Interaction* 30(1): 41–55.

Orlikowski, Wanda J. 1992. "The Duality of Technology: Rethinking the Concept of Technology in Organizations." *Organization Science* 3(3): 398–427.

Orlikowski, Wanda J. 2000. "Using Technology and Constituting Structures: A Practice Lens for Studying Technology in Organizations." *Organization Science* 11(4): 404–28.

Ornstein, Norman. 2008. "Our Broken Senate." *The American* March/April. Retrieved September 13, 2013, from http://www.american.com/archive/2008/march-april-magazine-contents/our-broken-senate.

Osborne, Thomas, and Nikolas Rose. 1999. "Do the Social Sciences Create Phenomena? The Example of Public Opinion Research." *British Journal of Sociology* 50(3): 367–96.

Overton, Spencer. 2007. *Stealing Democracy: The New Politics of Voter Suppression*. New York, NY: W.W. Norton.

Page, Benjamin I. 1983. *Who Gets What From Government*. Berkeley, CA: University of California Press.

Page, Benjamin I. 1996. *Who Deliberates? Mass Media in Modern Democracy*. Chicago, IL: University of Chicago Press.

Page, Benjamin I., and Robert Y. Shapiro. 1992. *The Rational Public: Fifty Years of Trends in Americans' Policy Preferences*. Chicago, IL: University of Chicago Press.

Pager, Devah, and Lincoln Quillian. 2005. "Walking the Talk? What Employers Say versus What They Do." *American Sociological Review* 70(3): 355–80.

Paley, Julia. 2001. *Marketing Democracy: Power and Social Movements in Post-Dictatorship Chile*. Berkeley, CA: University of California Press.

Patterson, Thomas E. 2002. *The Vanishing Voter: Public Involvement in an Age of Uncertainty*. New York, NY: Vintage.

References

Paxton, Pamela. 2002. "Social Capital and Democracy: An Interdependent Relationship." *American Sociological Review* 67(2): 254–77.

Pear Analytics. 2009. "Twitter Study." Retrieved March 25, 2013, from http://www.pearanalytics.com/wp-content/uploads/2012/12/Twitter-Study-August-2009.pdf.

Peer, Limor. 1992. "The Practice of Opinion Polling as a Disciplinary Mechanism: A Foucauldian Perspective." *International Journal of Public Opinion Research* 4(3): 230–42.

Perrin, Andrew J. 1995. "Election Fetishism: Perceptions of Southern African Democratization." Presented at the New York African Studies Association 19th Annual Conference, New York, April 21–2. Retrieved August 21, 2013, from http://perrin.socsci.unc.edu/perrin-election-fetishism.pdf.

Perrin, Andrew J. 2001. "Fast-Track to Trouble for Workers." *News & Observer* (Raleigh, NC), October 12.

Perrin, Andrew J. 2005. "Political Microcultures: Linking Civic Life and Democratic Discourse." *Social Forces* 84(2): 1049–82.

Perrin, Andrew J. 2006. *Citizen Speak: The Democratic Imagination in American Life*. Chicago, IL: University of Chicago Press.

Perrin, Andrew J. 2008. "Why You Voted." *Contexts* 7: 22–5.

Perrin, Andrew J. 2012. "'Since This Is the Editorial Section I Intend to Express My Opinion': The Public Sphere of Letters to the Editor." Unpublished manuscript.

Perrin, Andrew J., and Katherine McFarland. 2008. "The Sociology of Political Representation and Deliberation." *Sociology Compass* 2(4): 1228–44.

Perrin, Andrew J., and Katherine McFarland. 2011. "Social Theory and Public Opinion." *Annual Review of Sociology* 37: 87–107.

Perrin, Andrew J., and Jeffrey K. Olick. 2011. "Before the Public Sphere: Translators' Introduction." Pp. xv–lxi in *Group Experiment: The Frankfurt School on Public Opinion in Postwar Germany*, by Friedrich Pollock, Theodor W. Adorno et al.. Eds., trans., and intro. Andrew J. Perrin and Jeffrey K. Olick. Cambridge, MA: Harvard University Press.

Perrin, Andrew J., and Sondra J. Smolek. 2009. "Who Trusts? Race, Gender, and the September 11 Rally Effect Among Young Adults." *Social Science Research* 38(1): 134–45.

Perrin, Andrew J., and Stephen B. Vaisey. 2008. "Parallel Public Spheres: Distance and Discourse in Letters to the Editor." *American Journal of Sociology* 114(3): 781–810.

Perrin, Andrew J., Robin Wagner-Pacifici, Lindsay Hirschfeld, and Susan Wilker. 2006. "Contest Time: Time, Territory, and Representation in the Postmodern Electoral Crisis." *Theory and Society* 35: 351–91.

Perrin, Andrew J., Steven J. Tepper, Neal Caren, and Sally Morris. 2011. "Cultures of the Tea Party." *Contexts* 10: 74–5.

Perrin, Andrew J., J. Micah Roos, and Gordon W. Gauchat. 2014. "From

References

Coalition to Constraint: Modes of Thought in Contemporary American Conservatism." *Sociological Forum* 29(2).

Perrin, Andrew J., Steven J. Tepper, Neal Caren, and Sally Morris. Forthcoming. "From Identity to Caucus: The Tea Party Movement, 2009–2012." *Sociological Quarterly*.

Peters, Jeremy W., and Brian Stelter. 2012. "On Fox News, a Mistrust of Pro-Obama Numbers Lasts Late into the Night." *New York Times* November 6. Retrieved February 4, 2013, from http://www.nytimes.com/2012/11/07/us/politics/web-sites-and-networks-focus-on-claims-of-fraud-and-intimidation.html.

Peters, John Durham. 1999. *Speaking into the Air: A History of the Idea of Communication*. Chicago, IL: University of Chicago Press.

Petrocik, John R., William L. Benoit, and Glenn J. Hansen. 2003. "Issue Ownership and Presidential Campaigning, 1952–2000." *Political Science Quarterly* 118(4): 599–626.

Pincione, Guido, and Fernando R. Tesón. 2006. *Rational Choice and Democratic Deliberation: A Theory of Discourse Failure*. Cambridge, UK: Cambridge University Press.

Piven, Frances Fox, and Richard Cloward. 1988. *Why Americans Don't Vote*. New York, NY: Pantheon.

Poguntke, Thomas. 1993. *Alternative Politics: The German Green Party*. Edinburgh, UK: Edinburgh University Press.

Polletta, Francesca, and Kelsy Kretschmer. 1999. "Free Spaces." In *The Wiley-Blackwell Encyclopedia of Social and Political Movements*, eds. David A. Snow, Donatella della Portya, Bert Klandermans, and Doug McAdam. Hoboken, NJ: Wiley-Blackwell.

Pollock, Friedrich, Theodor W. Adorno, et al. 2011. *Group Experiment and Other Writings: The Frankfurt School on Public Opinion in Postwar Germany*. Eds., trans., and intro. Andrew J. Perrin and Jeffrey K. Olick. Cambridge, MA: Harvard University Press.

Posner, Richard A. 1999. *An Affair of State: The Investigation, Impeachment, and Trial of President Clinton*. Cambridge, MA: Harvard University Press.

Posner, Richard A. 2002. *Breaking the Deadlock: The 2000 Election, the Constitution, and the Courts*. Princeton, NJ: Princeton University Press.

Powell, G. Bingham. 1986. "American Voter Turnout in Comparative Perspective." *American Political Science Review* 80(1): 17–43.

Prasad, Monica, Andrew J. Perrin, Kieran Bezila, Kate Kindleberger, Steve Hoffman, Kim Manturuk, and Ashleigh Smith Powers. 2009a. "'There Must be a Reason': Osama, Saddam, and the Social Psychology of False Beliefs." *Sociological Inquiry* 79(2): 142–62.

Prasad, Monica, Andrew J. Perrin, Kieran Bezila, Steve Hoffman, Kate Kindleberger, Kim Manturuk, and Ashleigh Smith Powers. 2009b. "The Undeserving Rich: 'Moral Values' and the White Working Class." *Sociological Forum* 24(2): 225–53.

References

Press, Andrea L., and Bruce A. Williams. 2010. *The New Media Environment: An Introduction*. Malden, MA: Wiley-Blackwell.

Prior, Markus. 2007. *Post-Broadcast Democracy: How Media Choice Increases Inequality in Political Involvement and Polarizes Elections*. New York, NY: Cambridge University Press.

Putnam, Robert D. 2000. *Bowling Alone: The Collapse and Revival of American Community*. New York, NY: Simon & Schuster.

Quirk, Paul J. 2000. "Scandal Time: The Clinton Impeachment and the Distraction of American Politics." Pp. 118–41 in *The Clinton Scandal and the Future of American government*, eds.Mark J. Rozell and Clyde Wilcox. Washington, DC: Georgetown University Press .

Rapoport, R.B. 1982. "Sex Differences in Attitude Expression: A Generational Explanation." *Public Opinion Quarterly* 46: 86–96.

Reagan, Ronald. 1964. "Rendezvous with Destiny." Speech. Retrieved February 16, 2009, from http://www.reaganfoundation.org/reagan/speeches/rendezvous.asp.

Redlawsk, David P. 2002. "Hot Cognition or Cool Consideration? Testing the Effects of Motivated Reasoning on Political Decision Making." *Journal of Politics* 64(4): 1021–44.

Rehnquist, William H. 2004. *Centennial Crisis: The Disputed Election of 1876*. New York, NY: Knopf.

Reilly, Ryan J. 2012. "Pennsylvania GOP Leader: Voter ID Will Help Romney Win State." Retrieved November 26, 2012, from http://tpmmuckraker.talkingpointsmemo.com/2012/06/pennsylvania_gop_leader_voter_id_will_help_romney.php.

Richey, Brooks. 2012. *Does This News Make Me Look Fat? How America's Junk Food Diet Makes Us Mentally Obese. And the Diet Plan for Fitness*. n.p.: Omena.

Ridgeway, Cecilia, and Chris Bourg. 2004. "Gender as Status: An Expectation States Approach." Pp. 217–41 in Alice H. Eagly, Anne E. Beall, and Robert J. Sternberg, eds. *Psychology of Gender*. 2nd edn., eds. Alice H. Eagly, Anne E. Beall, and Robert J. Sternberg. New York, NY: Guilford Press.

Riesman, David, Nathan Glazer, and Reuel Denney. 1961. *The Lonely Crowd: A Study of the Changing American Character*. Abridged edn. New Haven, CT: Yale University Press.

Rock, Kid, and Sean Penn. 2012. *Americans: A Public Service Film*. Video recording. Retrieved February 24, 2013, from http://americansfilm.com.

Rolfe, Meredith. 2012. *Voter Turnout: A Social Theory of Political Participation*. New York, NY: Cambridge University Press.

Romney, Mitt. 2012. "Address Accepting the Presidential Nomination at the Republican National Convention in Tampa, Florida." August 30. Retrieved September 13, 2013, from http://www.presidency.ucsb.edu/ws/index.php?pid=101966.

References

Rosanvallon, Pierre. 2006. *Democracy Past and Future*. Ed. Samuel Moyn. New York, NY: Columbia University Press.

Rosenau, James N. 1974. *Citizenship Between Elections: An Inquiry into the Mobilizable American*. New York, NY: Free Press.

Rosenberry, Jack. 2010. *Public Journalism 2.0: The Promise and Reality of a Citizen-Engaged Press*. New York, NY: Routledge.

Rosenstone, Steven J., and John Mark Hansen. 1993. *Mobilization, Participation, and Democracy in America*. New York, NY: Macmillan.

Rousseau, Jean-Jacques. 1913. *The Social Contract and the Discourses*. Trans. G.D.H. Cole. London, UK: J.M. Dent.

Saad, Lydia. 2011. "Americans Would Swap Electoral College for Popular Vote." *Gallup Politics*, October 24. Retrieved February 22, 2013, from http://www.gallup.com/poll/150245/americans-swap-electoral-college-popular-vote.aspx.

Saad, Lydia. 2013. "Americans Call for Term Limits, End to Electoral College." *Gallup Politics*, January 18. Retrieved February 22, 2013, from http://www.gallup.com/poll/159881/americans-call-term-limits-end-electoral-college.aspx.

Saletan, William. 2012. "Cheer Up, Republicans. You're Going To Have a Moderate Republican President for the Next Four Years: Barack Obama." *Slate*, November 6.

Sanchez, Julian. 2010. "Frum, Cocktail Parties, and the Threat of Doubt." Blog entry, March 26. Retrieved August 21, 2013, from http://www.juliansanchez.com/2010/03/26/frum-cocktail-parties-and-the-threat-of-doubt.

Sanders, L.M. 1999. "Democratic Politics and Survey Research." *Philosophy of Social Science* 29: 248–80.

Sarfatti-Larson, Magali, and Robin Wagner-Pacifici. 2001. "The Dubious Place of Virtue: Reflections on the Impeachment of William Jefferson Clinton and the Death of the Political Event in America." *Theory and Society* 30: 735–74.

Sauder, Michael, and Wendy N. Espeland. 2009. "The Discipline of Rankings: Tight Coupling and Organizational Change." *American Sociological Review* 74(1): 63–82.

Saward, Michael. 2006. "The Representative Claim." *Contemporary Political Theory* 5(3): 297–318.

Saward, Michael. 2008. "Representation and Democracy: Revisions and Possibilities." *Sociology Compass* 2: 1000–13.

Scheppele, Kim Lane. 2001. "When the Law Doesn't Count: The 2000 Election and the Failure of the Rule of Law." *University of Pennsylvania Law Review* 149: 1361.

Scheppele, Kim Lane. 2006. "North American Emergencies: The Use of Emergency Powers in Canada and the United States." Symposium on North American Constitutionalism. *International Journal of Constitutional Law* 4(2): 213–43.

References

Scheufele, Dietram A. 2000. "Agenda-Setting, Priming, and Framing Revisited: Another Look at Cognitive Effects of Political Communication." *Mass Communication and Society* 3: 297–316.

Schlozman, Kay Lehman, Sidney Verba, and Henry E. Brady. 2012. *The Unheavenly Chorus: Unequal Political Voice and the Broken Promise of American Democracy.* Princeton, NJ: Princeton University Press.

Schudson, Michael. 1992a. "Was There Ever a Public Sphere? If So, When? Reflections on the American Case." Pp. 143–63 in *Habermas and the Public Sphere*, ed. Craig Calhoun. Cambridge, MA: MIT Press.

Schudson, Michael. 1992b. *Watergate in American Memory: How We Remember, Forget, and Reconstruct the Past.* New York, NY: Basic Books.

Schudson, Michael. 1997. "Why Conversation is Not the Soul of Democracy." *Critical Studies in Mass Communication* 14: 297–309.

Schudson, Michael. 1998. *The Good Citizen: A History of American Civic Life.* New York, NY: Free Press.

Schudson, Michael. 2002. "Review Essay: News, Public, Nation." *American Historical Review* 107: 481–95.

Schudson, Michael. 2003. *The Sociology of News.* New York, NY: W.W. Norton.

Schudson, Michael. 2013. "Would Journalism Please Hold Still!" Pp. 191–9 in *Rethinking Journalism: Trust and Participation in a Transformed News Landscape*, eds. Chris Peters and Marcel Broersma. London, UK: Routledge.

Schultz, Jennifer, and Ronald L. Breiger. 2010. "The Strength of Weak Culture." *Poetics* 38(6): 610–24.

Schultz, Stanley K. 1965. "The Morality of Politics: The Muckrackers' Vision of Democracy." *Journal of American History* 52(3): 527–47.

Schuman, Howard. 2008. *Method and Meaning in Polls and Surveys.* Cambridge, MA: Harvard University Press.

Schuman, Howard, and Stanley Presser. 1980. "Public Opinion and Public Ignorance: The Fine Line between Attitudes and Nonattitudes." *American Journal of Sociology* 85: 1214–25.

Schuman, Howard, and Stanley Presser. 1996. *Questions and Answers in Attitude Surveys.* 2nd edn. Thousand Oaks, CA: Sage.

Schumpeter, Joseph Alois. 1950. *Capitalism, Socialism, and Democracy.* 3d edn. New York, NY: Harper.

Schwartz, Barry. 2004. *The Paradox of Choice: Why More Is Less.* New York, NY: ECCO.

Schwartz, Evan I. 1994. "Direct Democracy: Are You Ready for the Democracy Channel?" *Wired.* Retrieved August 21, 2013, from http://www.wired.com/wired/archive/2.01/e.dem_pr.html.

Schweppenhäuser, Hermann, and Rainer Köhne. 2011. "From a Monograph on 'Aspects of Language.'" Pp. 161–76 in *Group Experiment and Other Writings: The Frankfurt School on Public Opinion in Postwar Germany*, by Friedrich

References

Pollock, Theodor W. Adorno, et al. Eds., trans., and intro. Andrew J. Perrin and Jeffrey K. Olick. Cambridge, MA: Harvard University Press.

Shelby County, Alabama v. Holder, Attorney General, et al. 570 US. 2013.

Shelley, Fred M. 1996. *Political Geography of the United States.* New York, NY: Guilford Press.

Sherkat, Darren E., Melissa Powell-Williams, Gregory Maddox, and Kylan Matthias de Vries. 2011. "Religion, Politics, and Support for Same-Sex Marriage in the United States, 1988–2008." *Social Science Research* 40(1): 167–80.

Sicinski, Andrzej. 1970. "'Don't Know' Answers in Cross-National Surveys." *Public Opinion Quarterly* 34(1): 126–9.

Silver, Brian D., Barbara A. Anderson, and Paul R. Abramson. 1986. "Who Overreports Voting?" *American Political Science Review* 80(2): 613–24.

Skocpol, Theda. 1996. "Unravelling from Above." *American Prospect* 25: 20–5.

Skocpol, Theda, and Morris P. Fiorina, with the assistance of Marshall Ganz, Ziad Munson, Bayliss Camp, Michele Swers, and Jennifer Oser. 1999. "How Americans Became Civic." Pp. 27–80 in *Civic Engagement in American Democracy*, eds. Theda Skocpol and Morris P. Fiorina. Washington, DC: Brookings Institution Press.

Smith, Christian. 2003. *Moral, Believing Animals: Human Personhood and Culture.* New York, NY: Oxford University Press.

Smith, Daniel A., and Carolina J. Tolbert. 2004. *Educated by Initiative: The Effects of Direct Democracy on Citizens and Political Organizations in the American States.* Ann Arbor, MI: University of Michigan Press.

Smith, Graham. 2009. *Democratic Innovations: Designing Institutions for Citizen Participation.* Cambridge, UK: Cambridge University Press.

Smith, Kevin, John R. Alford, Peter K. Hatemi, Lindon J. Eaves, Carolyn Funk, and John R. Hibbing. 2012. "Biology, Ideology, and Epistemology: How Do We Know Political Attitudes are Inherited and Why Should We Care?" *American Journal of Political Science* 56(1): 17–33.

Smith, Tom W. 1987. "That Which We Call Welfare by Any Other Name Would Smell Sweeter: An Analysis of the Impact of Question Wording on Response Patterns." *Public Opinion Quarterly* 51: 75–83.

Sniderman, Paul M., and Thomas Piazza. 1993. *The Scar of Race.* Cambridge, MA: Harvard University Press.

Sobieraj, Sarah. 2011. *Soundbitten: The Perils of Media-Centered Political Activism.* New York, NY: New York University Press.

Sobieraj, Sarah, and Jeffrey M. Berry. 2011. "From Incivility to Outrage: Political Discourse in Blogs, Talk Radio, and Cable News." *Political Communication* 28(1): 19–41.

Southall, Ashley. 2013. "A 102-Year-Old Face of Voting Delays at the State of the Union." *Caucus: The Politics and Government Blog of the Times. New York Times*, February 12. Retrieved February 17, 2013, from http://thecaucus.

References

blogs.nytimes.com/2013/02/12/a-102-year-old-face-of-voting-delays-at-the-state-of-the-union.

Spitzer, Robert J. 2012. "Comparing the Constitutional Presidencies of George W. Bush and Barack Obama: War Powers, Signing Statements, Vetoes." March 5. Paper for the "Change in the White House? Comparing the Presidencies of George W. Bush and Barack Obama" Conference, April 2012. http://ssrn.com/abstract=1980301 or http://dx.doi.org/10.2139/ssrn.1980301.

Starr, Paul. 2004. *The Creation of the Media: Political Origins of Modern Communications.* New York, NY: Basic Books.

Stephenson, Peter H. 1989. "Going to McDonald's in Leiden: Reflections on the Concept of Self and Society in the Netherlands." *Ethos* 17(2): 226–47.

Stroud, Natalie Jomini. 2011. *Niche News: The Politics of News Choice.* New York, NY: Oxford University Press.

Sturgis, Patrick, and Patten Smith. 2010. "Fictitious Issues Revisited: Political Interest, Knowledge, and the Generation of Nonattitudes." *Political Studies* 58: 66–84.

Sunstein, Cass R. 2000. "Deliberative Trouble? Why Groups Go to Extremes." *Yale Law Journal* 110(1): 71–119.

Sunstein, Cass R. 2007. *Republic.com 2.0.* Princeton, NJ: Princeton University Press.

Sunstein, Cass R. 2009. *Going to Extremes: How Like Minds Unite and Divide.* Oxford, UK; New York, NY: Oxford University Press.

Swidler, Ann. 1992. "Inequality and American Culture: The Persistence of Voluntarism." *American Behavioral Scientist* 35: 606–29.

Swidler, Ann. 2001. *Talk of Love: How Culture Matters.* Berkeley, CA: University of California Press.

Taylor, Charles. 1985. *Human Agency and Language: Philosophical Papers 1.* Cambridge, UK: Cambridge University Press.

Taylor, D. Garth. 1982. "Pluralistic Ignorance and the Spiral of Silence: A Formal Analysis." *Public Opinion Quarterly* 46(3): 311–35.

Tessler, Mark, and Eleanor Gao. 2005. "Gauging Arab Support for Democracy." *Journal of Democracy* 16(3): 83–97.

Tilly, Charles. 1983. "Speaking Your Mind Without Elections, Surveys, or Social Movements." *Public Opinion Quarterly* 47: 465–83.

Tilly, Charles. 1993. "Contentious Repertoires in Great Britain, 1758–1834." *Social Science History* 17(2): 253–80.

Tocqueville, Alexis de. 2004 [1835]. *Democracy in America.* Trans. Arthur Goldhammer. New York, NY: Library of America.

Toobin, Jeffrey. 2001. *Too Close to Call: The Thirty-Six-Day Battle to Decide the 2000 Election.* New York, NY: Random House.

Torpey, John. 2006. "Alexis de Tocqueville, Forgotten Founder." *Sociological Forum* 21(4): 695–707.

Tourangeau, Roger, and Kenneth A. Rasinski. 1988. "Cognitive Processes

References

Underlying Context Effects in Attitude Measurement." *Psychological Bulletin* 103(3): 299–314.

Tourangeau, Roger, Kenneth A. Rasinski, Norman Bradburn, and R.O.Y. D'Andrade. 1989. "Carryover Effects in Attitude Surveys." *Public Opinion Quarterly* 53(4): 495–524.

Tufekci, Zeynep, and Christopher Wilson. 2012. "Social Media and the Decision to Participate in Political Protest: Observations from Tahrir Square." *Journal of Communication* 62(2): 363–79.

Vaisey, Stephen. 2009. "Motivation and Justification: A Dual-Process Model of Culture in Action." *American Journal of Sociology* 114(6): 1675–715.

Valelly, Richard M. 1990. "Vanishing Voters." *American Prospect* 1: 140–50.

Valelly, Richard M. 1993. "Public Policy for Reconnected Citizenship." Pp. 241–65 in *Public Policy for Democracy*, eds. Helen Ingram and Steven Rathgeb Smith. Washington, DC: Brookings Institution Press.

Valelly, Richard M. 2004. *The Two Reconstructions: The Struggle for Black Enfranchisement*. Chicago, IL: University of Chicago Press.

Veenstra, Aaron S., Ben Sayre, and Kyerstin Thorson. 2008. "Sticking Together Online: Political Participation and Ideologically Homogeneous Blog Consumption." Conference presentation, American Association for Public Opinion Research, New Orleans, Louisiana.

Verba, Sidney, Kay Lehman Schlozman, and Henry Brady. 1995. *Voice and Equality: Civic Voluntarism in American Politics*. Cambridge, MA: Harvard University Press.

Verhulst, Brad, Lindon J. Eaves, and Peter K. Hatemi. 2012. "Correlation Not Causation: The Relationship Between Personality Traits and Political Ideologies." *American Journal of Political Science* 56(1): 34–51.

Vidich, Arthur J., and Joseph Bensman. 2000 [1958]. *Small Town in Mass Society: Class, Power, and Religion in a Rural Community*. Revised edn. Urbana, IL: University of Illinois Press.

Voss, Kim. 1993. *The Making of American Exceptionalism: The Knights of Labor and Class Formation in the Nineteenth Century*. Ithaca, NY: Cornell University Press.

Walsh, Katherine Cramer. 2004. *Talking About Politics: Informal Groups and Social Identity in American Life*. Chicago, IL: University of Chicago Press.

Walzer, Michael. 1983. *Spheres of Justice: A Defense of Pluralism and Equality*. New York, NY: Basic Books.

Wand, Jonathan N. et al. 2001. "The Butterfly Did It: The Aberrant Vote for Buchanan in Palm Beach County, Florida." *American Political Science Review* 95(4): 793–810.

Wang, Tova Andrea. 2012. "How GOP Voter Suppression Could Win Florida for Romney." *Salon*, October 25. Retrieved February 27, 2013, from http://www.salon.com/2012/10/25/how_gop_voter_suppression_could_win_florida_and_the_white_house_for_romney.

References

Warner, Michael. 1992. "The Mass Public and the Mass Subject." Pp. 377–401 in *Habermas and the Public Sphere*, ed. Craig Calhoun. Cambridge, MA: MIT Press.

Warner, Michael. 2002. "Publics and Counterpublics." *Public Culture* 14(1): 49–90.

Weber, Max. 1978. *Economy and Society: An Outline of Interpretive Sociology*. Berkeley, CA: University of California Press.

Wedeen, Lisa. 1999. *Ambiguities of Domination: Politics, Rhetoric, and Symbols in Contemporary Syria*. Chicago, IL: University of Chicago Press.

Wedeen, Lisa. 2008. *Peripheral Visions: Publics, Power, and Performance in Yemen*. Chicago, IL: University of Chicago Press.

Weiler, Joseph H.H. 1995. "Does Europe Need a Constitution? Demos, Telos and the German Maastricht Decision." *European Law Journal* 1(3), 219–58.

Westen, Drew, Pavel S. Blagov, Keith Harenski, Clint Kilts, and Stephan Hamann. 2006. "Neural Bases of Motivated Reasoning: An fMRI Study of Emotional Constraints on Partisan Political Judgment in the 2004 U.S. Presidential Election." *Journal of Cognitive Neuroscience* 18(11): 1947–58.

Whyte, William H. 1956. *The Organization Man*. Philadelphia, PA: University of Pennsylvania Press.

Wilentz, Sean. 2005. *The Rise of American Democracy: Jefferson to Lincoln*. New York, NY: W.W. Norton.

Wilson, David C., David W. Moore, Patrick F. McKay, and Derek R. Avery. 2008. "Affirmative Action Programs for Women and Minorities: Expressed Support Affected by Question Order." *Public Opinion Quarterly* 72: 514–22.

Wilson, William J. 1997. *When Work Disappears: The World of the New Urban Poor*. New York, NY: Vintage.

Wojcieszak, Magdalena E., and Diana C. Mutz. 2009. "Online Groups and Political Discourse: Do Online Discussion Spaces Facilitate Exposure to Political Disagreement?" *Journal of Communication* 59: 40–56.

Wolf, Michael R., J. Cherie Strachan, and Daniel M. Shea. 2012. "Forget the Good of the Game: Political Incivility and Lack of Compromise as a Second Layer of Party Polarization." *American Behavioral Scientist* 56, 1677–95.

Wolfinger, Raymond E., and Steven J. Rosenstone. 1980. *Who Votes?* New Haven, CT: Yale University Press.

Young, Michael Dunlop. 1959. *The Rise of the Meritocracy, 1870–2033: The New Elite of Our Social Revolution*. New York, NY: Random House.

Zaller, John R. 1992. *The Nature and Origins of Mass Opinion*. Cambridge, UK: Cambridge University Press.

Zernike, Kate. 2010. *Boiling Mad: Inside Tea Party America*. New York, NY: Times Books.

Index

Index

Bentsen, Lloyd, 65
Berger, Ben, 90, 185
Berinsky, Adam, 31, 123
Berlin Wall, 13, 72
Berman, Marshall, 40, 164–5
Bernstein, Carl, 147
Berry, Jeffrey M., 99
Bezila, Kieran, 66, 98
Bickford, Susan, 100
Bishop, Bill, 95, 146
Bishop, George F., 123, 124
Blagov, Pavel S., 67
Blee, Kathleen, 33, 177
Blokker, Paul, 13
Blumer, Herbert, 128, 130
Bobbitt, Randy, 97, 150
Bogart, Leo, 122, 135
Böhm, Franz, 119
Bonilla-Silva, Eduardo, 32
Borrelli, Stephen A., 126
Bourdieu, Pierre, 3, 123, 128, 130
Bourg, Chris, 86
Brady, Henry E., 4, 55, 92, 173
Breed, Warren, 98
Breiger, Ronald, 157
Brenner, Philip S., 123
Brinkley, Douglas, 173
Brokaw, Tom, 65
Brooks, Clem, 4, 137
Brown, Robert D., 111
Brown, Ryan, 33
Bryan, Frank, 45, 85, 93
Buchanan, Patrick, 55, 56
Burden, Barry C., 111
Burke, Edmund, 18
Burstein, Paul, 44, 137
Bush, George H.W., 65
Bush, George W., 2, 37, 55, 66–7, 127, 158, 172

Callon, Michel, 134
campaign financing, 2, 178, 181
Campbell, Andrea Louise, 139

Campbell, Angus, 48
Canon, David T., 111
Capella, Joseph N., 153
Caren, Neal, 39, 159
Carlson, Darren K., 179
Cassino, Dan, 160
Chaffetz, Jason, 101
Childs, Harwood, 121
Cicourel, Aaron, 129
Citizens United v. Federal Election Commission, 2, 39
citizenship, 49–50; choice-making, 53, 132, 134; concept of, 16
civil rights movement, 32, 34, 36, 72
civil society, 49–50, 57
Civil War (US), 23
civility, 99–102, 161, 183
Civil War (US), 23
Clinton, William J., 122, 162; impeachment of, 39, 108–9, 167
Cloward, Richard, 54, 111, 175
CNBC, 159
CNN, 94, 101, 145, 151, 160, 173
Coggins, Elizabeth, 137
Cohen, Joshua, 20
Cohen, Patricia, 95
Cohn, Alicia M., 101
Cold War, 13, 36, 59, 72
Congress, favorability of, 1
Conley, Dalton, 32
Conlon, Ian, 127, 135
Converse, Philip E., 48, 123
Cook, Fay Lomax, 4, 44, 137
Cook, James M., 98
Coontz, Stephanie, 33
Coser, Lewis A., 91
Coser, Rose Laub, 33
Cottrell, Robert J., 23
Crowley, Candy, 101
culture, 5–10, 38, 44, 49, 58, 60, 111, 120, 157, 172–5, 181–2
cynicism, 3, 44
Czechoslovakia, 59

Index

Index

Index

Index

Index

225

Index

publics, 6, 9, 48, 59, 61, 71, 73–5, 79, 83, 115, 133, 140, 141, 153, 157, 169, 185; attentive, 50, 69, 154, 170–1; issue, 157; mass, 149; types of, 171
Putnam, Robert D., 60, 157

Quillian, Lincoln, 32
Quirk, Paul J., 109

radio, 31, 94, 96, 130, 150; talk shows, 97, 145
Ramsay, Clay, 160
Rapoport, Ronald B., 123
Rasinski, Kenneth A., 126
reactivity, 132–3
Reagan, Ronald W., 65, 140
Reconstruction, 23–5
Reconstruction Amendments, 23–5, 29
Redlawsk, David P., 100
referenda, 28–9, 45, 108, 168, 176; in California, 75
Rehnquist, William, 173, 179
Reilly, Ryan J., 112
repertoires, 76, 120; see also culture
representation, 45, 81, 109, 112–13, 114–15, 167–8; as creative, 170
responsiveness, policy, 4, 44, 137
Richey, Brooks, 151
Ridgeway, Cecilia, 86
Riesman, David, 77, 117–18, 133
ritual, 56
Rock, Kid, 186
Rockwell, Norman, 84–5, 93, 96, 141
Rolfe, Meredith, 48, 54
Romney, Mitt, 73–4, 89–90, 98, 101–2, 112, 122, 158, 186
Roos, J. Micah, 65
Roosevelt, Franklin D., 30
Roper, Elmo, 118–19
Rosanvallon, Pierre, 6, 169

Rose, Nikolas, 134
Rosenau, James N., 75, 110
Rosenberry, Jack, 144
Rosenstone, Steve J., 48, 78
Rousseau, Jean-Jacques, 26
Rove, Karl, 158
Rucht, Dieter, 82

Saad, Lydia, 179, 180
Saletan, Will, 89
same-sex marriage, 135–6
Sanchez, Julian, 95, 98, 141
Sanders, Lynn, 129
Sanford, R. Nevitt, 119
Santelli, Rick, 159
Sarfatti-Larson, Magali, 109, 167
Sauder, Michael, 133
Saward, Michael, 134, 169
Sayre, Ben, 95
Scheppele, Kim Lane, 2, 173
Scheufele, Dietram A., 127
Schlozman, Kay Lehman, 4, 92
Schudson, Michael, 17, 20, 86, 90–1, 94, 147, 148, 161
Schultz, Jennifer, 157
Schultz, Stanley K., 147
Schuman, Howard, 122–6, 130
Schumpeter, Joseph A., 7
Schwartz, Barry, 157
Schwartz, Evan I., 86
Schweppenhäuser, Hermann, 60
secret ballot, 27–8, 51, 104, 176, 181–2
self-determination, 30
September 11 attacks, 2, 37, 66, 86
Shapiro, Robert Y., 32, 44
Sharon Statement, 35
Shaw, Bernie, 173
Shea, Daniel M., 161
Shelby County v. Holder, 39, 176
Shelley, Fred M., 52
Sherkat, Darren, 136
Sides, John, 75, 95

226

Index

Index